The COBOL Programmer's Handbook

Development standards, program analyses, and model programs

Paul Noll
Mike Murach

Mike Murach & Associates, Inc.

4697 West Jacquelyn Avenue
Fresno, California 93722
(209) 275-3335

Development Team

Originator/author:	Paul Noll
Director/writer:	Mike Murach
Writer/editor:	Anne Prince
Production director:	Steve Ehlers
Cover design:	Michael Rogondino

Related program development products

A textbook called *How to Design and Develop COBOL Programs*
Case Studies for *How to Design and Develop COBOL Programs*
Instructor's Guide for *How to Design and Develop COBOL Programs*
LISTMODS software for preparing structure listings from COBOL
     source programs

Related system development products

A textbook called *How to Design and Develop Business Systems*
Case Studies for *How to Design and Develop Business Systems*
Instructor's Guide for *How to Design and Develop Business Systems*

Related COBOL products

A textbook called *Structured ANS COBOL, Part 1*
A textbook called *Structured ANS COBOL, Part 2*
A textbook called *Report Writer*
Instructor's Guides for both parts of *Structured ANS COBOL*

20 19 18 17 16 15 14 13 12 11 10 9 8 7 6 5 4

Library of Congress Catalog Card Number: 84-61555

ISBN: 0-911625-21-6

Contents

Preface

This handbook is designed to help you improve the quality of your COBOL programs as well as your programming productivity. It is a reference book that can be used in conjunction with a textbook called *How to Design and Develop COBOL Programs*. But if you're already familiar with the principles of structured program development, you can use this handbook by itself.

What this book does

If you check the contents for this book, you can see that it consists of six sections. In general, the first two sections present standards for developing COBOL programs. The next two sections present analyses of COBOL programs. And the last two sections present model COBOL programs.

In section 1, you will find general standards that apply to both batch and interactive programs. Although we have no precise data on how many companies use these standards, we estimate that several thousand companies use standards that are based on the version of these standards that we published in 1978. In our opinion and in the opinion of many of our customers, if you adopt the standards in this section for your shop, you will have a standards manual that is more complete and useful than the vast majority of those used in other shops.

In section 2, you will find specific standards for developing CICS programs in COBOL for an IBM mainframe. If you use CICS, these standards can make dramatic improvements in both program quality and programmer productivity in your shop. They are extracted from our best-selling CICS book, *CICS for the COBOL Programmer (Part 1)*, which was written by Doug Lowe. If you don't use CICS, of course, you can skip this section. But you may find that you can use this section as a guide for preparing interactive development standards that are specific to your system.

In section 3, you will find analyses of four typical batch programs: an edit program, a report-preparation program, a sequential update or file-maintenance program, and a random update or file-maintenance program. Then, in section 4, you will find analyses of three interactive file-maintenance programs. In these sections, we present the basic functions and structures for each type of program. We also analyze the model programs that are presented in sections 5 and 6. In brief, sections 3 and 4 should answer many of the questions that you might have as you develop new programs.

In sections 5 and 6, we present seven complete programs that are intended to be used as models for developing programs of your own. For each program, you will find complete program specifications: program overviews, COPY members for record layouts, screen flow diagrams, screen layouts, print charts...whatever is necessary to give a complete specification. In addition, you will find a structure chart for each program that represents the design of the program; the COBOL listing for the tested program; and the test run output. For the CICS model program, you will also find the mapset listing and the CICS translator listing. In other words, these sections present the program documentation for seven programs, and this documentation conforms to the standards presented in sections 1 and 2 of this handbook. Although the specifications for these programs are simplified somewhat so the coding won't get unwieldy, the design and code of these programs can be applied to a wide range of production programs.

How to use this book

If this handbook is available to you while you are studying *How to Design and Develop COBOL Programs*, it can aid your studies in four ways. First, by referring to the model programs in sections 5 and 6 of this handbook while you read the textbook, you can cut down on page flipping as you move your eye from text to illustration. In other words, this handbook can act as the illustration book for many of the major illustrations referred to by the textbook. Second, after you read the chapters on program design and COBOL coding in the text, you can read the program analyses in sections 3 and 4 of this book for additional insight and perspective. Third, you will probably reach a point in the reading of the text at which you will want to stop and study the complete documentation for a program. Since complete documentation is only given for the edit program in the textbook, this handbook gives you the opportunity to study other programs referred to by the text. Finally, sections 1 and 2 of this book can act as a study guide. Since they summarize the important aspects of each chapter, they provide efficient summaries for review.

Similarly, this handbook can be an important study aid to a student taking a COBOL course. Since it presents professional standards and techniques, it can enhance the coverage of most COBOL courses. And the model programs present the kind of professional program documentation that isn't presented in most COBOL courses. As a result, we recommend that you try this book as a supplement to any COBOL course you offer; it may have a dramatic effect on your training results.

Once you understand the principles presented in *How to Design and Develop COBOL Programs*, this handbook becomes your reference for developing programs of your own. If, for example, you need to refresh your memory on how to code certain COBOL elements, read the standards for COBOL programming in section 1 or 2. If you are using one of the model programs as a guide for a program you are developing and you don't understand some aspect of it, read the program analyses in section 3 or 4 and you may solve your problem. But most important, use the programs in sections 5 and 6 as models for the next programs you develop. Borrow portions of structure charts and segments of COBOL code. Borrow anything that relates to the program you're developing. If you do this for just a short time, you will soon have a library of model programs of your own. And that can lead to major improvements in program quality and programmer productivity.

If you are a programming manager, you probably won't use this handbook yourself. So your main task is to make sure that your programmers use it. In most cases, you can do this by simply making sure that copies of this handbook are available to your programmers. Because the handbook really does work, most programmers will make use of its standards and model programs. But if you want some ideas on enforcing its standards and encouraging the use of its techniques, by all means read *How to Design and Develop COBOL Programs*; one of its chapters is especially for managers.

Some related products

If you want to run a course on the standards and techniques presented in this handbook, we offer a complete training package. It consists of the text, *How to Design and Develop COBOL Programs*, *Case Studies* that go with the text, and an *Instructor's Guide* that makes it easy for an instructor to administer a course using the case studies and text. This package not only teaches a student how to apply modern programming methods to the development of COBOL programs, but it also motivates experienced programmers to use these methods.

If you're concerned about systems design and development as well as program development, we offer a comparable training package for systems design and development. It is called *How to Design and Develop Business Systems*. And it too consists of text, case studies, and advisor's guide. If you get this package, you will see that its methods for designing and developing business systems complement our methods for designing and developing COBOL programs.

Finally, if you train programmers in COBOL, we offer a complete package in *Structured ANS COBOL*. It consists of three textbooks and an advisor's guide. In this package, the case studies are included in the advisor's guide so they can be copied and distributed to the students. If you get this package, you will see that it is closely coordinated with our package for designing and developing COBOL programs. So your COBOL students will learn to develop programs the right way from the start.

How we developed this handbook

Maybe you recognize this handbook as a revision and expansion of *The Structured Programming Cookbook* that we published in 1978. Well, that's what it is. Although we feel that the contents of the *Cookbook* are still useful, we decided that we could make some major improvements to it if we revised it.

Since we published the *Cookbook*, we have had many personal experiences with its methods because we have used them in our own COBOL shop. Similarly, Paul Noll has had many experiences in teaching and enforcing the methods of the *Cookbook* since he has been consulting in COBOL shops throughout the country for the last six years. Finally, we have sold many thousands of copies of the *Cookbook* since its publication, and dozens of our customers wrote to us with comments and questions about it. As a result of these experiences, we felt that we were able to make some important changes to the standards, analyses, and programs of the *Cookbook*. So if you compare sections 1, 3, and 5 of this handbook with the three sections of the *Cookbook*, I think you'll find many improvements in the handbook.

More important, though, sections 2, 4, and 6 of this handbook present standards, analyses, and model programs for interactive programs. Since interactive programs weren't covered at all in the *Cookbook*, I think this coverage alone makes the handbook a major improvement over the *Cookbook*. In our own shop, we've developed hundreds of thousands of lines of high-quality interactive programs using the methods presented in this handbook. So we're confident that the interactive sections will justify the cost of the handbook many times over.

In case you're interested, Paul Noll wasn't able to help with the development of this handbook because he is teaching at a university in Chengdu, China, this year. However, we were able to get his ideas for this revision before he left for China. That left me to develop this revision with some outstanding technical help from one of our staff members, Anne Prince.

Conclusion

Since I entered the data processing industry in 1965, I've listened to many people discuss the need for programming standards. But few shops have adequate standards. Now, I hope you'll find that sections 1 and 2 provide the standards that you're looking for.

Similarly, since 1965 I've continually heard data processing people say that we have to "stop re-inventing the wheel." But most programmers re-invent it everytime they write a program. So now I hope sections 5 and 6 of this book help you stop program re-invention. I'm not saying that these sections will provide models for all the programs you will ever write in the future...that's not our intention. But I do hope that our model programs will help you start your own libraries of model programs...because that can have a major effect on program quality and programmer productivity.

If you have comments, criticisms, or suggestions, we'd love to hear from you. If you do, you'll find a comment form in the back of this book. And thanks much for being our customer.

Mike Murach
Fresno, California
October, 1984

Section 1

Standards for program development

This section presents standards for developing COBOL programs. It starts with a recommended development procedure and continues with standards for each of the tasks in the development procedure. These standards apply to both batch and interactive programs.

In section 2, you will find specific standards for developing interactive COBOL programs using CICS. If you don't use CICS in your shop, you may find section 2 useful as a guide for developing interactive standards that are specific to your system.

A program development procedure

The preferred sequence for program development is given in figure 1-1. Although practical considerations may force a slightly different development sequence upon you, you should try to follow this sequence as much as possible. At the least, you should make sure that you analyze the programming problem before you design it and that you design the program before you start to implement it.

In figure 1-1, you can see that task 8 assumes top-down coding and testing. For short programs, however, you may code the entire program in one step and test it in another. In general, though, you should use top-down coding and testing on any program that takes longer than a day to code.

Within the analysis, design, and implementation phases, you may rearrange the development tasks somewhat. During the implementation phase, for instance, you obviously need to have the job-control procedure, test data, and code for a test run before you can start to test a program. But whether you should develop the job-control procedure and test data before or after the code is a debatable point. To some extent it depends on the program you're writing and your personal preferences.

If you use walkthroughs in your shop, they should become part of your preferred development sequence. If, for example, design walkthroughs are required, the preferred development sequence becomes this:

1. Analyze the programming problem.
2. Design the program.
3. Conduct a design walkthrough.
4. Implement the program.

Analysis
1. Get complete program specifications.
2. Get related programs, COPY members, and subprograms.

Design
3. Design the program using a structure chart.
4. If necessary, plan the modules of the program using pseudocode or HIPO diagrams.

Implementation
5. Plan the testing of the program by creating a test plan.
6. If necessary, code the job-control procedures for the test runs.
7. If necessary, create the test data for the test runs.
8. Code and test the program using top-down testing.
9. Document the program.

Figure 1-1   The preferred sequence of tasks for developing a program

Developing program specifications

Getting complete specifications

When you receive specifications for a program, they may already be complete. On the other hand, they may be quite sketchy. In any case, it's your job to make sure that the program specifications are complete.

A checklist for program specifications

Complete specifications consist of at least the components illustrated in the specifications for the model programs in this book. A checklist of basic components follows:

1. A program overview
2. A listing of COPY members for all files used by the program
3. Print charts for all documents created by a program
4. Screen layouts for each screen used in an interactive program.
5. Screen flow diagrams for interactive programs that use more than one screen, but only when the flow from one screen to another isn't obvious.

In addition, your specifications may include decision tables, editing rules, and so on. Try to look beyond the obvious to make sure you have all the information you need to develop a program.

Program overviews

The program overview can be one or more pages as illustrated by the overviews for the model programs. The top portion of the first overview page lists the files used by the program. The remainder of the form lists the major functions required by the program. If necessary, you can use subsequent pages of this form to record details you feel are necessary for a complete understanding of the program's requirements.

Keep in mind that the overview is not supposed to indicate the sequence in which the functions of the program are to be performed. Instead, it is intended to specify the requirements of the program in enough detail so a professional programmer can design the program using only the

```
Program:  INV2100  EDIT INVENTORY TRANSACTIONS        Page:  1

Designer:  Anne Prince                                Date:  08-17-84


Input/output specifications

File            Description                              Use


INVTRAN         Inventory transaction file               Input

PARTNUM         Part number file                         Input

VINVTRAN        Valid inventory transaction file         Output

IINVTLST        Print file:  Invalid inventory transaction    Output
                             listing


Process specifications


This program edits a file of transaction records consisting of two
record types:  sales transactions and return transactions.  Although
the formats for these records are similar, they are not exactly alike.

For efficiency, since the company has less than 100 inventory items,
load a part-number table at the start of the program that can be used
to check for valid part numbers throughout the program.  The part
numbers can be read from the part-number file.  The records in this
file are in order of transaction frequency; the first part number has
the most activity, the last part number has the least.

Print the output listing in the same order that the transactions are
read.  And print the editing totals on a separate page on the invalid
transaction listing.

The records in the valid transaction file have the same format as the
records in the input transaction file.
```

Figure 1-2   The first overview page of the edit program as prepared by a word
              processing system

overview and its supporting documents. In other words, the
overview shows *what* the program is supposed to do, but not
how the program is supposed to do it.

If you have access to a word processing system, it's best
to develop the program overviews using this system. That
way, you can make modifications and enhancements to the
overviews as you develop the program with a minimum of
effort. Figure 1-2, for example, shows the first overview page
for the model edit program as prepared by a word processing
system. In this case, the headings and rules in the overview
are part of the word processing document so they print along
with the specifications.

COPY members

COPY members should be available for all files that are used by a program on the assumption that any file is likely to be used by more than one program. So if COPY members have not yet been created for a file used by a program, you must either create them yourself or make sure that they get created.

In general, there should be one COPY member for the SELECT statement of a file, one for its FD statement, and one for each of the record formats of the file. Since the SELECT and FD statements for sequential files tend to be short and straightforward, it isn't essential that these be available in COPY members. But, at the least, there should be one COPY member for each of the record formats of a file.

Print charts

Every report should have a standard heading that gives the preparation date, the preparation time (if appropriate), and the report number. So make sure you use the standard heading format.

Also, as much as possible, all reports should be self-explanatory. This means that all data items on the report should be identified on the report itself; the user shouldn't be confused by codes that aren't fully explained or by data items that aren't identified. If you are forced to use codes to identify data items due to space limitations, make sure you use codes that are familiar to the user. Or, explain the codes on the bottom of each page of the report.

Screen layouts

If all screens in a system are formatted in a standard way, two benefits will result. First, the users will find that the interactive programs are easier to use. Second, it will be easier to create and maintain the programs that display and accept the screens. With this in mind, a list of reminders for preparing screen layouts follows:

1. Divide your screens into three zones: the heading zone, the data zone, and the communication zone. The *heading zone* (usually, lines 1 and 2 of a screen) should be used to display information like the program name, the date, and the screen number. As much as possible, this should

follow a standard format. The *data zone* should display
all data relevant to the program. And, the *communication zone* (usually, lines 23 and 24 of a screen) should
be used to display error messages and operator
instructions.

2. As much as possible, the screens should be self-
explanatory. In other words, the user shouldn't require
an extensive user manual in order to use a program.

3. Whenever possible, data elements should be aligned vertically to make them easier to read.

4. Data elements should be grouped logically to make the
screen easier to understand.

5. A screen shouldn't be unnecessarily crowded. Instead, use
multiple screens.

6. If you use highlighting, use it consistently within the
program and from one program to another.

7. Indicate errors in a useful and consistent way. At the
least, an error message for a user entry should identify
the field in error and indicate what's wrong with it.

8. If an operator uses a dedicated source document for
making entries to a program, the screen should be pat-
terned after the source document.

9. When an entry program doesn't have a dedicated source
document, you should try to pattern the screen after a
related output document or a primary input document.

Figure 1-3 shows a screen layout for an interactive
program. The heading zone of this screen is just line 1; it
displays the program function and the date. The communication zone is lines 23 and 24 of the screen with line 23 used
for error messages and line 24 used for standard operator
instructions.

Screen flow diagrams

If a program requires two or more screens, the program
specifications should include a screen flow diagram that shows
how the screens are to be used. In figure 1-4, for example,
you can see a screen flow diagram for a program that uses
two screens: an entry screen and a verification screen. To
relate this diagram to the screen layouts, the screen names
used on the screen flow diagram should be the same as the
names used on the screen layout forms.

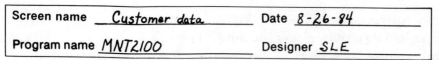

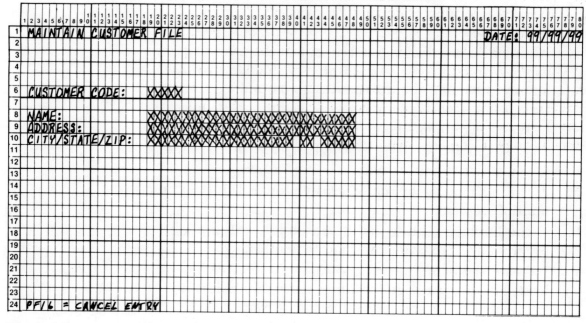

Figure 1-3   A screen layout for an interactive program

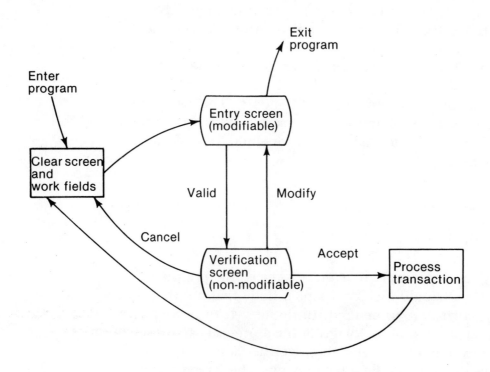

Figure 1-4   A screen flow diagram for a single-entry screen program with verification

If practical from an operational point of view, all entry
programs should use a minimum of two screens: one to accept
the data entered by the operator, another with expanded data
that gives the operator a chance to sight verify the entered
data. If, for example, the operator enters a product code in
the entry screen, the verification screen can give the complete
product description. Then, the operator can sight verify this
data to make sure that it is correct. A two phase entry process
like this can improve the accuracy of the data that is processed by the system, and it is particularly valuable when the
entry is done in the user department.

Using related programs,
COPY members, and subprograms

Using related programs

One of the most important techniques for improving your productivity is to reuse structural elements or segments of code from programs you've done in the past. With that in mind, you should get the structure charts and COBOL listings for any programs you've done similar to the program you're about to do. And you should get these before you start to design your program.

When you review the structure charts for these programs, you are likely to find that portions of the charts can be used in your new program. So you won't have to design your new program from scratch. Similarly, you may find that certain groups in the Data Divisions and certain paragraphs in the Procedure Divisions of the old programs can be used in the new program, probably with just minor modifications. So you won't have to start your coding from scratch either.

When you first start using the standards presented in this handbook, you won't have a collection of programs to use as a basis for new programs. So that's the purpose of the model programs: to help get you started. By borrowing structural elements and COBOL code from these programs, you can start your own library of model programs.

Using COPY members

At the least, the COPY library should contain a COPY member for each record description used within a file within a system. And you should always use these in your programs. Then, if a change must be made to these descriptions, a single change to the COPY members makes it possible for all programs using the COPY members to be changed by recompiling them.

In addition, unless system limitations make this impossible, you may want to use COPY members for the SELECT statements and FD statements of the files within a system. This reduces the chance of clerical error and makes it easier for you to convert your programs from one system to another.

```
*
 01   INVOICE-RECORD.
*
     05     IR-INVOICE-NUMBER              PIC X(6).
     05     IR-INVOICE-DATE.
            10     IR-INVOICE-MONTH        PIC 99.
            10     IR-INVOICE-DAY          PIC 99.
            10     IR-INVOICE-YEAR         PIC 99.
     05     IR-PURCHASE-ORDER-NUMBER       PIC X(10).
     05     IR-CUSTOMER-NUMBER             PIC X(6).
     05     IR-BILLING-ADDRESS.
            10     IR-BILL-NAME            PIC X(31).
            10     IR-BILL-ADDRESS         PIC X(31).
            10     IR-BILL-CITY            PIC X(18).
            10     IR-BILL-STATE           PIC XX.
            10     IR-BILL-ZIP-CODE        PIC X(5).
     05     IR-SHIPPING-ADDRESS.
            10     IR-SHIP-NAME            PIC X(31).
            10     IR-SHIP-ADDRESS         PIC X(31).
            10     IR-SHIP-CITY            PIC X(18).
            10     IR-SHIP-STATE           PIC XX.
            10     IR-SHIP-ZIP-CODE        PIC X(5).
     05     IR-PRODUCT-DATA                OCCURS 5 TIMES.
            10     IR-QUANTITY             PIC S9(3).        COMP-3.
            10     IR-PRODUCT-CODE         PIC X(5).
            10     IR-LIST-PRICE           PIC S9(5)V99      COMP-3.
            10     IR-NET-PRICE            PIC S9(5)V99      COMP-3.
     05     IR-TOTAL-DATA.
            10     IR-PRODUCT-TOTAL        PIC S9(5)V99      COMP-3.
            10     IR-CASH-DISCOUNT        PIC S9(5)V99      COMP-3.
            10     IR-SALES-TAX            PIC S9(5)V99      COMP-3.
            10     IR-FREIGHT              PIC S9(5)V99      COMP-3.
            10     IR-INVOICE-TOTAL        PIC S((5)V99      COMP-3.
```

Figure 1-5   A COPY member with an acceptable structure

After you find the COPY members for the SELECT
statements, FD statements, and record descriptions that you
will use, you should check your COPY libraries to see whether
you want to use any other COPY members in your program.
For instance, you might have COPY members for standard
report headings, screen headings, screen-control fields, screen-
handling messages, and so on. You might also have COPY
members for code that is meant for a specific application.

If you think your program could use a COPY member
that would be useful in other programs and the COPY
member isn't available, find out whether you should create
this COPY member. If you are assigned this task, organize the
COPY member as logically as possible. In figure 1-5, for
example, you can see a COPY member that has an acceptable
structure. Because related fields are grouped and because all
fields have meaningful names, it's easy to find the fields
you're looking for. So the extra time you spend to organize a
COPY member can pay for itself many times over.

When you find COPY members that you are going to use in your program, you can make listings of these members and file them along with your program specifications. Then, you can refer to them when you start to code your program. At the least, you should record the names of the COPY members you are going to use so you can use them in your COPY statements. Then, you can code a preliminary version of your program using the COPY member names, compile the program, and get the program listing so you'll be able to refer to the data names in the COPY members when you code the rest of the program.

In general, you shouldn't use COPY members for processing modules because the paragraph names and data names must be modified to suit your program. Instead, you should copy processing modules that are of use to you from other programs into your program. Then, you can edit the modules so the names are appropriate for your program. Since most modern computer systems make it easy for you to copy segments of code from one program to another, there's no need to keep processing modules in the COPY library.

Using subprograms

Figure 1-6 lists some general subprogram functions that should be available in your subprogram library. In addition, your subprogram library is likely to contain functions that are specific to your installation or to the application you're working on. So check your library to see if it contains any subprograms that you can use in your program.

If you think your program could use a subprogram that would be useful in other programs and the subprogram isn't available, find out whether you should write this subprogram. If the subprogram becomes available, show it on your structure chart and use it in your program.

If you decide to use one or more subprograms in your program, you can note the subprogram names on the program overview. Then, you will have a record of the names to use in your structure chart and in your COBOL code.

Date and time-handling functions

Convert a Gregorian date to a Julian date (and vice versa)
Compute the elapsed time in days between two dates
Determine the day of the week from the date
Resequence the elements in a date
Convert 24-hour time to a.m./p.m. time (and vice versa)
Compute elapsed time

Editing functions

Validate a date
Validate a state code
Validate a zip code

Character-manipulation functions

Center a left-justified character string in a field

Figure 1-6   Some general subprogram functions

Program design

General information

Use top-down design for the development of all programs. As documentation for your design, use a structure chart as shown in figure 1-7. This is the structure chart for the model edit program.

The basic principles of program design

1. Each module of a program should represent one and only one function.
2. The function of a called module must be logically contained in the function of its calling module.
3. You must be able to code each module in a single COBOL paragraph.

Four steps for creating structure charts

1. Create a rough draft of the structure chart.
2. Review and analyze the structure chart and revise it as necessary.
3. When you're satisfied with the structure chart, number the modules in it.
4. Draw a refined draft of the structure chart.

Level 0

This level should contain one module that represents the entire program. For most business programs, it will repeatedly execute at least one of the modules at level 1.

Level 1

This level should contain at least one primary module that represents the processing for one input record, one set of input records, or one interactive transaction. For instance, module 300 in figure 1-7 represents the processing for one input record.

In addition, this level should contain modules that represent *functions* that must be done before or after the primary modules are executed. In figure 1-7, modules 100 and 200 are done before module 300 is executed, and module 500 is done afterwards.

Level 2 and below

Level 2 should contain the subordinates for each level-1 module. To make sure that all subordinates are shown, you may want to list the functions that you feel make up each level-1 function. Then, make sure that there is one module for each of these functions. This idea is continued for levels 3 and below.

Left-to-right module placement

In general, you place the subordinates at each level from left to right in the sequence in which you think they are likely to be executed. This does not mean, however, that they must be executed in that sequence. And in many cases, they won't be executed in the implied sequence.

Module names

1. In most cases, module names should consist of one verb followed by one or two adjectives followed by one object. Occasionally, however, it is acceptable to name a module with only a verb and an object. For instance, "edit address" is acceptable as a module name if it is subordinate to a module named "edit customer data." In this case, it's obvious that the address is a customer address. But if the customer data provides for both a bill-to and a ship-to address, "edit address" is *not* an acceptable module name. In general, then, use an adjective whenever there's any chance for confusion. Remember that the module name should clearly indicate the function of the module.

2. Because the module number together with the module name will make up the paragraph name for the module in the COBOL program, the module name combined with the module number and separating hyphens must not exceed 30 characters. So you should try to keep your module names within these COBOL limitations.

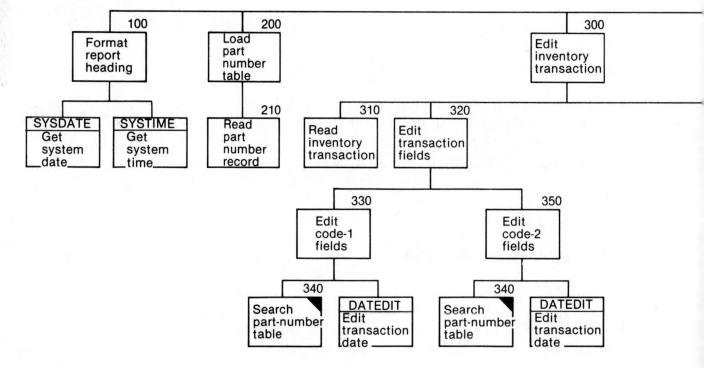

Figure 1-7   The structure chart for the edit program

From a practical point of view, though, you often won't discover that a module name is too long until you code it in COBOL. Then, you can shorten the module name in your COBOL program, even though you leave it unchanged on your structure chart. For instance, module 300 named "edit inventory transaction" may become 300-EDIT-INVENTORY-TRAN in your COBOL code. But that shouldn't cause any confusion. On the other hand, if you want to shorten the name on your structure chart so it conforms to your COBOL code, that's okay too.

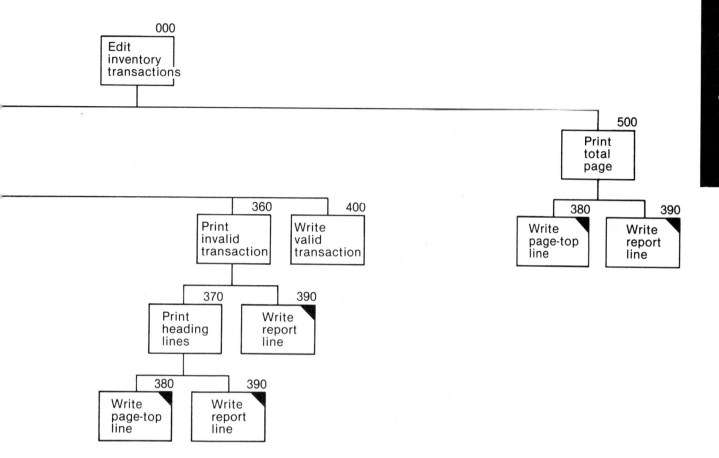

Verb list

Figure 1-8 is a list of module verbs broken down by type
(input, output, or processing). We have suggested meanings
for all of them; and these meanings conform to the way the
verbs are used in the programs presented in this handbook. If
you add verbs to this list or modify the meaning of some of
the verbs in the list, make sure the other programmers in your
shop agree with your use of the verbs. In other words, all of
the programmers in your shop should use the verbs in the
same way.

Input verbs	Suggested meaning
Accept	In interactive programs, physically accept the data from one field in a screen or from one full screen.
Get	Obtain an acceptable record or set of records. This can be used in a batch or an interactive program. In a batch program, subordinate modules might read a record, edit a record, and dispose of an invalid record. In an interactive program, subordinate modules might accept the data from a screen, edit it, and accept the operator's indication that the data is okay for processing.
Read	Physically read records from a file or data base; count records if required.
Return	Sort language that means to make a record available in an output procedure; count records if required.

Output verbs

Delete	Two related meanings: (1) Physically remove a record from a file or database; (2) Mark a record to indicate that it is deleted.
Display	In interactive programs, physically display the data in one field of a screen or in one full screen.
Print	Do everything associated with preparing a line to be printed on paper. This may include: (1) calling a module to read one or more related records that contain needed data for the print function, (2) formatting the output line or lines, (3) moving a proper spacing value into a space-control field before a line is printed, (4) calling a module to physically write a line, (5) resetting total fields to zero in preparation for the next group of records, and (6) setting up control or data fields in preparation for the next group of records.
Punch	Punch output cards; count records if required. This verb is becoming obsolete.
Put	Two meanings: (1) Format output record and call a module to physically write it on the output file or display it on an interactive screen; (2) Store an entry in a table; count entries if required.
Release	Sort language that means to make a record available in an input procedure; count records if required.
Rewrite	Physically write an output record in a file or data base in the same location on a direct-access device from which the last record was read; count records if required.
Write	Physically write an output record on the output device; count records if required.

Processing verbs

Accumulate	Develop totals by successive addition of intermediate totals.

Figure 1-8   A verb list (part 1 of 3)

Processing verbs (cont.)

Add	Add a record to a file. Subordinate modules might format the output record and physically write the record.
Apply	Apply a transaction to a record that is being updated or maintained without actually writing, rewriting, or deleting the record on the file. This verb is used in update and maintenance programs.
Calculate	Develop results by using any combination of arithmetic operations.
Change	Modify a record in a file. Subordinate modules might format the changed record and physically write the record.
Clear	In an interactive program, return data fields on a screen to blanks or zeros so the operator can enter the data for the next transaction.
Compare	Compare two fields or records.
Convert	Change something from one form to another.
Create	Develop a record, table, or file.
Determine	Find out; may include arithmetic computation.
Edit	Check one or more fields or records for validity.
Format	Prepare output records to be written, but this shouldn't include a call to a module that actually writes them.
Load	Read and store entries in a table; sort them if necessary.
Maintain	Add records to, change records in, or delete records from a master file based on data maintenance transactions as opposed to operational transactions. (See **update**.)
Prepare	This is a general verb that should only be used in control modules. It means to prepare output by doing whatever needs to be done. Subordinate modules might read records, accumulate or calculate new data fields, and prepare the output.
Process	This is a general verb that should only be used in control modules. It means operate on the input fields to do whatever needs to be done. Subordinate modules might read records, accumulate or calculate new data fields, and prepare output. Avoid using this verb whenever you can use a more specific verb.
Produce	This is a general verb that should only be used in control modules. It means produce some output by doing whatever needs to be done. Subordinate modules might read records, accumulate or calculate new data fields, and produce output.

Figure 1-8   A verb list (part 2 of 3)

Processing verbs (cont.)

Search	Look for in a table or a file.
Sort	Arrange records in a specified order.
Store	Place entries in a table or fields in storage.
Update	The primary meaning is to change records in a master file based on data in an operational transaction as opposed to a maintenance transaction. Sometimes, however, an update function will require adding records to a file or deleting records from a file based on operational data. (See **maintain**.)
Validate	In an interactive program, check the user's sign-on codes to make sure he or she is a valid user of the system.
Verify	In an interactive program, ask the user to give a response that indicates whether or not he or she has sight-verified the data on the screen and is ready to release it for processing.

Figure 1-8   A verb list (part 3 of 3)

Module numbers

1. All module numbers should be written outside of the module box on the structure chart at the upper righthand corner.

2. The top-level module should be given the number 000 or 0000.

3. The level-1 modules should be given numbers that are multiples of 100 or 1000. Start numbering with the left module and proceed to the right.

4. From level 2 on down, the modules should be numbered by 10s or 100s. Often, it's most efficient to number down the legs by 10s. That way, all of the COBOL code for a leg will be found in consecutive paragraphs in the COBOL listing.

5. When a module is added to a structure chart after numbering, it should be given a number that indicates its logical placement in the structure chart. If, for example, you add a module to a chart that logically comes between modules 330 and 340, the new module should have a number between 330 and 340, like 335.

One read or write statement per file

Since I/0 statements have a significant effect on the design
and execution of a program, you should code only one read or
write statement per file. The primary exceptions to this standard follow:

1. Because a print file generally requires one WRITE state-
    ment that will skip to the top of a page before printing
    and another that will skip as many lines as are indicated
    by a space-control field, a print file can have two write
    modules. Furthermore, if a program requires skipping to
    the channels in a carriage-control tape, there can be one
    write module for each carriage-control channel that is
    used.

2. Because a variable-length file may require one WRITE
    statement for each record length, a variable-length file
    can have as many write modules as there are record
    lengths for the file.

3. Because an indexed file can be accessed dynamically, it
    may require one READ statement for random access (a
    READ statement) and another for sequential access (a
    READ NEXT statement).

4. Because interactive COBOL compilers for multi-user
    systems may provide one READ statement for input only
    and another for reading with the intent to update, a file
    used in an interactive program may require two READ
    modules. This, of course, varies from one system to
    another.

5. Because you can both add records to and change records
    in an indexed or relative file that is accessed on a random
    basis, an indexed file can have one I/O statement for
    writing (adding) records and another for rewriting
    (changing) records.

**Isolate file-handling I/O statements
by putting them in separate I/O modules**

To make sure that you use only one read or write statement
per file with the exceptions noted above, you must put each
I/O statement in its own I/O module. If necessary, then, each
I/O module can be called by more than one calling module.
But no matter how many different modules call the I/O
module, the program still contains only one read or write
statement for that file.

An I/O module will consist primarily of the READ, WRITE, or REWRITE statement for a file. But it may also contain closely related code such as code to count the number of records read from a file or the number of records written to a file. And a read module for a sequential file will have code that handles the end-of-file condition. If you check the verb list in figure 1-8, you can see the type of code that is acceptable in a typical I/O module.

**Isolate screen-handling I/O statements
by putting them in separate I/O modules**

When you develop interactive programs, you should think of the screen-handling operations as input and output operations. When data is received from a screen, for example, it is an input operation. And when data is sent to a screen, it is an output operation.

As a standard practice, then, you should isolate screen-handling I/O statements by putting them in their own modules. For most compilers, this means that you will have one screen-handling I/O module for each screen layout used by a program. This is illustrated by two of the three interactive programs presented in the model program section of this handbook. By obeying this standard, your programs will be easier to develop and maintain.

**Isolate search functions
by putting them in separate search modules**

Like an I/O operation, a search function has a significant effect on the design of a program. Also, search functions tend to be called from more than one place in a program. As a result, you should isolate search functions by putting them in their own modules. This is illustrated by module 340 in figure 1-7, which is called by two different modules.

Shade common modules

1. When a module is called by more than one module, it is referred to as a common module. Each common module should be shown as subordinate to all modules that call it. And the upper righthand corner of each common module should be shaded as illustrated by modules 340, 380, and 390 in figure 1-7.

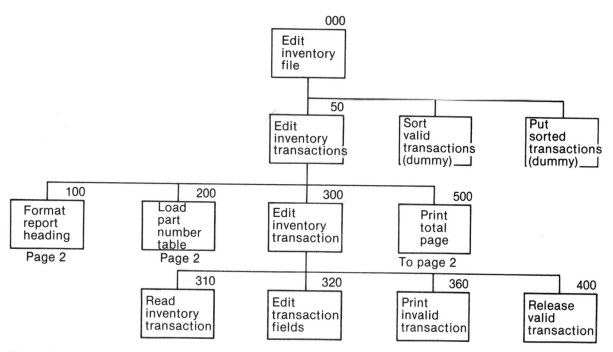

Figure 1-9   The top four levels of a structure chart for an edit program that sorts the valid
transactions using a SORT statement in module 000

2.   If a common module has subordinates, the subordinates
     do not have to be shown each time the common module
     is drawn. If, for example, module 480 is a common
     module with two subordinates, you don't have to repeat
     the subordinates the second time you show module 480
     on the structure chart. Obviously, module 480 will call
     its subordinates everytime it is executed.

Using more than one page for large charts

Most production programs will contain so many modules that
they can't all be drawn on a single structure chart page. In
this case, you use one page of a structure chart to refer to
subsequent pages as in figure 1-9. In this example, you will
find the modules for the format-report-heading leg of the
program on page 2. You will also find the modules for the
load-part-number table leg and the print-total-page leg on
page 2. The use of more than one page for a single chart is
illustrated by several of the model programs in this book.

Subprogram modules

If a module on a structure chart is to be implemented as a subprogram, the subprogram name should be given at the top of the module box with a line below it. Then, the function of the module can be stated in the remaining space using a verb, one or two adjectives, and a noun. This is illustrated in figure 1-7 by the subprogram module DATEDIT.

Declarative modules

1. In general, you don't have to show any modules that will be coded in the declaratives section of a program on the structure chart. But if you think they will improve the clarity or logic of the structure chart, feel free to show them on it.
2. If you do show declarative modules on the structure chart, the module numbers should be preceded by the letter D. And the modules should be placed logically on the chart. For instance, a declarative module for error processing should be shown on the main structure chart as subordinate to the modules that contain the related OPEN, CLOSE, READ, or WRITE statements. And a declarative module related to a Report Writer function should be shown as subordinate to the module that contains the GENERATE verb.
3. If declarative processing that is not shown on the structure chart involves more than one module, you should create a separate structure chart for it. Then, you can be sure that its processing will be structured in a way that is consistent with the structure of the rest of the program.

Sort modules

When you use the sort feature of COBOL, it implies an input procedure, the sort, and an output procedure. Normally, then, the main portion of the program is in either the input or the output procedure. And sometimes, both the input and the output procedures are extensive.

In any event, the use of the SORT statement forces you to use another level of structure in your structure chart. This is illustrated by the structure chart in figure 1-9, which shows the design of an edit program that sorts the valid transactions after they have been edited. Otherwise, the structure of this program is the same as the structure in figure 1-7.

In figure 1-9, the sort module is a dummy module (because the SORT statement calls the system's sort program), and the output procedure is a dummy module (the programmer coded GIVING in the SORT statement). As a result, the main portion of the program that has to be coded by the programmer is the input procedure. In this case, then, the top-level module of the input procedure (module 50) is equivalent to the 000 module of the program that is charted in figure 1-7. Notice that you don't have to number the dummy modules when using the sort feature although it's okay if you do.

As you can see from this example, you should always show the input module, the sort module, and the output module of the SORT statement on your structure chart, whether or not they are dummy modules. That way your structure charts will always be logical. By marking them as dummy modules, you will remind yourself that you don't actually have to code these modules later on.

Checklist for review and analysis of a structure chart

1. Is the structure chart complete? (Does each module have all of its subfunctions represented by subordinate modules?)

2. Does each module name represent only one function? (Does the module name correspond to a single imperative sentence?)

3. Is proper subordination shown? (Is the function of each called module logically contained in the function of the calling module?)

4. Can each module be coded in a single COBOL paragraph?

5. Are the control spans reasonable?

6. Are the modules independent? (Are control codes only passed to the calling module?)

7. Are the verbs consistent? (Do the same verbs always imply the same functions?)

Module planning

General information

To plan the coding of the modules you have drawn on your structure chart, you can use either pseudocode or HIPO diagrams. Because it's more efficient to use pseudocode, though, you should only use HIPO diagrams when they are required.

As you get experience with the programming techniques presented in *How to Design and Develop COBOL Programs*, you may find that you don't need to plan your coding at all. Since COBOL code is similar to pseudocode, particularly when it comes to control code, you may find that you can code directly from your structure chart without any loss in terms of program quality or programmer productivity. This is particularly true if you are working from a COBOL listing for a similar program.

In any event, if you have to or want to use pseudocode or HIPO diagrams to plan your modules, remember that they are working papers. They do not become a part of your final program documentation. They are intended to help you code your program more efficiently or to let other people review your coding ideas before you actually implement them. Normally, then, these papers are handwritten in pencil. But if you can prepare them more efficiently using a typewriter or a word processing system, that's okay too.

When you plan the modules of a program, you can plan all of the modules or just the control modules. In general, the control modules are the ones that are most critical to your coding and testing efforts, while the work modules tend to be trivial. As a result, you should be able to code a program with maximum efficiency if you plan only the control modules.

Some general principles for module planning

Whether you use pseudocode or HIPO diagrams to plan your modules, there are some general principles you should keep in mind:

1. *Keep the modules independent.* When you're planning one module, it's okay to check your plans for other modules if you're just checking trivial points: proper data

names, whether a switch has been set, whether a field
has been moved, and so on. But if you continually need
to refer to the processing steps in one module in order to
plan a later module in the same program, something's
wrong. Perhaps you should go back to your structure
chart and make sure your modules are independent. In
some cases, you will find that you can divide modules
that are giving you trouble into more clearly defined
functions.

2. *Document only the function specified by the module name.*
   In some cases, you and the other members of your
   programming group will agree that certain verbs will
   have conventional meanings in your shop; that is, the
   verbs will include certain subfunctions not normally
   implied by their definitions. In the absence of such
   conventions, however, document only the function
   named by the module. It's better to create a separate
   module for a function that doesn't conform to any
   convention than to put it in a module where it will be
   difficult to find later on.

3. *In general, move subfunctions down the line.* Some subfunctions, like counting records or resetting total fields,
   are trivial enough that they don't require separate
   modules, yet they're hard to place in the existing
   modules. In such cases, move the subfunctions down the
   line in the structure chart and make them part of some
   low-level module. For example, we suggest that you
   count records in read or write modules and that you reset
   totals in print modules. Remember, however, that it's
   sometimes illogical to move subfunctions down the line.
   This is particularly true in interactive programs. For
   instance, it's often better to clear a terminal screen in a
   control module for getting an interactive transaction than
   it is to clear it in a lower-level module. So you can't
   always follow this down-the-line principle.

4. *In general, move control code up the line.* Sometimes you
   can logically put certain elements of control code in more
   than one module of a program. For instance, the code
   that modifies a control field in a report preparation
   program can be put in the primary level-1 control
   module or it can be put in one of the lower-level print
   modules. In this case, we recommend that you move the
   code up the line into the control module so the control
   module makes sense without referring to the lower-level
   modules.

Using pseudocode

When you use pseudocode to plan the modules of a program, you can record your pseudocode on any kind of paper you prefer, ruled or unruled. Remember, pseudocode is your own planning code. It will normally not be subjected to any kind of formal review.

The language of pseudocode   Because it is a personal language, you can use your own form of pseudocode. But here are some general recommendations for using pseudocode:

1. Capitalize all of the structure words of your plans; that is, words like DO, UNTIL, IF, and ELSE.
2. Indent your code using the same basic principles for indentation that you use for COBOL coding.
3. For functions that don't require control constructs, it is often best to express the purpose of the module in abbreviated English. Later on, you can worry about the coding details that will be required by COBOL.

How detailed should your pseudocode be   Since pseudocode is a personal language, we recommend this simple rule: Code as much detail as you need to convince yourself that you can code the module in COBOL. What you want to do is to avoid coding the program twice, once in pseudocode and again in COBOL.

Using HIPO diagrams

When you use HIPO diagrams, the implication is that they will be submitted for formal review or walkthrough. As a result, the standards for preparing HIPO diagrams are somewhat rigorous.

The basic form for HIPO diagrams is shown in figure 1-10. This is the HIPO diagram for the top-level module of the edit program, the first model program of this handbook.

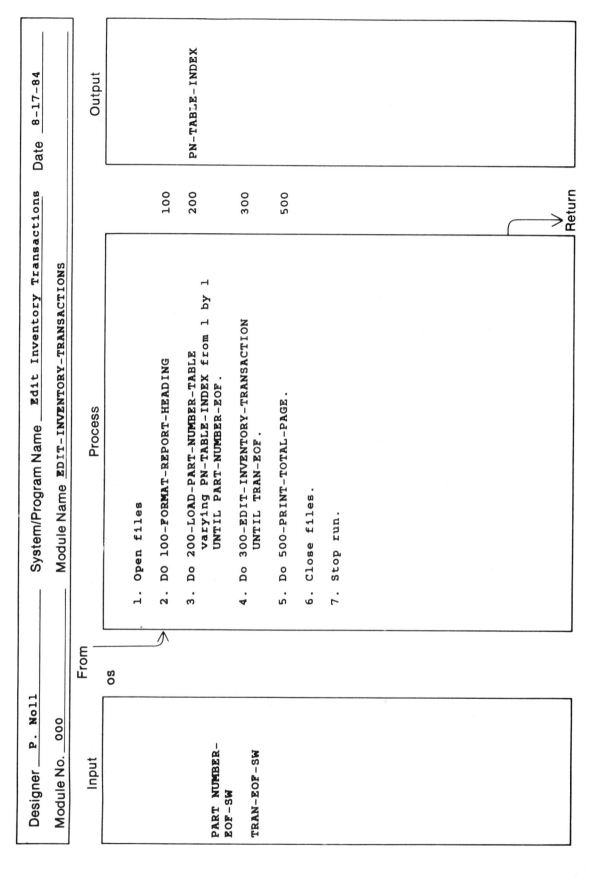

Figure 1-10 A HIPO diagram for module 000 of the edit program

Six steps for preparing HIPO diagrams

1. Complete the heading.
2. Record the processing requirements.
3. Record the input and output requirements.
4. Set off the numbers of the called modules.
5. List the calling modules.
6. Use extended description when necessary.

How detailed should your HIPO diagrams be   Since HIPO diagrams will be subjected to public review, we recommend this rule: Develop as much detail as you feel you would need if you had to pass your diagrams onto another professional programmer for coding.

Module numbers and names

1. The module number used in the heading of the HIPO form is the same as the one used on the structure chart.
2. The module name used in the heading of the HIPO form is created by hyphenating the module description that is used in the module box on the structure chart.

Called and calling modules

1. Indicate what modules will be called by the module you're documenting. To do this, write the numbers of all called modules in the space between the process and output boxes to the right of the steps that call the modules. In figure 1-10, for example, module 000 calls module 100 in step 2, module 200 in step 3, module 300 in step 4, and module 500 in step 5.
2. Indicate the calling modules for the module you are documenting. To do this, write the numbers of all calling modules near the upper lefthand corner of the process box. For example, you can see in figure 1-11 that module 330 is called by module 320. If module 330 were a common module, the numbers of its other calling modules would be written underneath 320. In figure 1-10, the calling module is OS. This means that control is passed to the module from the operating system, since module 000 is the top-level module of the program.

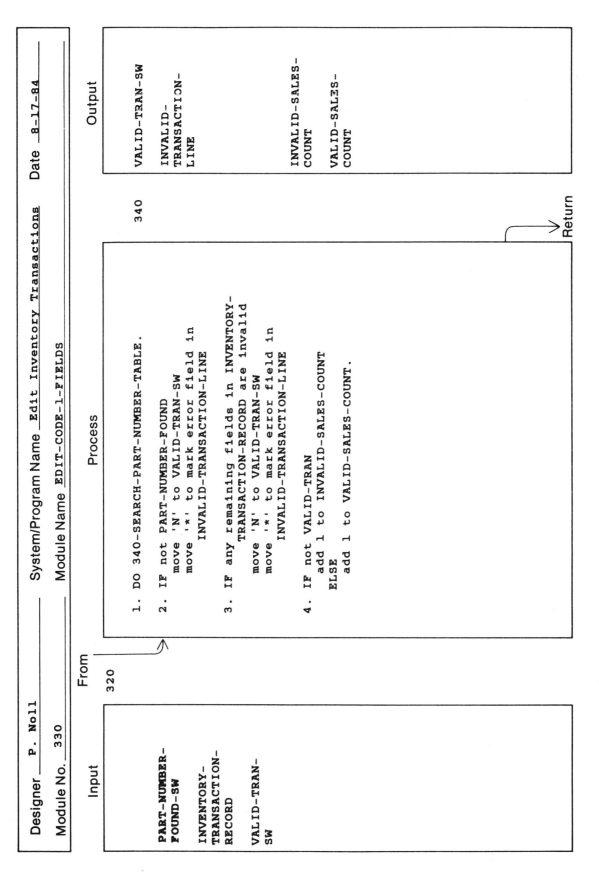

Figure 1-11   A HIPO diagram for module 330 of the edit program

Using two or more HIPO diagrams for one module   Often, when the processing steps for a single module require more than one HIPO diagram, the module itself will require more than 50 lines of COBOL code and should be broken down into two or more modules. However, if after analysis you feel that the module size will be acceptable, use a second or third HIPO form to finish the processing steps.

Language in the process box

1. Use a combination of pseudocode and COBOL when recording the processing steps in a HIPO diagram. Use COBOL for all file, record, and data names that you will need to code in the program. Use structure words like DO, UNTIL, IF, and ELSE to specify the structures you need. Use everyday English to clearly explain whatever else will happen in the processing steps. (This is illustrated in figures 1-10 and 1-11.)
2. If a module consists of *only* one or two statements, it's okay to code it in COBOL itself.
3. Don't code the program twice! Don't use so much COBOL in the process box that the documentation turns out to be a coded module on a HIPO form.

Using extended description

1. When the processing in a module is complicated and you need to go into some detail to clarity one or more of the steps, use an extended description form. For example, figure 1-12 is an extended description for the module in figure 1-11. It gives the rules for determining the validity of each input field. When using an extended description form, the HIPO diagram should indicate the overall logic of the module; the extended description form should document the details.
2. Use the reference column on the form to relate each entry in the extended description to a step or steps in the HIPO diagram. For example, in figure 1-12 there is a 3 in the reference column opposite ITR-UPDATE-CODE, since checking the validity of ITR-UPDATE-CODE is part of step 3 in the HIPO diagram.
3. Because the extended description form consists of an area for notes and a column for references, you can use it to record or refer to any documentation that will clarify the

Extended Description

| Designer **P. Noll** | System/Program Name **Edit Inventory Transactions** Date **8-17-84** |
| Module No. **330** | Module Name **EDIT-CODE-1-FIELDS** |

	Notes	Ref.
Validity is:		
ITR-UPDATE-CODE	Must be 'C'	3
ITR-REF-DATE	Use DATEDIT subprogram: must be a valid date in the form MMDDYY	3
ITR-BRANCH-NO	Numeric and less than 25 and > 0	3
ITR-SALESMAN-NO	Numeric and > 0	3
ITR-CUST-NO	Numeric and > 0	3
ITR-QUANTITY	Numeric and > 0	3
ITR-PART-NUMBER	Match in the part -number file	1

Notes	Ref.

Figure 1-12   The extended description form used for module 330 of the edit program

requirements of a module. In other words, you can use it to summarize processing requirements (as in figure 1-12), to record a specification table, to refer to a table that is found somewhere else, and so on.

Indentation in the process box Use indentation in the process box to make your documentation clear and easy to follow. In particular, do the following:

1. When a statement is too long for one line in the process box, break it up at a sensible place and indent the second and subsequent lines. For example, step 3 in figure 1-10 is too long for one line. So the programmer broke it up at the varying and UNTIL clauses and indented these clauses on the next two lines.

2. Indent phrases starting with words that indicate some condition must be met: UNTIL, AT END, INVALID KEY, etc.

3. Indent statements that tell what to do when a condition is met. For example, in a READ statement, the statement that tells what to do when the AT END condition is met is indented from AT END.

4. In an IF statement, indent the statements that are to be done if the condition is met. If the IF statement has an ELSE clause, line up the IF and ELSE and indent the statements in the ELSE clause. This is shown in figure 1-11.

5. Be consistent in your indentation. You will use the same statements again and again, so indent them the same way every time.

6. Be logical in your indentation. Use indentation as a tool to make your documentation understandable to yourself and to anyone else who might have to read it.

COBOL coding

General information

Coding a module on the structure chart   The three principles that follow are essential to the quality of a program:

1. Each module in the structure chart is coded in a single paragraph in the COBOL program. Exception: An input or output procedure in a SORT statement must be a section that ends with an EXIT paragraph.
2. The paragraph name for each module consists of the module's number and name taken from the structure chart. The number and name are separated by hyphens with the number first.
3. The modules (paragraphs) are placed in the program in the order specified by their module numbers.

Blank comment lines in the source program   Use blank comment lines (an asterisk in column 7 and blanks in the rest of the line) to vertically format the program listing. To do this, place blank comment lines before and after division headers, declarative headers, section headers, and paragraph headers as shown in figure 1-13. In addition, use them to highlight the logical groupings in the Data Division by putting them before and after FD statements and 01-level items as shown in figure 1-14.

Skipping to the next page in a source listing   You can use occasional skips to the top of a page in a source listing to make your listing more readable. For instance, you may want to skip to the top of the page at the start of the Procedure Division. You should avoid the unnecessary use of skipping, however, because it wastes paper. Skip to the top of a page only when it improves readability.

Environment Division

Sequence of SELECT statements   SELECT statements should be coded in this sequence: (1) input files, (2) I-O files, (3) output files with print files last, (4) sort files, and (5) if

```
      IDENTIFICATION DIVISION.
  *
          .
          .
          .
  *
      DATA DIVISION.
  *
          .
          .
          .
  *
      PROCEDURE DIVISION.
  *
      DECLARATIVES.
  *
          .
          .
  *
      END DECLARATIVES
  *
      MAIN SECTION.
  *
      000-UPDATE-INVENTORY-MASTERS.
  *
          .
          .
  *
      100-UPDATE-INVENTORY-MASTER.
  *
          .
          .
          .
```

Figure 1-13   Proper use of blank comment lines to space the source listing

```
      DATA DIVISION.
  *
      FILE SECTION.
  *
      FD   TRANSACTION-FILE
           LABEL RECORDS ARE STANDARD
           RECORD CONTAINS 28 CHARACTERS.
  *
      01   TR-INPUT-AREA                PIC X(28).
  *
      FD   PRINTER-FILE
           LABEL RECORDS ARE STANDARD
           RECORD CONTAINS 132 CHARACTERS.
  *
      01   PRINT-AREA                   PIC X(132).
  *
```

Figure 1-14   A structured Data Division (part 1 of 2)

```
WORKING-STORAGE SECTION.
*
01   SWITCHES.
*
     05   TRAN-EOF-SW           PIC X            VALUE 'N'.
          88   TRAN-EOF                          VALUE 'Y'.
     05   VALID-TRAN-SW         PIC X.
          88   VALID-TRAN                        VALUE 'Y'.
*
01   PRINT-FIELDS              COMP             SYNC.
*
     05   LINE-COUNT            PIC S999         VALUE +57.
     05   LINES-ON-PAGE         PIC S999         VALUE +56.
     05   SPACE-CONTROL         PIC S9.
*
01   COUNT-FIELDS             COMP-3.
*
     05   VALID-RECORD-COUNT    PIC S9(5)        VALUE ZERO.
     05   INVALID-RECORD-COUNT  PIC S9(5)        VALUE ZERO.
*
01   TOTAL-FIELDS             COMP-3.
*
     05   CUSTOMER-TOTAL        PIC S9(7)V99     VALUE ZERO.
     05   SALESMAN-TOTAL        PIC S9(7)V99     VALUE ZERO.
     05   GRAND-TOTAL           PIC S9(9)V99     VALUE ZERO.
*
01   SUBSCRIPT-FIELDS         COMP             SYNC.
*
     05   COMMISSION-LEVEL-SUB  PIC S99.
     05   YEARS-SERVICE-SUB     PIC S99.
*
01   TR-RECORD.
*
     05   TR-TRAN-CODE          PIC X.
          88 TR-DELETE                           VALUE 'D'.
          88 TR-ADD                              VALUE 'A'.
          88 TR-CHANGE                           VALUE 'C'.
     05   TR-BRANCH-NO          PIC XX.
     05   TR-SALESMAN-NO        PIC XXX.
     05   TR-CUSTOMER-NO        PIC X(5).
     05   TR-TRAN-DATE.
          10 TR-TRAN-MONTH      PIC 99.
          10 TR-TRAN-DAY        PIC 99.
          10 TR-TRAN-YEAR       PIC 99.
     05   TR-QUANTITY           PIC 9(5).
     05   TR-ITEM-NO            PIC X(6).
```

Figure 1-14   A structured Data Division (part 2 of 2)

your compiler treats a terminal screen as a file, the screen
file. Then, if the FD statements in the file section of the Data
Division are coded in the same sequence used for the
SELECT statements, the SELECT statements are an index to
the FD statements.

Data Division

Sequence of code   To start, the FD statements in the file section of the Data Division should be coded in the same sequence used for the SELECT statements. Then, the fields in the working-storage section should be coded in a regular pattern. In general, this pattern should consist of:

1.   Groups of work fields such as switches, flags, and counters
2.   Record descriptions in the same order as the related files are listed in the SELECT statements
3.   Screen handling fields, if they are defined within the COBOL program, ending up with the screen definitions themselves

In addition, you should code line descriptions for print files in this order: (1) heading lines, (2) body lines, (3) total lines. If you use regular coding sequences like these, it will be easier for you to locate code as you go from one program to another.

If you are likely to refer frequently to some of the working-storage definitions, you may want to put them at the start of the working-storage section. If, for example, you are writing a program that creates and processes a related set of tables, you may want to put the table definitions at the start of working storage. That way you will be able to find them easily.

Data names   Use hyphens to separate the parts of data names so the names are clear and easy to read. Also, use a two- or three-letter prefix in the names of all the fields in a single input or output record to show that the fields are related. For example, in figure 1-14 all the fields in the transaction record start with the prefix TR.

Meaningful names   Give meaningful names to all data items and 88-level items. A COBOL name can be up to 30 characters long, so don't skimp. Use as many of the 30 characters as you need to make the names in your program easy to understand—not only easy for yourself, but for others as well.

Grouping data items   Do not use any 77-level items. Instead, group items under general 01-level headings. For example, you can group all total fields under an 01 item called TOTAL-FIELDS as shown in figure 1-14. If all the items in a group have the same USAGE, specify this at the group level as shown for SUBSCRIPT-FIELDS in figure 1-14.

Switches   When condition names are used for a field that has only two possible conditions, the field is called a switch. Here are the basic rules that apply to switches:

1. All switch names end in SW.
2. The condition represented by the switch should be self-explanatory if you drop the SW from the switch name. Thus, VALID-TRAN-SW would be the switch name for the condition named VALID-TRAN, which would indicate a valid transaction.
3. The switch is on if it has a value of Y (for yes) and off if it has a value of N (for no).
4. If a switch must have a starting value, initialize it by giving it a VALUE in working storage.

Flags   When condition names are used for a field that has more than two possible conditions, the field is called a flag. The condition names for a flag may be closely related to the flag name, like GROUP-1, GROUP-2, and GROUP-3 for a flag named GROUP-FLAG; or they can be unrelated, like TRAINEE, SALESMAN, and ASSOCIATE for a flag named STATUS-FLAG.

Indentation   Indent the entries in the Data Division as follows:

1. Leave two spaces between the level number and the data name.
2. Indent each successive level four spaces from the previous level.
3. Align PIC, VALUE, and USAGE clauses.

These indentation standards are illustrated in figure 1-14.

Condition names   Use condition names whenever appropriate because they can improve the readability and the maintainability of your programs. In particular, condition names should be used for switches, for flags, for codes that are likely to change during the life of the program, and for codes that have obscure meanings.

Defining a constant print line   To define a print line in working storage that consists primarily of constants, it is often

```
*
 01  HDG-LINE-2.
*

     05  FILLER          PIC X(20)    VALUE 'BRANCH   SLSMN   CUST '.
     05  FILLER          PIC X(20)    VALUE ' SALES AMOUNT         '.
     05  FILLER          PIC X(20)    VALUE '                     '.
     05  FILLER          PIC X(20)    VALUE '                     '.
     05  FILLER          PIC X(20)    VALUE '                     '.
     05  FILLER          PIC X(20)    VALUE '                     '.
     05  FILLER          PIC X(12)    VALUE '
```

Figure 1-15   A technique for defining a constant line of printer output

efficient to divide the line into a carriage-control field, FILLER fields of 20 characters each, and a final FILLER field of as many characters as are needed to complete the line. Then place the literals wherever you want them to print in the line. This technique is illustrated in figure 1-15. If you start the VALUE clauses in column 44, the periods for the 20-character literal lines will fall in column 72, the last legal coding position.

Procedure Division

Sequence of code   The paragraphs in the Procedure Division are placed in the sequence given by the module numbers that are the first characters of the paragraph names. If declaratives are used, these paragraphs are placed in sequence by module number within the declaratives section. As a result, all paragraphs within the Procedure Division should be easy to locate.

Forbidden usages   Do *not* use the following in the Procedure Division, except as noted:

1. ALTER
2. EXIT (*except* when using the sort feature)
3. GO TO (*except* when using the sort feature)
4. GO TO DEPENDING (use linear IFs for implementing the case structure)
5. PERFORM THRU
6. Sections (*except* when using the sort feature or declaratives)

One STOP or GOBACK statement   A program may have only one ending statement. It can be either a STOP RUN statement or a GOBACK statement.

Section names   Do not divide your program into sections except when you are required to do so; that is, when you are using the sort feature or declaratives. Even when section names are required, they should not be used in PERFORM statements.

Indentation   Figure 1-16 shows the proper use of indentation in the Procedure Division:

1. If a statement is longer than one line, break it up at the start of a clause or phrase (never in the middle of a word) and indent the succeeding lines by four spaces. (See how example 4 in figure 1-16 is broken at INTO, example 5 at AFTER ADVANCING, example 7 at GIVING, and example 8 at VARYING.)

2. In statements like the OPEN, CLOSE, and MOVE, align similar elements such as file or data names. (See examples 1, 2, 3, and 4.)

3. Indent conditional clauses, such as AT END, INVALID KEY, and ON SIZE ERROR, by four spaces. (See examples 4, 6, 7, 8, and 9.)

4. Imperative statements that are executed when a condition is met are indented four spaces from their related conditional clauses. (See examples 4, 6, 7, 9, 10, and 11.)

5. In general, indent the IFs in nested IF statements four spaces from the previous level. (See example 10 in figure 1-16.) If there are several levels of nested IF statements, however, each subsequent level may be indented only two more spaces instead of the usual four. Then, you won't run out of coding space by the time you reach the fourth or fifth level.

6. The ELSE that goes with a previous IF is aligned directly under the IF. Be careful, though. The compiler will pair an ELSE with the first previous IF that doesn't have an ELSE, regardless of your indentation. So check to make sure all IFs and ELSEs are properly paired. (See example 10.)

7. In linear nesting, the ELSE and IF clauses aren't indented. Instead, each ELSE clause is aligned under the first IF clause, and the IF contained in the ELSE follows on the same line. The imperative statements that are to be executed if the condition is met are still indented four spaces. (See example 11 in figure 1-16.)

Example 1:

```
OPEN INPUT   TRANSACTION-FILE
             OLD-MASTER-FILE
      OUTPUT NEW-MASTER-FILE
             REPORT-FILE
             ERROR-FILE.
```

Example 2:

```
CLOSE TRANSACTION-FILE
      OLD-MASTER-FILE
      NEW-MASTER-FILE
      REPORT-FILE
      ERROR-FILE.
```

Example 3:

```
MOVE SPACE        TO PR-RECORD.
MOVE TP-ITEM-NO   TO PR-ITEM-NO.
MOVE TP-ITEM-DESC TO PR-ITEM-DESC.
```

Example 4:

```
READ TRANSACTION-FILE
    INTO TR-INPUT-AREA
    AT END
        MOVE 'Y'        TO TRAN-EOF-SW
        MOVE HIGH-VALUE TO TR-ITEM-NO.
```

Example 5:

```
WRITE PR-OUTPUT-AREA
    AFTER ADVANCING SPACE-CONTROL LINES.
```

Example 6:

```
WRITE NM-OUTPUT-AREA
    INVALID KEY
        PERFORM 420-PRINT-ERROR-MESSAGE.
```

Example 7:

```
MULTIPLY TR-QUANTITY BY TB-UNIT-PRICE
    GIVING IL-SALES-AMOUNT
    ON SIZE ERROR
        PERFORM 360-PROCESS-INVALID-TRAN.
```

Figure 1-16   Proper use of indentation in the Procedure Division (part 1 of 2)

Example 8:

```
PERFORM 110-READ-ITEM-CODE-TABLE
    VARYING TABLE-SUB FROM 1 BY 1
    UNTIL TABLE-EOF.
```

Example 9:

```
SEARCH ITEM-CODE-TABLE-ENTRY
    AT END
        PERFORM 320-PRINT-ERROR-MESSAGE
    WHEN IT-ITEM-NO (IT-INDEX) EQUAL TO TR-ITEM-NO
        MOVE IT-UNIT-PRICE (IT-INDEX) TO TP-UNIT-PRICE.
```

Example 10:

```
IF CR-CUST-CODE EQUAL TO 1
    MOVE .020 TO DISCOUNT-PERCENT
ELSE
    IF CR-CUST-CODE EQUAL TO 2
        MOVE .050 TO DISCOUNT-PERCENT
    ELSE
        MOVE .000 TO DISCOUNT-PERCENT.
```

Example 11:

```
IF CR-CUST-CODE EQUAL TO 1
    MOVE .020 TO DISCOUNT-PERCENT
ELSE IF CR-CUST-CODE EQUAL TO 2
    MOVE .050 TO DISCOUNT-PERCENT
ELSE
    MOVE .000 TO DISCOUNT-PERCENT.
```

Figure 1-16   Proper use of indentation in the Procedure Division (part 2 of 2)

Compound conditions   Use compound conditions when they closely relate to the decisions that have to be made by the program. When you use them, align the parts as shown in figure 1-17. In addition, whenever NOT, AND, and OR are mixed in a compound condition, use parentheses to dictate which part of the condition should be evaluated first. (The compiler starts with the innermost set of parentheses and works outward.)

You may use implied subjects and relational operators as long as the conditional statements are easy to understand. Once it becomes unclear what the implied subject or operator refers to, though, you should state the complete condition.

Example 1:

```
PERFORM procedure-name
    UNTIL condition-1
      AND condition-2.
```

Example 2:

```
IF        condition-1
      OR condition-2
    statement-group-1
ELSE
    statement-group-2.
```

Figure 1-17   Proper indentation when using compound conditions

If there is any confusion about how the compiler interprets a compound condition, don't hesitate to rewrite the code using two or more IF statements rather than the compound condition. Remember that the goal of your coding is clarity, not only for yourself, but for anyone else who may have to maintain the program.

NEXT SENTENCE   Whenever possible, avoid using NEXT SENTENCE in IF statements.

Comments   Comments should only be used to tell what's going on in a segment of coding, not to tell how it's being accomplished. The main reasons for using comments are (1) to relate a block of code to other documentation (such as a decision table), and (2) to explain an abstruse segment of code that can't be coded in a straightforward manner because of language restrictions. *Never* use comments to explain something the code should make clear by itself.

Linear nesting   If an IF statement tests one field repeatedly for a series of values, linear nesting can be used. An example of linear nesting is shown in figure 1-18.

Levels of nesting   When you have to go beyond five levels of nesting in nested IF statements, check your program design. Maybe you can simplify the problem by revising the structure chart.

The case structure   The case structure should be implemented by using linear IF statements. For example, figure 1-18 is equivalent to a case structure with nine cases.

```
PROCEDURE DIVISION.
*
        .
        .
        .
    IF TR-ACTIVITY-CODE EQUAL TO 1
        PERFORM CODE-1-FUNCTION
    ELSE IF TR-ACTIVITY-CODE EQUAL TO 2
        PERFORM CODE-2-FUNCTION
    ELSE IF TR-ACTIVITY-CODE EQUAL TO 3
        PERFORM CODE-3-FUNCTION
    ELSE IF TR-ACTIVITY-CODE EQUAL TO 4
        PERFORM CODE-4-FUNCTION
    ELSE IF TR-ACTIVITY-CODE EQUAL TO 5
        PERFORM CODE-5-FUNCTION
    ELSE IF TR-ACTIVITY-CODE-EQUAL TO 6
        PERFORM CODE-6-FUNCTION
    ELSE IF TR-ACTIVITY-CODE EQUAL TO 7
        PERFORM CODE-7-FUNCTION
    ELSE IF TR-ACTIVITY-CODE EQUAL TO 8
        PERFORM CODE-8-FUNCTION
    ELSE IF TR-ACTIVITY-CODE EQUAL TO 9
        PERFORM CODE-9-FUNCTION
    ELSE
        PERFORM DEFAULT-FUNCTION.
```

Figure 1-18   Nested IF statements in linear form (the recommended
implementation of the case structure)

The sort feature   When you use the sort feature with an
input or output procedure, you will have to use section
names, a GO TO statement, and an EXIT paragraph consisting only of the EXIT statement. This is one case in which all
three are acceptable. And this is illustrated by the fourth
model program, the random-update program.

Because the sort module shown on a structure chart for a
program that uses the sort feature is always a dummy
module, you don't have to code it. Similarly, if the SORT
statement specifies USING or GIVING instead of an input or
output procedure, these modules are dummy modules. So,
again, you don't have to code them.

Paragraph length   In general, you should try to keep the
length of your COBOL paragraphs at around 50 lines or less.
If a paragraph is over 50 lines, you should check it for readability. If the paragraph is easy to read and understand, no
changes are necessary. If not, you should consider revising the
structure chart for the program so the paragraph can be
divided into two or more modules, thus increasing readability.

Testing

General information

1. A test plan such as the one in figure 1-19 should be prepared for each program before any test data is developed. This plan will indicate (1) the sequence in which the modules will be tested if top-down testing is used, (2) the sequence in which the test data will be supplied to the program, and (3) the source of the test data.

2. Your primary objective during testing should be to make your program fail. If that isn't your objective, you aren't likely to do an adequate job of testing. And a major problem in program development is inadequate program testing.

3. If you are developing a program that will take more than a day to code, you should use top-down coding and testing. That way you can code and test a portion of the program each day. And this should help you reduce the total amount of time you spend coding and testing the program.

Creating a test plan

1. If top-down testing is used, decide the sequence in which the modules will be tested.

2. List all the conditions in your program that need to be tested. You can make sure your list is complete by reviewing the planning you've done for each of the modules of your program; that is, you can review your HIPO diagrams or pseudocode for the modules. If you are going to code the program without planning the modules, you must develop your list from the program specifications and structure chart.

3. Decide the sequence in which the conditions that you listed in step 2 should be tested. The guiding rule here is to test in a sequence that will point up major errors first. A general sequence that can be used is this: (1) valid conditions only, (2) independent error conditions, (3) contingencies (error conditions that result when two or more conditions are combined), and (4) volume conditions like page overflow or exceeding the maximum size of a table.

Program: INV2100 EDIT INVENTORY TRANSACTIONS		Page: 1
Designer: Anne Prince		Date: 08-18-84

Test phase	Data	Data source
1. Modules 000, 200, and 300	None	Not applicable
2. Add modules 210, 310, 320, 330, 340, and 350	Three part-number records; two valid transactions: one for each transaction code, and one with the first part number in the table, one with the last part number	Self
3. Add modules 100, 360, 370, 380, 390, 400, and 500	Invalid transactions that will test all possible causes of invalid fields	Self
4. Contingencies	Mixed data from steps 2 and 3; any new records that might cause contingent errors	Self
5. Page overflow and maximum table size	As many part-number records as the program is supposed to provide for; 150 transactions with enough invalid transactions to cause page overflow	Test data generator

Figure 1-19   A test plan for the edit program using top-down coding and testing

4. Decide where the test data will come from: Will you enter it yourself for an interactive program? Will you create it yourself? Will "live data" be available? Or what?

The sequence of top-down testing

When top-down testing is used, you normally can test the modules of your program in many different sequences. When planning the sequence, you should keep these points in mind:

1. Try to find the major errors first. So if you have any doubts about some portion of your design or its implementation, test that portion first.
2. Outside pressures may influence your testing sequence. For instance, a user or operations group may be concerned about some phase of the program. If so, test that phase first.
3. When there are no other considerations, you should test the major control modules of your program first. After that, it is logical to test the program one leg at a time. But, to a large extent, you can select the sequence that you feel is most efficient.

Creating job-control procedures for test runs

When you code job-control procedures for test runs, you should try to make the job-control language as easy to read as possible. This makes it easier to modify if you have to change it for subsequent test runs.

Within the limits of your job-control language, then, you should try to code only one parameter per line. You should try to align the parameters in each job-control statement. You should present the required parameters for each statement in consistent sequences. And so on.

Although this will vary significantly from one system, figure 1-20 shows both an organized and an unorganized job-control listing for a user of MVS on an IBM mainframe. In the first job-control listing, you can see that the programmer has coded only one parameter per line; that he has tried to present the parameters for the DD statements in the same sequence each time; and that he has aligned the parameters as much as the syntax of the job-control language permit. Because the second listing doesn't do these things, it is much more difficult to read and modify.

A job-control listing that's easy to read

```
//ARSTMTS   JOB   HE66YFNH,
//               'W. CLARY'
//EXTRACT1 EXEC  PGM=AGEDSEL,
//               REGION=120K,
//               PARM=010980
//STEPLIB   DD   DSN=MMA.USERLIB,
//               DISP=SHR
//ACCTREC   DD   DSN=ARMAST,
//               DISP=OLD
//AGEDACCT  DD   DSN=&&AGEDACCT,
//               DISP=(NEW,PASS),
//               UNIT=SYSDA,
//               SPACE=(TRK,(10,1),RLSE),
//               DCB=(LRECL=120,BLKSIZE=2400,RECFM=FB)
//DELSTMTS EXEC  PGM=ARSTMTS,
//               REGION=60K
//STEPLIB   DD   DSN=MMA.USERLIB,
//               DISP=SHR
//AGEDACCT  DD   DSN=&&AGEDACCT,
//               DISP=(OLD,DELETE)
//STMTS     DD   SYSOUT=A,
//               DCB=BLKSIZE=133
//
```

A job-control listing that's difficult to read

```
//ARSTMTS   JOB   HE66YFNH,'W. CLARY'
//EXTRACT1 EXEC   PGM=AGEDSEL,REGION=120K,PARM=010980
//STEPLIB   DD   DSN=MMA.USERLIB,DISP=SHR
//ACCTREC   DD   DSN=ARMAST,DISP=OLD
//AGEDACCT  DD   DSN=&&AGEDACCT,DISP=(NEW,PASS),UNIT=SYSDA,
//   SPACE=(TRK,(10,1),RLSE),DCB=(LRECL=120,BLKSIZE=2400,RECFM=FB)
//DELSTMT  EXEC   PGM=ARSTMTS,REGION=60K
//STEPLIB   DD   DSN=MMA.USERLIB,DISP=SHR
//AGEDACCT  DD   DSN=&&AGEDACCT,DISP=(OLD,DELETE)
//STMTS   DD   SYSOUT=A,DCB=BLKSIZE=133
//
```

Figure 1-20   Examples of job-control listings

Creating the test data

1. For the early test runs, be sure to keep the volume of data low. Otherwise, it will be difficult to locate bugs and the cause of the bugs.

2. Always determine in advance what the output for each test run should be.

3. For interactive programs, you don't actually create the test records that you will use for the interactive transactions. But you should plan the entries you are going to make in your interactive test runs.

Using debugging statements

1. If you encounter a bug that is difficult to isolate, you may want to insert debugging statements such as DISPLAY, TRACE, and EXHIBIT into the modules of your program. These will help show what is happening as the program executes.
2. To indicate what modules have been executed during the test run, you can use a DISPLAY statement at the start of each of the critical paragraphs in the program. For instance,

```
DISPLAY '200-LOAD-PART-NUMBER-TABLE'
```

could be the first statement in module 200 of the edit program.

Coding program stubs

1. A program stub should contain a few statements that simulate the processing the module will do when it is coded completely.
2. Do not develop elaborate program stubs. At some point, it becomes easier to code the module itself than to simulate it.
3. The first statement in each stub should be a debugging statement that indicates the number or name of the module (see step 2 in "Using Debugging Statements"). These statements will help you determine whether the stubs were called properly.

A checklist for testing interactive programs

When you test an interactive program, it is often difficult to keep track of all that happens during a test run. As a result, you should use a checklist like the one in figure 1-21 to make sure that you have detected all errors.

What to check for as you examine the appearance of the screen:

Are all headings and captions placed correctly?
Is there any garbage on the screen?
Are there any misspellings?
Do all the fields have the correct attributes?
Is the cursor in the correct initial location?
Does the cursor move correctly from field to field?

What to check for as you enter valid data:

Are all program screens displayed in the correct sequence?
Do all control keys work correctly?
Are the operator messages always correct?
Are the functions of all control keys shown?
Does the program properly acknowledge receipt of valid data?
Are work fields properly cleared after each valid transaction?
Are control totals accumulated properly?
Are files updated properly?

What to check for as you enter single errors:

Does each case of invalid data for each field yield a correct error message?
Do lookup routines work properly?
When you correct the error, does the error message go away?
Does the program post transactions even though errors are detected?

What to check for as you enter compound errors:

Are all errors detected, or does the program only detect the first error in a transaction?
Are all errors properly indicated?

Figure 1-21   A checklist for testing an interactive program

Documentation

Required program documentation

1. Program specifications including program overview, print charts, screen layouts, and screen flow diagrams
2. Structure chart or structure listing showing all of the modules of the program
3. COBOL compiler listing

Other items that may be required

1. Job-control listings, test data listings, and test run output for each test run in the systems or acceptance tests
2. User guide prepared by the programmer

Find out what is required in your shop.

Subprogram documentation

If you write a subprogram that will be used by the programming staff, you must prepare user instructions that tell the other programmers what your subprogram does and how to use it. This usually can be done on a single sheet of paper as illustrated in figure 1-22. One copy of these instructions must then be kept as part of the documentation for the subprogram. Another copy must be filed with the documentation for all subprograms that shows the programmers what's available.

Structure listing software

If you have a structure listing program in your shop, use it to document the structure of your program. A structure listing program prepares a structure listing like the one in figure 1-23 from your COBOL code. This is a simple listing of the modules of a program with indentation used to show the levels of the modules. The one shown in figure 1-23 corresponds to the structure chart for the model edit program.

Subprogram name: DATEDIT

Programmer: Steve Eckols

Date: 6-30-83

Function: This program evaluates a six-character date in the format MMDDYY (month-day-year) and sets a one-character switch field to "Y" if the date is logically valid or to "N" if it is not.

Editing: All three fields within the date must be numeric.

                     The month field must have one of these values:
                     01, 02, 03, 04, 05, 06, 07, 08, 09, 10, 11, or 12.

                     If the month field has value 02, then the day field value must be between 01 and 28 if it is not a leap year (i.e., if the year field value is not evenly divisible by 4).

                     If the month field has value 02, then the day field value must be between 01 and 29 if it is a leap year (i.e., if the year field value is evenly divisible by 4).

                     If the month field has value 01, 03, 05, 07, 08, 10, or 12, then the day field value must be between 01 and 31.

                     If the month field has value 04, 06, 09, or 11, then the day field value must be between 01 and 30.

                     If all of these editing criteria are met, the switch field value is set to "Y". Otherwise, the switch field is set to "N".

Use: To use this program, code these (or similarly named) fields in the WORKING-STORAGE SECTION of your COBOL program:

```
05   VALID-DATE-SW       PIC X.
     88  VALID-DATE                VALUE 'Y'.
              .
              .
              .
05   CURRENT-DATE.
     10   CURRENT-MONTH  PIC XX.
     10   CURRENT-DAY    PIC XX.
     10   CURRENT-YEAR   PIC XX.
```

                     Then, code this CALL statement in your PROCEDURE DIVISION:

```
CALL 'DATEDIT' USING VALID-DATE-SW
                     CURRENT-DATE.
```

Figure 1-22   An acceptable user's guide for a subprogram

```
✿
  000-EDIT-INVENTORY-TRANS
✿
      100-FORMAT-REPORT-HEADING
✿
          'SYSDATE'
          'SYSTIME'
✿
      200-LOAD-PART-NUMBER-TABLE
✿
          210-READ-PART-NUMBER-RECORD
✿
      300-EDIT-INVENTORY-TRAN
✿
          310-READ-INVENTORY-TRAN
          320-EDIT-TRANSACTION-FIELDS
      ✿
              330-EDIT-CODE-1-FIELDS
          ✿
                  'DATEDIT'                        C
                  340-SEARCH-PART-NUMBER-TABLE     C
              ✿
              350-EDIT-CODE-2-FIELDS
          ✿
                  'DATEDIT'                        C
                  340-SEARCH-PART-NUMBER-TABLE     C
                  ✿
      ✿
          360-PRINT-INVALID-TRANSACTION
      ✿
              370-PRINT-HEADING-LINES
          ✿
                  380-WRITE-PAGE-TOP-LINE          C
                  390-WRITE-REPORT-LINE            C
              ✿
              390-WRITE-REPORT-LINE            C
          ✿
          400-WRITE-VALID-TRANSACTION
      ✿
      500-PRINT-TOTAL-PAGE
      ✿
          380-WRITE-PAGE-TOP-LINE      C
          390-WRITE-REPORT-LINE        C
          ✿
✿

C = COMMON MODULE
```

Figure 1-23   A structure listing for the edit program that is charted in figure 1-7

If you don't have a structure listing program, you can get
one from us. This is an inexpensive program written in
structured ANS COBOL that we supply in source code form.
As a result, you can easily modify it to run on your system.
Write or call us for details.

Walkthroughs

General information

Formal walkthroughs can be conducted at several different times during the development of a program. Some typical times for walkthroughs follow:

1. After the program specifications have been developed (a *program specification walkthrough*)
2. After the program is designed (a *design walkthrough* covering structure chart only or structure chart and HIPO diagrams)
3. After the test plan and test data have been developed (a *test plan walkthrough*)
4. After the program or selected modules of a program have been coded, but before they have been tested (a *coding walkthrough*)
5. After the program or selected modules of a program have been coded and tested (a *coding walkthrough*)
6. After the user guide has been prepared (a *user guide walkthrough*)

Find out what kinds of walkthroughs, if any, are required in your shop.

In addition, informal walkthroughs can be held at any time during the development of a program. This can simply mean, for example, that one programmer reviews your coding and user guides, and you do the same for him. If you are concerned about any phase of development, you should at least initiate an informal walkthrough.

Walkthrough format

1. A walkthrough is initiated by a programmer when he's ready for a public review of some phase of his work.
2. The programmer invites from two to six colleagues to participate in the walkthrough (two or three is usually better than five or six).
3. No managers are allowed at a walkthrough—this is a time for finding errors, not for evaluating programmers.

4. At least 48 hours before the meeting, the programmer gives an agenda like the one in figure 1-24 to the participants. Besides giving general information about when and where the meeting will be held, the agenda specifies the program name, the type of walkthrough that will be held, the material that will be reviewed, and the walkthrough objectives (that is, what the materials are to be reviewed for).

5. Along with the agenda, the programmer hands out copies of the materials listed on the agenda to each participant. The participants then have at least 48 hours to review the materials so they will be prepared for the actual walkthrough.

6. At the walkthrough, an action list is made of all the questions, errors, and possible trouble spots raised during the meeting. However, no attempt is made at this time to correct anything. The purpose of the walkthrough meeting is error detection, not correction.

7. The programmer follows up the meeting in two ways. First, within an hour of the meeting, he makes and distributes copies of the action list to each of the walkthrough participants. Second, within two days of the meeting, he lets each of the participants know in writing what he did to resolve each of the items on the action list.

The meeting

1. Select one participant to be moderator and one to be recorder. In general, the programmer should be neither moderator or recorder. The moderator's job is to keep the meeting on track; it's up to him or her to make sure the comments don't become too trivial or too personal. The recorder is in charge of writing down items on the action list.

2. The main part of the walkthrough consists of detecting errors. Sometimes, however, the meeting begins with the programmer giving an overview of his program. Since the materials given to the participants are usually self-explanatory, a walkthrough should *not* begin with an overview unless there is a solid reason for having one.

3. When a question is raised, the programmer should be given a chance to explain his work. If it's agreed that the point is or could be a problem, it goes on the action list.

Walkthrough Agenda

Notice date: August 25, 1984

Originator: Paul Noll

Meeting date and time: Friday   August 27   1:30 P.M.

Location: Room 578

Program: Produce sales report

Type of Walkthrough: Design

Materials:

1 Specifications

2 Structure chart

3 HIPO diagrams for all control modules

4

5

Objectives:
Please review for

1 Completeness and logic

2 Meaningful names

3 Naming consistency

4

5

Team:

	Name	Present	Resolution Initials	Date
Moderator	Mike Murach	Yes		
Recorder	Doug Lowe	Yes		
Member 1	Judy Taylor	Yes		
Member 2				
Member 3				
Member 4				

Date of resolution August 30, 1984   **Originator's signature**

Figure 1-24   A walkthrough form that serves as an agenda and as a record of followup

Action List

Originator: Paul Noll
Program: Produce sales report
Type of walkthrough: Design

Questions:

1. Is there an unnecessary level in the structure chart? Can modules 130, 140, and 150 be moved from level 3 to level 2?

2. Will module 120 process the first record in the file?

3. Should control field changes be made in module 120 (the major control module) rather than in the print modules?

4. Is the module name for module 120 meaningful?

5. Inconsistency in use of TR and TRAN in several HIPO diagrams (marked in red and returned).

Resolution:

Changed. The modules have been moved to level 2. See attached structure chart.

Changed. It didn't work. See attached HIPO diagram

Changed. I moved the control field changes from the print modules to module 120. See attached HIPO diagram.

Changed. From "process sales record" to "produce sales line."

Changed. All references are now TRAN.

Figure 1-25   An action list for a design walkthrough including resolution of the questions raised

4. Avoid pointing up trivial errors (such as syntax errors, missing punctuation, or inconsistent names) at the walkthrough. Instead, a participant should mark these errors in red on his own materials and hand them to the programmer at the end of the meeting.

5. All of the walkthrough members should participate actively in the meeting. To do this, they have to prepare ahead of time by going through the walkthrough materials the programmer gave them and listing any problem areas and errors they find. Then at the meeting, they'll be able to raise their own questions, as well as intelligently discuss the points raised by the other participants.

Followup

1. The easiest way for a programmer to tell the other walkthrough members what he did about the items on an action list is to simply write his resolutions on the action list itself. (This is shown in figure 1-25.) Then he can

make copies and distribute them. Notice that the explanations aren't long, but they say enough so the other participants know what action was taken on each point.

2. If a major error is found in a walkthrough, the best resolution may be for the programmer to redo the material and hold another walkthrough.

3. Anytime a formal walkthrough is held, a report should be made to management. The easiest way to do this is to use an agenda form like the one in figure 1-24. After the participants are satisfied with the programmer's resolution of the points on the action list, they initial the form; then the originator signs it and turns it in. Notice that the form simply gives the agenda and states that all the problems were solved. It doesn't give any indication of who found how many errors, how many errors there were in all, how crucial or trivial the errors were, etc.

Checklist for effective walkthroughs

1. No manager present
2. Error detection only
3. Two hour time limit
4. The right participants
5. Vested interests
6. Show results
7. No counting
8. Professional behavior only

Section 2

Standards for CICS program development

This section presents standards for developing CICS programs on an IBM system. As a result, if you don't use CICS in your shop, you can skip this section. On the other hand, you may want to use this section as a guide for developing interactive standards that are specific to your system.

In general, you should think of this section as an extension to and modification of the standards in section 1. In other words, this section only presents those standards that specifically apply to CICS programs. As a result, a CICS user should combine the general standards of section 1 with the specific standards of section 2.

The standards in this section were developed by Doug Lowe as presented in his book, *CICS for the COBOL Programmer (Part 1)*. If you are interested in knowing more about CICS or about the background behind these standards, we recommend that you read Doug's book.

A program development procedure

The preferred sequence for CICS program development is given in figure 2-1. Of the ten tasks, only two apply specifically to CICS programs. In task 6, you must be sure that the appropriate CICS tables are updated before you try to test your program. In task 7, you must create the mapsets required by your program before you can code the program in COBOL.

Within the analysis, design, and implementation phases, you may rearrange and overlap the development tasks somewhat. During the implementation phase, for example, you obviously need to update the CICS tables, create the test data, and code a portion of the program before you can start to test the program. But to some extent the sequence in which you do these tasks depends upon the program you're writing and your personal preferences.

If you use walkthroughs in your shop, they should become part of your development sequence. If, for example, you use both specification and design walkthroughs, the preferred development sequence becomes this:

1. Analyze the programming problem.
2. Conduct a specification walkthrough.
3. Design the program.
4. Conduct a design walkthrough.
5. Implement the program.

Analysis

1. Get complete specifications.
2. Get related programs, COPY members, and subprograms.

Design

3. Design the program using a structure chart.
4. If necessary, plan the modules of the program using pseudocode or HIPO diagrams.

Implementation

5. Plan the testing of the program by creating a test plan.
6. Make sure that the appropriate CICS tables are updated so you will be able to run your program later on.
7. Create the BMS mapsets required by your program. Instead of using the symbolic mapset generated by BMS, create your own symbolic mapset.
8. If necessary, create the test data for the test runs.
9. Code and test the program using top-down testing.
10. Document the program.

Figure 2-1   The preferred sequence of tasks for developing a CICS program

Developing program specifications

When you develop a CICS program, you start by making sure you have complete program specifications just as you must do for any program you're developing. In many cases, this will mean that you must develop screen layouts for all of the screens used by the program as well as a screen flow diagram that shows the sequence in which these screens are used.

Screen flow diagrams

You should develop a screen flow diagram for a CICS program whenever you have trouble visualizing it. For instance, figure 2-2 shows a screen flow diagram for a typical CICS program in which the operator is given a chance to sight-verify the data he has entered after he enters it. As you can see, the flow lines indicate the keys on the 3270 keyboard that initiate certain actions. For instance, the use of the CLEAR key when the order-entry screen is in operation causes the program to send a termination message and end the session. And the use of the PA1 key when the order-verification screen is in operation causes the order-entry screen to be sent to the terminal so the operator can modify his entries.

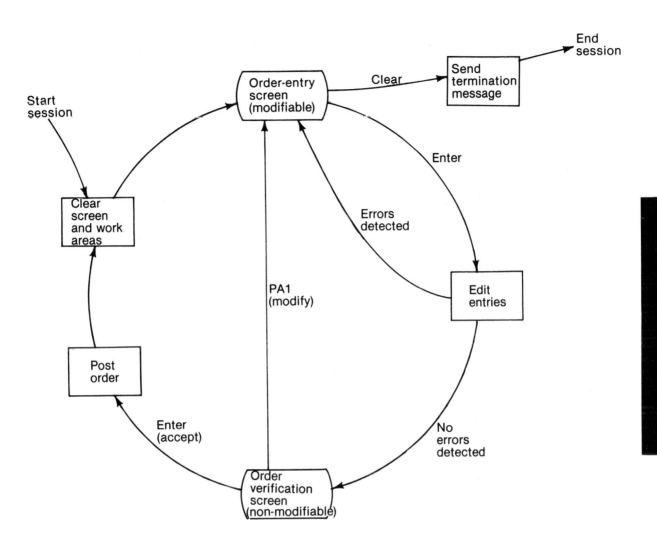

Figure 2-2   A screen flow diagram for an order-entry program

Using related programs,
COPY members, and subprograms

Using related programs

Since most CICS programs have the same general structure,
you should be able to make effective use of old CICS
programs when you develop new ones. In the design and
COBOL portions of this section, for example, you can see
some typical design and coding elements. By reusing these
from one program to the next, you can improve your
development productivity considerably.

When you first start developing CICS programs using the
methods presented in *How to Design and Develop COBOL
Programs*, you won't have a collection of programs that you
can use as a basis for new programs. So you can use model
program 7 in this book to help you get started. In a short
time, however, you should be able to develop your own
library of effective CICS programs.

Using COPY members

To start, the COPY library should include a COPY member
for each record format for each file that your program
requires. In addition, it should include a COPY member for
the field attribute characters required for screen handling. At
the least, then, you should make sure that you find and use
these members.

Because the IBM-supplied COPY member for field
attribute characters isn't very good, we recommend that you
develop your own. For instance, figure 2-3 shows the COPY
member that we use for field attribute characters.

After you find the COPY members for record descriptions
and field attribute characters, you should check to see
whether you want to use any other COPY members in your
program.

```
BKEND    C.FACDEFN

*
 01  FIELD-ATTRIBUTE-CHARACTERS.
*
     05  FAC-UNPROT                      PIC X       VALUE ' '.
     05  FAC-UNPROT-MDT                  PIC X       VALUE 'A'.
     05  FAC-UNPROT-BRT                  PIC X       VALUE 'H'.
     05  FAC-UNPROT-BRT-MDT              PIC X       VALUE 'I'.
     05  FAC-UNPROT-DARK                 PIC X       VALUE '<'.
     05  FAC-UNPROT-DARK-MDT             PIC X       VALUE '('.
     05  FAC-UNPROT-NUM                  PIC X       VALUE '&'.
     05  FAC-UNPROT-NUM-MDT              PIC X       VALUE 'J'.
     05  FAC-UNPROT-NUM-BRT              PIC X       VALUE 'Q'.
     05  FAC-UNPROT-NUM-BRT-MDT          PIC X       VALUE 'R'.
     05  FAC-UNPROT-NUM-DARK             PIC X       VALUE '*'.
     05  FAC-UNPROT-NUM-DARK-MDT         PIC X       VALUE ')'.
     05  FAC-PROT                        PIC X       VALUE '-'.
     05  FAC-PROT-MDT                    PIC X       VALUE '/'.
     05  FAC-PROT-BRT                    PIC X       VALUE 'Y'.
     05  FAC-PROT-BRT-MDT                PIC X       VALUE 'Z'.
     05  FAC-PROT-DARK                   PIC X       VALUE 'x'.
     05  FAC-PROT-DARK-MDT               PIC X       VALUE ' '.
     05  FAC-PROT-NUM                    PIC X       VALUE '0'.
     05  FAC-PROT-NUM-MDT                PIC X       VALUE '1'.
     05  FAC-PROT-NUM-BRT                PIC X       VALUE '8'.
     05  FAC-PROT-NUM-BRT-MDT            PIC X       VALUE '9'.
     05  FAC-PROT-NUM-DARK               PIC X       VALUE 'a'.
     05  FAC-PROT-NUM-DARK-MDT           PIC X       VALUE QUOTE.

BKEND
```

Figure 2-3   A COPY member for field attribute characters

Program design

General information

Use top-down design for the development of all programs. As documentation for your design, use a structure chart as shown in figure 2-4. This is the structure chart for an order-entry program.

Because you should use pseudo-conversational programming techniques when you develop CICS programs, the design of a CICS program differs from that of a non-CICS program. In particular, the top-level module of a CICS program calls all of the major processing modules of the program. In a non-CICS program, the top-level module calls a level-1 module that repeatedly executes the major processing modules of the program. So a CICS program has one less level of structure than a comparable non-CICS program.

Level 0

This level should contain one module that represents the entire program. In a pseudo-conversational program, the

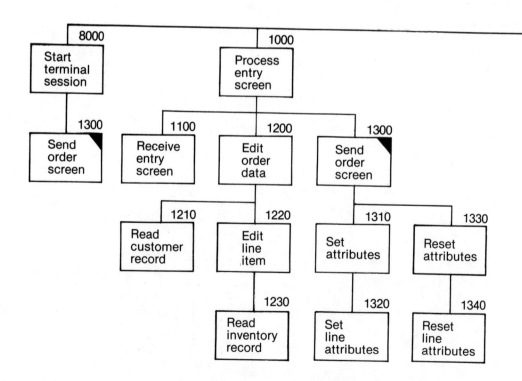

Figure 2-4　　A structure chart for an order-entry program

program ends each time a screen is sent to a terminal awaiting a response from the operator. Then, when the operator presses one of the attention-identifier keys (AID keys), CICS restarts the program by calling the top-level module. As a result, this module is repeatedly executed as the operator uses the screens of the program.

Level 1

In general, this level consists of one module for each screen used by the program. In addition, it should include one start-terminal-session module that properly formats the first screen. And it may include a send-termination-message module that's only executed at the end of the terminal session.

The structure chart in figure 2-4 uses all of these level-1 modules. From left to right, it has a start-terminal-session module, one module for each of the screens shown in the screen flow diagram in figure 2-2, and a send-termination-message module.

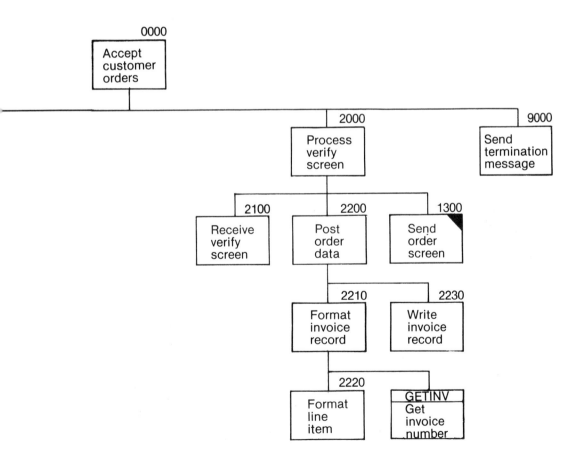

Level 2 and below

For each screen your program processes, you must provide for at least three functions: (1) receiving the data from the screen, (2) processing the data, and (3) sending the next screen. As a result, most of your programs will have level-2 modules like those shown in the structure chart in figure 2-4. As you can see, each of the screen-handling modules calls a receive-screen module, a processing module, and send-screen module. If necessary, however, a level-1 module can call more than one processing or send-screen module at level 2 of the structure chart.

Below level 2, the structure of the program depends on the program specifications. In general, you design these levels just as you would in a non-CICS program. However, all I/O statements will be coded as CICS commands rather than COBOL statements.

Verb list

Figure 1-8 in section 1 is a list of module verbs broken down by type (input, output, or processing). We have suggested meanings for all of them; and these meanings conform to the way the verbs are used in the programs presented in this handbook.

When you use CICS, you will want to add two I/O verbs to this list. The first, *receive*, is an input verb that means to accept data from a screen. The second, *send*, is an output verb that means to display data on a screen, but it also implies the setting or resetting of field attribute characters before the screen is actually sent to the terminal.

Module numbers

1. The top-level module should be given the number 0000.
2. The level-1 modules should be given numbers that are multiples of 1000. For object-program efficiency, the start-terminal-session module should be numbered 8000, and the send-termination-message module, if there is one, should be numbered 9000. Then, from left to right, the screen-handling modules should be numbered by 1000 starting with 1000. In a large program, if you have more screens than you can handle with this numbering system, you can number the level-1 modules using smaller increments, such as increments of 500.

3. From level 2 on down, the modules should be numbered by 10s or 100s. Often, it's most efficient to number down the legs as illustrated in figure 2-4. That way, all of the COBOL code for a leg will be found in consecutive paragraphs in the COBOL listing.

Isolate I/O functions by putting them in separate I/O modules

When you develop CICS programs, you should isolate both file and terminal I/O functions for two reasons. First, they have a significant effect on the structure of your programs. Second, in most cases, CICS requires you to use branching logic within a module to process exceptional conditions. By obeying this standard, your programs will be easier to design, develop, and maintain.

Checklist for review and analysis of a structure chart

1. Is the structure chart complete? (Does each module have all of its subfunctions represented by subordinate modules?)
2. Does each module name represent only one function? (Does the module name correspond to a single imperative sentence?)
3. Is proper subordination shown? (Is the function of each called module logically contained in the function of the calling module?)
4. Are the I/O functions in separate modules so they can be coded as COBOL sections?
5. Are the control spans reasonable?
6. Are the modules independent? (Are control codes only passed to the calling module?)
7. Are the verbs consistent? (Do the same verbs always imply the same functions?)

Creating BMS mapsets

When you develop CICS programs, you should use Basic Mapping Support (BMS), which is a component of CICS. To use BMS, you have to write an assembler-language program called a mapset. This program will define the screens used by your program.

After you've coded the mapset in assembler language, it must be assembled. When it's assembled, it transforms your mapset into two mapsets, a physical mapset and a symbolic mapset. The physical mapset is a load module that is used by BMS. The symbolic mapset is a COPY member that you use in your COBOL program.

If your shop has a mapset generator, you will probably want to use it. Once you get used to it, it should help you increase your productivity.

Creating your own symbolic maps

Because the symbolic maps generated by the assembler are not easy to read and use, we recommend that you create your own symbolic maps for the screens used by your program. For instance, figure 2-5 shows a symbolic map created by a programmer as opposed to one generated by BMS.

Some rules for creating symbolic maps follow:

1. Code only one 01 item for each map, and choose a name for it that corresponds to the screen name you used on the layout form for the screen. For instance, a map named CUSTOMER-DATA-MAP corresponds to a layout form for a screen named *customer data screen*.

2. Don't forget to code a 12-byte FILLER item at the beginning of each map.

3. For each map field, code three data names using these rules:

    a. Start each data name with a two- or three-character prefix that's an abbreviation of the map name. For instance, CDM could be the prefix for the CUSTOMER-DATA-MAP.

    b. Include one character to define the field's function: L for length, A for attribute, or D for data.

    c. Create a meaningful name for each field such as CDM-L-CUSTOMER-NUMBER. To do so, you should separate each component of the name with a hyphen.

```
BKEND    C.ORDSET1

01  ORDER-ENTRY-MAP.
*
    05  FILLER                        PIC X(12).
*
    05  OEM-L-CUSTOMER-NUMBER         PIC S9(4)    COMP.
    05  OEM-A-CUSTOMER-NUMBER         PIC X.
    05  OEM-D-CUSTOMER-NUMBER         PIC X(5).
*
    05  OEM-L-NAME                    PIC S9(4)    COMP.
    05  OEM-A-NAME                    PIC X.
    05  OEM-D-NAME                    PIC X(30).
*
    05  OEM-L-PO-NUMBER               PIC S9(4)    COMP.
    05  OEM-A-PO-NUMBER               PIC X.
    05  OEM-D-PO-NUMBER               PIC X(10).
*
    05  OEM-LINE-ITEM                 OCCURS 10.
*
        10  OEM-L-ITEM-NUMBER         PIC S9(4)    COMP.
        10  OEM-A-ITEM-NUMBER         PIC X.
        10  OEM-D-ITEM-NUMBER         PIC 9(5).
*
        10  OEM-L-QUANTITY            PIC S9(4)    COMP.
        10  OEM-A-QUANTITY            PIC X.
        10  OEM-D-QUANTITY            PIC 9(5).
*
        10  OEM-L-ITEM-DESCRIPTION    PIC S9(4)    COMP.
        10  OEM-A-ITEM-DESCRIPTION    PIC X.
        10  OEM-D-ITEM-DESCRIPTION    PIC X(20).
*
        10  OEM-L-UNIT-PRICE          PIC S9(4)    COMP.
        10  OEM-A-UNIT-PRICE          PIC X.
        10  OEM-D-UNIT-PRICE          PIC ZZ,ZZ9.99
                                      BLANK WHEN ZERO.
*
        10  OEM-L-EXTENSION           PIC S9(4)    COMP.
        10  OEM-A-EXTENSION           PIC X.
        10  OEM-D-EXTENSION           PIC ZZ,ZZ9.99
                                      BLANK WHEN ZERO.
*
    05  OEM-L-INVOICE-TOTAL           PIC S9(4)    COMP.
    05  OEM-A-INVOICE-TOTAL           PIC X.
    05  OEM-D-INVOICE-TOTAL           PIC ZZ,ZZ9.99
                                      BLANK WHEN ZERO.
*
    05  OEM-L-OPERATOR-MESSAGE        PIC S9(4)    COMP.
    05  OEM-A-OPERATOR-MESSAGE        PIC X.
    05  OEM-D-OPERATOR-MESSAGE        PIC X(79).
*
    05  OEM-L-ERROR-MESSAGE           PIC S9(4)    COMP.
    05  OEM-A-ERROR-MESSAGE           PIC X.
    05  OEM-D-ERROR-MESSAGE           PIC X(77).
*
    05  OEM-L-DUMMY                   PIC S9(4)    COMP.
    05  OEM-A-DUMMY                   PIC X.
    05  OEM-D-DUMMY                   PIC X.
*

    BKEND
```

Figure 2-5   A symbolic map that was created by the programmer for an order-entry screen

COBOL coding

Data Division

Sequence of code   In general, you should code the elements in the Data Division in the same sequence that you would use for a non-CICS program: (1) groups of work fields, (2) record descriptions, and (3) screen-handling fields. Within the screen-handling portion of the Data Division, we recommend the sequence of code shown in figure 2-6.

The communication area   When a pseudo-conversational program ends after sending a screen to a terminal, the data in its Working-Storage Section is lost unless it's explicitly saved. In most programs, however, you will want to pass some data from one execution of the program to the next. One way to do this is to save fields in the communication area.

When you use a communication area in your program, you should name it COMMUNICATION-AREA, and you should code it at the 01 level. Then, code the major groups of the communication area starting at the 05 level in the same sequence that you'd use in a non-CICS program: switches, then flags, and so on. All field names in the communication area should start with CA-, but otherwise follow the basic rules for naming any field in the Data Division.

Field attribute characters   If your program is going to change any field attributes, you will probably want to include a working-storage group that contains the values of commonly used attribute bytes. If you do, you should use your shop's COPY member for this purpose, such as the one shown in figure 2-3.

Symbolic maps   You use a COPY statement to copy a symbolic mapset into your program. As explained in the section on BMS mapsets, we recommend that you create your own COPY members rather than use those generated by the assembler. If you do, you will improve the readability of your program.

Linkage-Section fields   Although the CICS command translator will automatically generate a one-byte entry for DFHCOMMAREA if you don't code one, you should always code it yourself. This entry should be the same length as the communication area you coded earlier.

Communication area
    Switches
    Flags
    Control total fields
    Record descriptions

Field attribute characters (COPY member)

Symbolic maps (COPY members)

Linkage section
    DFHCOMMAREA
    Execute Interface Block

Figure 2-6   The coding sequence for CICS fields in the screen-handling portion of the Data Division

Procedure Division

Coding a module on the structure chart   The three principles that follow are essential to the quality of a CICS program:

1. Each module in the structure chart is coded as a COBOL section.
2. The section name for each module consists of the module's number and name taken from the structure chart. The number and name are separated by hyphens with the number first. The section name, of course, must be followed by the word SECTION.
3. The sections are placed in the program in the order specified by their module numbers.

Forbidden usages   When you code a CICS program, you code each module as a section. Then, you can use more than one paragraph within a section to handle the implied GOTOs of a CICS command. This in turn leads you to the use of GO TO statements and an EXIT paragraph that makes use of the EXIT statement. As a result, the list of forbidden usages in a CICS program is shorter than the list for non-CICS programs.

The forbidden usages follow:

1. ALTER
2. GO TO DEPENDING (use linear IFs for implementing the case structure)
3. PERFORM THRU

Operator communication statements	ACCEPT
	DISPLAY
File I/O statements	OPEN
	CLOSE
	READ
	WRITE
	REWRITE
	DELETE
	START
Program termination statements	STOP RUN
	GOBACK
Sort statements	SORT
	RELEASE
	RETURN
Debugging statements	EXHIBIT
	TRACE
String manipulation statements	INSPECT
	UNSTRING
Segmentation feature	
Report Writer feature	

Note: The shaded verbs will be supported by the COBOL II compiler when using CICS.

Figure 2-7   COBOL elements not supported under CICS

Usages that aren't supported under CICS   Figure 2-7 lists the COBOL elements that aren't currently supported when you're running a program under CICS. However, some of these elements will be supported under COBOL II. These include the STOP, GOBACK, INSPECT, and UNSTRING statements.

Coding CICS commands   When you code a CICS command, you should separate the options by blanks, not commas. In addition, you should code each option on a separate line. In other words, your commands will have this general format:

```
000-MAINTAIN-CUSTOMER-FILE SECTION.
*
     EXEC CICS
         ADDRESS CWA(BLL-CWA)
     END-EXEC.
     IF EIBCALEN = ZERO
         PERFORM 8000-START-TERMINAL-SESSION
     ELSE
         MOVE DFHCOMMAREA TO COMMUNICATION-AREA
         IF PROCESS-ACTION-SCREEN
             PERFORM 1000-PROCESS-ACTION-SCREEN
         ELSE IF PROCESS-CUSTOMER-SCREEN
             PERFORM 2000-PROCESS-CUSTOMER-SCREEN
         ELSE
             PERFORM 3000-PROCESS-VERIFY-SCREEN.
     IF END-SESSION
         EXEC CICS
             XCTL PROGRAM('MNT2000')
         END-EXEC
     ELSE
         EXEC CICS
             RETURN TRANSID('MT21')
                    COMMAREA(COMMUNICATION-AREA)
                    LENGTH(2)
         END-EXEC.
*
```

Figure 2-8   The level-0 module of the CICS model program

```
EXEC CICS
     command option-1(value)
             option-2(value)
                 .
                 .
             option-n(value)
END-EXEC.
```

Coding the level-0 module   Figure 2-8 gives the coding for
the level-0 module of the CICS model program in this
handbook. It illustrates the basic coding structure that a
level-0 module should have. A module like this should start by
checking the value of one of the fields in the Linkage Section
(EIBCALEN) to see if this is the first time the program is
invoked. If it is (EIBCALEN = ZERO), the module should
call the start-terminal-session module. If it isn't, it should
check the values in the communication area to see which of
its screen-handling modules it should call.

After the appropriate screen-handling module has been
executed, the program should end its current execution. If the
operator has indicated that the session should end, the
program should call a send-termination-message module if
there is one and then transfer control to another program.

```
xxxx-module-name SECTION.

    HANDLE AID or HANDLE CONDITION command.
    CICS command that requires the HANDLE AID or HANDLE CONDITION
        command.
    GO TO xxxx-EXIT.


xxxx-routine-1.

    COBOL statements for key-or-condition-1.
    GO TO xxxx-EXIT.


xxxx-routine-2.

    COBOL statements for key-or-condition-2.
    GO TO xxxx-EXIT.


        .
        .
        .


xxxx-routine-n.

    COBOL statements for key-or-condition-n.
    GO TO xxxx-EXIT.


xxxx-EXIT.

    EXIT.
```

Figure 2-9   The general structure of a module containing a HANDLE AID or HANDLE CONDITION command

Otherwise, it should issue a RETURN command that specifies (1) how the program should be restarted the next time the operator presses an AID key and (2) that the communication area should be saved for the next program execution.

Coding I/O modules that require branching   Figure 2-9 gives the general structure you should use for an I/O module that requires branching. You start by coding a paragraph within the section that contains the HANDLE CONDITION or HANDLE AID command and its associated CICS command. For instance, the first paragraph of a read module would contain a CICS READ command and its associated HANDLE CONDITION command. Similarly, the first

```
IF error-condition-1 for field-1
    MOVE attribute-character TO attribute-field for field-1
    MOVE -1                  TO length-field for field-1
    MOVE error-message       TO error-message-field
ELSE IF error-condition-2 for field-1
    .
    .
    .

IF error-condition-1 for field-2
    .
    .
    .

IF error-message-field NOT = LOW-VALUE
    MOVE 'N' TO VALID-DATA-SW.
```

Note: Fields should be tested in the reverse order of how they appear on the screen.

Figure 2-10   An effective structure for an edit module

Standards for CICS program development

paragraph of a receive module would contain a RECEIVE
MAP command and its associated HANDLE AID command.
Before or after the CICS commands, the first paragraph may
contain other CICS commands or COBOL statements, but in
most cases it won't need to. The first paragraph ends with a
GO TO statement that branches to the last paragraph in the
section, an EXIT paragraph.

Between the first and last paragraphs of the section, you
code one paragraph for each option you coded in the
HANDLE AID or HANDLE CONDITION command in the
first paragraph. Each of these paragraphs is named using the
module number and the name of the condition or key being
processed. For instance, you would code a paragraph named
1200-NOTFND in a section named 1200-READ-CUSTOMER-
RECORD to process the NOTFND condition. The last
statement in each of these intermediate paragraphs is a
GO TO statement that branches to the EXIT paragraph.
However, a GO TO statement in the last intermediate
paragraph is optional since control falls through to the EXIT
paragraph anyway.

Coding an edit module   Figure 2-10 gives a general
structure for an edit module in a CICS program. Basically,
you edit each field with a series of nested IF statements.
When you detect an error, you (1) modify the attribute field
so the error is highlighted, (2) move -1 to the length field so

the cursor will be placed under the field in error, and (3) move an appropriate error message to the error-message field. In general, you should edit the fields from the bottom of the screen to the top, so the error message will relate to the first error field on the screen and the cursor will be moved to this field.

Naturally, if the editing you're doing is complicated, you may want to divide the editing up into subordinate modules. Otherwise, the structure shown in figure 2-10 leads to highly readable code.

After all of the fields have been edited, the error-message field is tested for a value other than low-value. Since the error-message field is initialized to low-value before any editing is done, a value other than low-value means that the edit module detected an error. In that case, N is moved to VALID-DATA-SW so the calling module knows that an error was detected.

Testing

Updating CICS tables

Before you can test a CICS program, the appropriate CICS tables must be updated. For most programs, at least the processing program table (PPT) and the program control table (PCT) must be updated before you can run your program. In addition, your program may require changes in one or more other tables such as the file control table (FCT).

As an applications programmer, you probably won't update these tables yourself. However, you should be able to supply the table information that the systems programmer needs to update the tables.

The sequence of top-down testing

When top-down testing is used, you normally try to find the major errors first. When you develop CICS programs, the major errors often are related to your program's relationship with CICS itself. As a result, your test plan should provide for testing the CICS interface early.

For instance, the structure chart in figure 2-11 might represent the first phase of testing for the order-entry program charted in figure 2-4. Since the shaded modules are dummy modules, this tests the CICS interface without testing any of the processing modules. Once you're sure that the CICS interface works, you can continue testing just as you would for a non-CICS program.

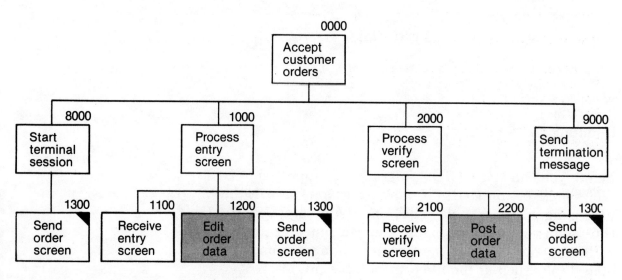

Note: The shaded modules are dummy modules.

Figure 2-11   Testing the CICS interface in an order-entry program

A checklist for CICS test runs

When you test a CICS program, it is often difficult to keep track of all that happens during a test run. As a result, you should use a checklist like the one in figure 2-12 to make sure that you have detected all errors.

What to check for as you examine the appearance of the screen:

Are all headings and captions placed correctly?
Is there any garbage on the screen?
Are there any misspellings?
Do all the fields have the correct attributes?
Is the cursor in the correct initial location?
Does the cursor move correctly from field to field?

What to check for as you enter valid data:

Are all program screens displayed in the correct sequence?
Do all AID keys work correctly?
Are the operator messages always correct?
Are the functions of all AID keys shown?
Does the program properly acknowledge receipt of valid data?
Are work fields properly cleared after each valid transaction?
Are control totals accumulated properly?
Are files updated properly?

What to check for as you enter single errors:

Does each case of invalid data for each field yield a correct error message?
Do lookup routines work properly?
Is the field in error highlighted?
Is the cursor positioned at the field in error?
When you correct the error, does the error message go away?
Does the program post transactions even though errors are detected?

What to check for as you enter compound errors:

Are all errors detected, or does the program only detect the first error in a transaction?
Is the cursor positioned under the first field in error, and is the corresponding error message displayed?
Are all errors highlighted?

Figure 2-12   What to check for when you test a CICS program

Documentation

Required program documentation

1. Program specifications including program overview, print charts, screen layouts, and screen flow diagrams
2. Structure chart or structure listing showing all of the modules of the program
3. Assembler-language source listing for the mapsets
4. Programmer-created symbolic mapset if you create your own
5. CICS translator listing
6. COBOL compiler listing

Other items that may be required

1. Test data listings and test run output for each test run in the systems or acceptance tests
2. User guide prepared by the programmer

Find out what is required in your shop.

Section 3

Batch program
analyses

This section presents analyses of the batch programs in section 5 of this handbook. For each of the four batch programs (model programs 1 through 4), this section gives additional perspective about the type of programming problem that the model program represents. Then, it gives additional information about the model program itself.

The four batch programs in section 5 represent the four basic types of batch programs: edit, report-preparation (or extract), sequential update or maintenance, and random update or maintenance. Although the trend in the data processing industry is to develop more interactive systems and fewer batch systems, batch programs will continue to be used for many years to come. And once you understand the programs for these basic batch functions, you will be better able to understand interactive programs that provide for these functions.

The edit program

General information

An edit program checks the records in a transaction file to make sure they contain valid data. If the edit program detects an invalid field within a record, the record is not released for further processing. In addition, the error record is usually listed on an error listing so the errors can be corrected and the data can be resubmitted for processing. If the edit program does not detect any invalid fields for a record, it releases the record for further processing. It usually does this by writing the valid records on a sequential transaction file that will be used to update and maintain master files.

In some installations, you will find an edit program referred to as a *validation*, or *verification*, *program*. However, these terms have taken on new meanings in interactive programming environments. As a result, we prefer the term *edit* to either of these other terms.

The basic structure of an edit program

Figure 3-1 presents a structure chart that shows the basic structure of an edit program. As you can see, the level-2 modules read a transaction record, edit the fields in the record, and either print an invalid transaction record on the invalid transaction listing or write a valid transaction on the valid transaction file.

At level 3, subordinate to the edit-transaction-fields module, you can have one or more modules to edit specific fields within the transaction record. For many fields, you won't need separate editing modules, because the field editing can be done in a few lines of code using IF statements. For some fields, however, you have to have separate editing modules. If, for example, a field must match a value in a table in order to be valid, the table search should be done in a separate module. Similarly, if a field like a date field is to be edited by a subprogram, this becomes a separate module on the structure chart. In general, you can create a separate module for any field that requires complex editing, and you should always create a separate module for a field that requires a table search or a subprogram.

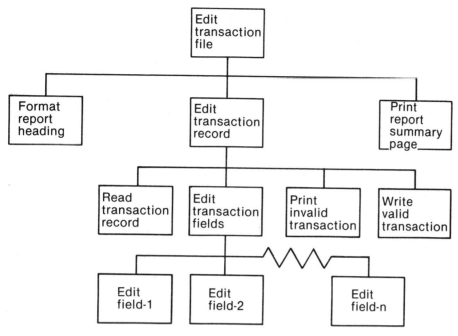

Figure 3-1   The basic structure of an edit program

I/O requirements

The basic I/O requirements of an edit program are (1) an input file of unedited transaction records and (2) an output file of valid transaction records. In addition, however, an edit program may require one or more files that contain data that is to be loaded into tables at the start of a program. Later, these tables are used by the editing routines for individual fields.

Sometimes, an edit program will edit the data in more than one file so it has to edit more than one type of record. For instance, a single edit program may edit the data in three files: a file of sales (issues from inventory), a file of receipts to inventory, and a file of returns from customers. A program like this may combine the valid transactions into a single file of transaction records that is processed in a subsequent file-updating job.

Some editing programs will also be required to sort either the input file or the output file. Normally, the transaction records come to an edit program in the sequence created by the entry operator. This sequence is often by date or time. But before the transactions can be processed by a sequential update or maintenance program, they must be sorted into the sequence of the master file that is going to be updated or maintained. So the edit program may have to sort the valid transactions into the appropriate sequence for updating or maintenance.

Fortunately, these variations in I/O requirements don't change the basic structure of an edit program. You should see them instead as minor variations that you can accommodate quite easily using the basic edit structure.

Printing requirements

The normal printing requirement of an edit program is a listing of the invalid transactions. Usually, this listing is in the same sequence as the input transaction file so the entry operators can locate the source documents for the invalid records more easily. By analyzing the listing and the source document, an entry operator should be able to correct the errors and reenter the transactions for processing.

To make it easier for operations people to correct invalid records, the error fields are usually highlighted on the error listing. This can be done by printing a message to the right of the error line indicating the fields in error. Or it can be done by printing an error code next to the fields that are in error. In some cases, it may be impossible to indicate all errors within a record, so the error listing only indicates the first error that is detected.

Editing requirements

The editing requirements, or rules, for the fields in a record may be simple or complex. For instance, they may be as simple as checking to make sure a field contains something (that it isn't blank); they may be as complex as looking a value up in a two-level table to make sure that the value falls within a certain range; and they may be more complex than that.

Perhaps the most common type of checking that is done within an edit program is making sure numeric fields contain numeric data. This type of checking will catch one of the most common types of entry errors—that is, skipping a required field so it contains blanks. Since attempting to perform an arithmetic operation on a blank field will often cause an abnormal program termination, *numeric checking* can save many reruns.

Beyond numeric checking, an edit program may do many other types of checks such as code checking, limit checking, and logical checking. *Code checking* refers to a test that makes sure a code is valid. For instance, 2, 3, 5, P, and T may be valid transaction codes, while L, 2, 3, 4, and 5 are valid customer-classification codes. *Limit checking* refers to a test that makes sure that the data in a field is within acceptable limits. For instance, the month in a date field shouldn't be over 12, and the day shouldn't be over 31. Finally, *logical checking* refers to a test for conditions that logically should never occur. For example, it is illogical that an hourly employee will work over 80 hours in one week.

In general, editing routines of more than a line or two of code that are common to many programs should be implemented in the form of subprograms. For instance, you should use subprograms for editing date fields, state codes, and zip codes. On the other hand, a simple test for valid numeric data takes only one COBOL statement so there's no point in implementing this test as a subprogram.

Combining program functions

For a couple of reasons, it's common to package one basic program function per program...particularly, on small systems. In this case, one program will do the edit function, another program will do the update function, and a third will do the file-maintenance function. This form of program packaging can simplify program development (the more functions per program, the more complex the program). And on systems with limited storage capacity, it may be the only way that a series of functions can be packaged.

On large systems, however, it's common to combine two or more functions in a single program. For instance, an edit program may be combined with the update or file-maintenance function. In model program 4, for example, a file of transaction records is sorted into master file sequence, the sorted records are edited, the master file is updated by the valid transactions, and a listing is printed for the invalid transactions. In most cases, combining functions like this can improve the operational efficiency of the computer system. And you shouldn't have much trouble combining editing functions with other program functions.

The model edit program

The edit program in this book is designed to show you some of the typical requirements of an edit program. On the other hand, it is quite straightforward so you shouldn't have much difficulty adapting its structure and code to other editing programs.

The program specifications

If you check the program specifications, you can see that this edit program edits two types of records: sales and return records. However, the record formats are so similar that one output line format can be used to list both types of invalid transactions. The error fields are highlighted on the error listing by printing an asterisk (*) to the left of each error field.

    If you check the editing rules in the program overview, you can see that all numeric fields are to be checked to make sure that they contain valid numeric data that is greater than zero. In addition, the date field must be edited using the subprogram DATEDIT, the branch number field must contain a number less than 25, and the part-number field must contain a number that can be found in the table of valid part numbers.

    Although loading a part-number table to check the validity of a part-number field may seem unrealistic, it depends on the company. For instance, we have thousands of customers but less than two dozen products, so in our company it may make sense to use a product-code table like the one in this edit program. On the other hand, if you had 40,000 parts, you probably wouldn't want to do a table-lookup like this. Then, if you absolutely had to make sure that the part-number was valid, you could look up the part-record in the part file on a random basis.

The structure chart

Since this program is limited in complexity, there aren't too many different ways that the structure chart can be structured. Obviously, the part-number table has to be read and loaded before starting to edit the transaction records. The report headings must be formatted before any printing can be done. And the total page must be printed after the records are edited. Moreover, all of the level-1 functions

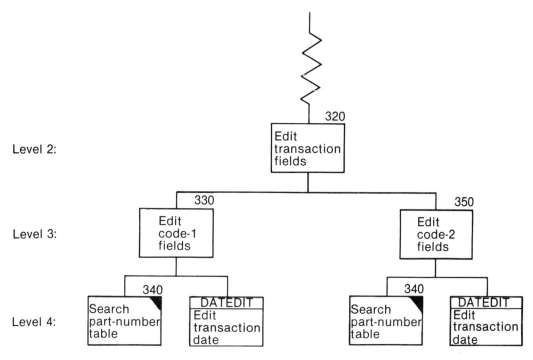

Figure 3-2   The edit leg of the structure chart for the model edit program

break down into clearly defined subfunctions. In my opinion, then, there isn't much that can be debated in the first three levels of the structure chart shown in section 5.

If there is room for debate, it concerns the edit leg of the structure chart as shown in figure 3-2. For instance, the first question my students usually raise is, why are two edit-fields modules needed at all? Since only four fields in the sales record differ from those in the return record, why shouldn't one module do the editing for both records?

My answer here is that one of the goals of structured programming is to provide for future changes (maintenance). And though it may be true that only four fields differ today, what about five years from now? Also, what if someone decides that this program should edit a third record type such as a receipt transaction? That's why I designed my structure chart to accommodate any changes in either the sales or the return record and to provide for the editing of any number of record types.

The next question that usually comes up is, why not add an edit-common-fields module to level 3 as shown in figure 3-3? My objection to this structure is that it would increase the complexity of module 320 since a count must be kept of valid and invalid transactions by transaction type. What's worse, however, the structure shown in figure 3-3 doesn't

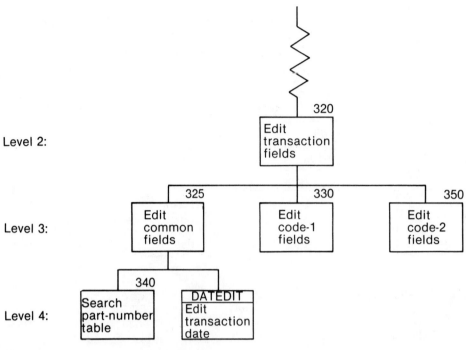

Figure 3-3   An unacceptable structure for using a module that edits the fields that are common to both record types

logically represent the program specifications. So if you want to use a common editing module, I recommend a structure like the one shown in figure 3-4.

The question now becomes, when should you use a common module for editing the fields that are found in both types of records and when should you simply duplicate the code? To me this depends on the amount of code that has to be duplicated. If the records have 20 fields in common, by all means use a common module. If only 3, why not duplicate the coding. In my opinion, this edit program with its 6 duplicate fields is on the borderline.

The COBOL code

To start, I want you to note how the use of the standards and guidelines in this book has led to an extremely readable program. By grouping switches, count fields, and print fields, the programmer has made it easy to find things in the working-storage section of the Data Division. Because the Procedure Division is structured and because indentation and blank comment cards are used within it, it is easy to read and understand from the top down.

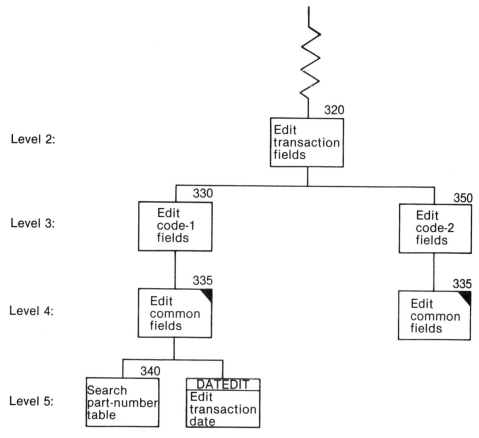

Level 2:

320
Edit
transaction
fields

Level 3:

330
Edit
code-1
fields

350
Edit
code-2
fields

Level 4:

335
Edit
common
fields

335
Edit
common
fields

Level 5:

340
Search
part-number
table

DATEDIT
Edit
transaction
date

Figure 3-4   An acceptable structure for using a module that edits the fields that are common to both record types

000-EDIT-INVENTORY-TRANS   In the Procedure Division, notice that the top-level module consists of an OPEN statement, four PERFORM statements, a CLOSE statement, and a STOP RUN statement. In many shops, however, a module like this would also send messages to the system operator indicating whether or not the program ran to a normal end of job.

On an IBM system, for example, this DISPLAY statement might be placed before the STOP RUN statement to indicate that the program ran to a normal end of job:

```
DISPLAY 'INV2100  I  1   NORMAL EOJ'
```

In this message, INV2100 is the program name; I means the message is for Information only; 1 means that this is the first message for this program; and NORMAL EOJ is the message itself. If you use messages like this in your shop, find out what the format is and make sure you use one in the top-level module of each of your programs.

In actual practice, the top-level module might also test to make sure that the required table has been loaded properly before the main processing routine begins. For instance, this module might test the value of PN-ENTRY-COUNT after the part-number table has been loaded to make sure that the file contains more than zero records and less than 101 records. If it doesn't, the table is either empty or it has overflowed the limits of its table definition. Then, an appropriate error message should be sent to the system operator and the end-of-file switch for the transaction file should be turned on so the program won't try to process the transaction file. To some extent, though, this depends on the design of the system rather than the program as discussed in the notes for module 200.

100-FORMAT-REPORT-HEADING   This module calls one subprogram to get the system date and another to get the system time. Since a COPY member is used for the standard portion of the heading, this module moves company name, report number, and report title into the standard areas defined by this COPY member. Otherwise, this heading data could be coded as constant values in the definitions for the heading lines in the Data Division.

200-LOAD-PART-NUMBER-TABLE   In module 200, you should realize that a value of zero will be put in the entry-count field (PN-ENTRY-COUNT) if the table file is empty (contains no records). Nevertheless, the program will continue, since module 000 doesn't stop if the table isn't loaded properly. And this means that all input transactions will be considered invalid because the part numbers will not be found in the part-number table.

This raises the question, should module 000 test for an empty table (PN-ENTRY-COUNT equal to zero) and stop if the table is empty? I think the answer depends on the design of the system. In a good system, the table file is printed at the time it is created, and later on it is checked by user personnel. As a result, the likelihood of an empty table file is low. In fact, even if the table file is not created properly and the mistake isn't caught by the user, the file will probably contain some records. For instance, it may contain some but not all of the records, or all of the records but not in the right sequence. So a test for an empty file really doesn't protect against the possibility of a faulty table file. Nevertheless, in the interest of eliminating one possible source of trouble, I do recommend checking for an empty table file in module 000.

We didn't do it in the model program, because we wanted to emphasize the essential code of a program like this.

Along the same lines, neither module 000 nor module 200 checks to make sure that no more than 100 part numbers are loaded into the part-number table. If the part-number file has been edited in a previous program so you can be sure there won't be more than 100 part-number records, this is no problem. Nevertheless, it can't hurt to check. As a result, I recommend changing module 000 so the PERFORM statement will stop executing module 100 (1) when the part-number file reaches EOF or (2) when PN-TABLE-INDEX is greater than 100. Here again, we didn't include this code in the model program because we wanted to emphasize the essential code of the program.

300-EDIT-INVENTORY-TRAN   In module 300, you might notice that nothing is done if module 310 detects the end-of-file condition for the transaction file. As a result, the program will not abort if the transaction file is empty.

310-READ-INVENTORY-TRAN   In module 310, the number of transaction records is counted after the READ statement is executed. This follows the principle of moving subfunctions down the line.

320-EDIT-TRANSACTION-FIELDS   In module 320, linear nesting is used to perform a different edit module for each valid transaction code. If the transaction code isn't valid, the linear nest executes the default code, which (1) highlights the transaction-code field as invalid, (2) moves N to the valid-transaction switch, and (3) adds one to the invalid-transaction-code count.

330-EDIT-CODE-1-FIELDS   Module 330 illustrates why the design shown in figure 3-3 shouldn't be used. If the editing for code-1 records is divided over two modules at the same level, it becomes more difficult to keep the count of valid and invalid sales transactions.

As you can see, the code in this module is as straight-forward as possible. The fields are edited in the same sequence as the fields within the record. If any field is found to be invalid, a value of N is moved to the valid-transaction switch and the error indicator (*) is moved into the print-line to highlight the field in error. To make the code even easier to follow, the programmer could have used blank comment lines to separate the editing code for each of the fields in the record, but I don't think it's necessary in this case.

340-SEARCH-PART-NUMBER-TABLE   Module 340 is the module that searches the part-number table. A search routine should always be coded in its own module since (1) the code it generates isn't trivial and (2) it is likely to be called from several parts of the program.

350-EDIT-CODE-2-FIELDS   This module is analagous to module 330.

360-PRINT-INVALID-TRANSACTION   In module 360, note that a data name (LINES-ON-PAGE) is used to indicate the number of lines that should be printed on each page, including all of the heading lines. Because this number may have to be changed due to operational changes, you should never use a literal for this purpose. Also, because page overflow takes place when LINE-COUNT is greater than LINES-ON-PAGE, LINES-ON-PAGE should have a value that is one less than the number of lines to be printed on each page.

380-WRITE-PAGE-TOP-LINE   Note that LINE-COUNT is set to 1 in this module to indicate that one line has been printed on the current page. Although this could also be done in module 370, it is logical here and it follows the principle of moving subfunctions down the line.

390-WRITE-REPORT-LINE   Module 390 writes all the lines on the invalid-transaction listing except the first line on each page (the PAGE-TOP line). After each line is printed, the SPACE-CONTROL value is added to LINE-COUNT. Thus, LINE-COUNT contains a value equal to the total number of lines printed on a page. Then, in module 360, LINE-COUNT is compared to LINES-ON-PAGE to determine when page overflow should take place. Since SPACE-CONTROL can be used in all WRITE statements for a print file except when skipping to the top of a page, this technique for counting the lines per page and testing for page overflow can work for all print files.

500-PRINT-TOTAL-PAGE   You can see that this module has computed two of the fields required on the total page. This is consistent with our loose definition of the verb "print." In short, a print module can do everything associated with printing one or more lines. If the computations were extensive, I would recommend that they be put in a separate module that is called by this module, but in this case they consist of only two COMPUTE statements.

The report-preparation program

General information

A report-preparation program reads one or more input files and prepares a report from the data in these files. At least one of these input files is read sequentially during the execution of the program, and this file usually drives the logic of the program. Because the data for a report is extracted from the input records, some people refer to a report-preparation program as an *extract program*.

When intermediate totals must be accumulated in a report-preparation program, the input file must be in sequence based on the data in a *control field*. For instance, customer number is the control field if totals must be accumulated by customer number, so the input file that drives the program must be in customer-number sequence. Similarly, a file must be in sequence by a control field within a control field if totals are to be accumulated at two different levels.

In order to print one level of intermediate totals, the control field from one record must be compared with the control field from the previous record. If the new control field is greater than the old control field, it indicates that an intermediate-total line should be printed. If the control fields are equal, it means that the data from the new record should be applied to the group being processed, so no total line should be printed. And if the new control field is less than the old control field, it indicates that the input file is not in sequence (an error condition). Needless to say, if more than one level of intermediate totals must be printed, the problem is complicated because comparisons must be done based on more than one control field (like customer number and salesman number).

The basic structure of a report-preparation program

Figure 3-5 presents a structure chart that shows a basic structure for a report-preparation program. As you can see, the level-2 modules read a record sequentially and print one or more lines based on the contents of this record. If intermediate or final totals are accumulated by the program, an accumulate module is also needed at level 2.

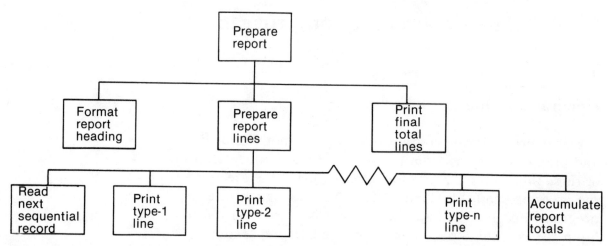

Figure 3-5   The basic structure of a report-preparation program

Because report-preparation programs vary greatly in size and complexity, I'm not saying that the structure in figure 3-5 applies to every report-preparation program. In fact, some programs may require a structure that is quite unique. So when you encounter a report format that is unusual, you should be prepared to develop a program structure that is unusual. And sometimes you will end up with a structure that is quite creative. For most report-preparation programs, however, the structure in figure 3-5 should be a good starting point for you.

Figure 3-6 shows some modules that might be called by a typical print module. First, if the program must read other records in order to get all the data required for a print line, the print module may call a read module; if the program must get data from more than one secondary file, it may call more than one read module. Second, if the operations or calculations required to develop the required data are complicated, the print module may call a module to develop the data. Third, if the statements required for formatting the print line are extensive, the print module may call a format module. Fourth, if the print module must provide for page overflow, it must call a print-report-heading module when overflow is required. And fifth, the print module must always call a module that actually writes the line on the printer (or to a print file).

In many print programs, however, the print modules are relatively simple. Then, a print module may not require subordinates to read other records, develop data, or format data. As a result, it may only require the module to write a report line, and, if the module must provide for page overflow, the module

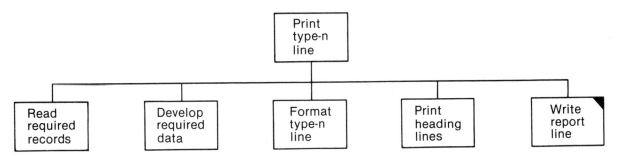

Figure 3-6   Possible subordinate modules for a print module

to print the report heading. You should keep in mind, though, that you can create subordinates like those in figure 3-6 to simplify a print module whenever it becomes cumbersome.

Figure 3-7 shows the structure of a general-purpose print leg that you can use in any report-preparation program. In this case, the print-report-line module uses code that is something like this:

```
IF LINE-COUNT GREATER THAN LINES-ON-PAGE
    PERFORM XXX-PRINT-HEADING-LINES.
MOVE NEXT-REPORT-LINE TO PRINT-AREA.
PERFORM XXX-WRITE-REPORT-LINE.
```

Since this module tests for page overflow, it simplifies the code in the calling module. However, this means that the calling module must format the next print line in a NEXT-REPORT-LINE area rather than in the print area itself. You can see how this works in the model program.

I/O requirements

The basic I/O requirements of a report-preparation program are the input files that contain the data from which the report is prepared. When the program is executed, its logic is driven by one of the input files that is read sequentially. As a result, at least one of the input files must be read sequentially. For instance, a report-by-item program will normally be driven by an item file that is read sequentially during the execution of the program.

Some report-preparation programs may be required to sort one of the input files to get it into the sequence required by the program. If, for example, a sales-by-customer report is to be prepared from a file of customer master records and a file of transaction records, the transaction file may need to be

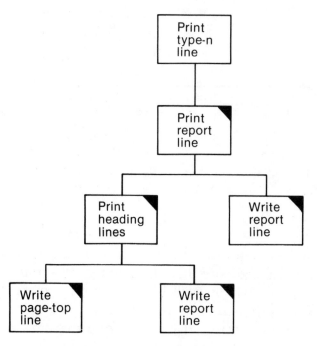

Figure 3-7   A general-purpose print-report-line leg that can be called by all other print modules

sorted into customer-number sequence. In this case, the program may sort the transaction file before it starts to prepare the report.

Printing requirements

The printing requirements for report-preparation programs vary considerably. At the simplest level, a *listing* is a report in which one line is printed for each input record. In a listing, each of the lines is called a *detail line*, so the report can be called a *detail report*.

In an *exception listing*, one line is printed for an input record, but only when that record indicates some special, or exceptional, condition. In the edit program, for example, the invalid transaction listing is an exception listing. Other reports that can be classified as exception listings are: a listing of inventory items that need to be reordered, a listing of students with 4.0 grade point averages, and a listing of bank customers with negative account balances.

In a *summary report*, one summary line is printed for each group of input records; for instance, in a sales-by-salesman report, one line is printed for each group of records that relates to one salesman. In some summary reports, one line is printed for each input record so detail lines are

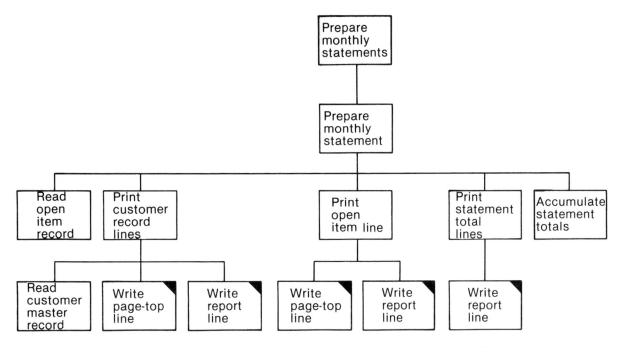

Figure 3-8 A structure chart for a program that prepares five lines from each customer record, one line from each open-item record, and two total lines for each customer

interspersed with *summary lines* throughout the report. When summary lines are printed based on changes in *more than one* control field, a summary report can be referred to as a *multilevel report*.

Within these general classifications, reports can vary immensely. For instance, a listing, or detail report, can print more than one detail line for each input record. And it can print detail lines for records read from more than one input file. In our shop, we prepare a monthly sales summary that prints five different kinds of detail lines for each record in our product file. And we have a customer listing program that prints up to 10 detail lines for each customer based on data taken from three different files.

Fortunately, these variations in printing requirements don't usually cause changes in the basic structure of a report-preparation program. You should see them instead as minor variations that you can accommodate using the basic report-preparation structure. Yes, the more types of lines your program prints, the more print modules your structure chart will have. But the basic structure of your program shouldn't change.

To illustrate this point, look at the structure chart in figure 3-8. This is the basic design for a program that prints monthly statements from a file of open items and a file of customer master records, both in customer number sequence.

On the monthly statement, up to six lines are printed based on the data in the customer master record, as many open-item lines are printed as there are open-item records for a customer, and two different total lines are printed when the customer number (the control field) changes. Although another level of subordination is used to keep the span of control manageable, I think you can see that the basic report-preparation structure remains intact.

Combining program functions

Reports are often prepared as byproducts of other program functions such as editing and updating. For instance, both the edit program and the sequential file-maintenance program in this handbook prepare listings of invalid transactions. Normally, however, these reports are simple listings. So it's usually quite easy to combine the report-preparation function with the primary function.

To improve the efficiency of a system, some programs prepare more than one report from a single reading of a group of files. For instance, a program may prepare a summary report by salesman as well as summary report by customer in a single reading of a customer file. In contrast, if two programs were used, it would mean that the customer file would have to be read twice to prepare the two reports. Then, if the customer file contains thousands of records, this might make a significant difference in report-preparation time. Although we don't recommend this type of program packaging because it makes a system more difficult to maintain, it sometimes makes sense.

In most cases, if you have to develop a program that prepares more than one report, you can start with the structure shown in figure 3-9. Here, in level 2, you still start by reading the next sequential record of the file that drives the logic of the program. But you think in terms of preparing more than one report from it. As a result, if the program requires more than one input file, all related records that will be used to prepare more than one of the reports must be read before you start to print the appropriate lines for the reports.

The model report-preparation program

The report-preparation program in this book is designed to show you some of the typical requirements of a report-preparation program. Because it uses the basic report-

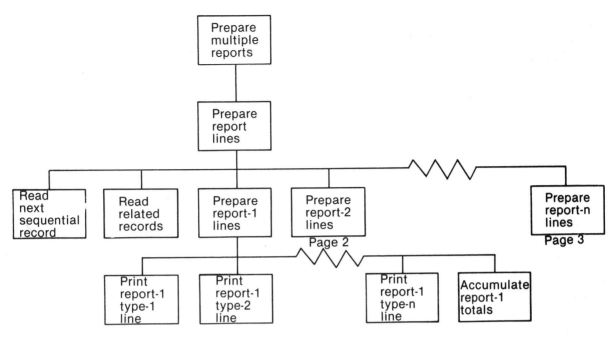

Figure 3-9 A basic structure for a program that prepares more than one report

preparation structure shown in figure 3-5, you shouldn't have much trouble adapting its structure and code to other report-preparation programs.

The program specifications

The report-preparation program in this book prepares a report from an input file of customer master records and an input file of salesman master records. The customer master file is in sequence by customer within salesman within branch. The salesman master file is indexed by salesman within branch. Since the program accumulates totals at two levels (by salesman and by branch), it can be called a two-level summary report. Note, however, that it also prints one detail line for each customer master record.

The specifications for this program are unrealistic in several ways. For instance, both customer and salesman master records consist of only a few fields. In actual practice, of course, these records would probably contain many more fields. Similarly, the report might contain more items of data. Even though the program is simplified, however, it provides a good model for developing other report-preparation programs.

The structure chart

If you look at the structure chart for the model program, you can see that it uses the basic structure shown in figure 3-5. In addition, it uses a general print-report-line leg as shown in figure 3-7.

When you use a general print routine (modules 240 through 270 in this program) to print all of the lines of a report, you assume that it's okay to skip to the next page at any point in the printing of the report. In some programs, however, you may not want to skip between the printing of related total lines. In this program, for example, you may not want to skip between the printing of a customer total line and a salesman total line or between a salesman total line and a branch total line. In other words, you may not want the last customer line for a salesman on one page and the salesman total on the next. And you may not want a salesman total on one page and the branch total on the next.

You can adjust the page overflow in a program like this, however, by making only a minor change to the structure chart. Quite simply, you substitute module 270 (the write-report-line module) for module 240 as the subordinate module for modules 290 and 300. Then, the program won't skip to the next page before printing a salesman or branch total line. In this case, of course, you must make sure that you have room on the page for printing the four extra lines required by both a salesman and a branch total line. But you can make sure of this by adjusting the LINES-ON-PAGE constant. This illustrates how easy it is to modify a well-structured program.

If you have written programs like this using traditional methods, you know that the first record read by the program has to be treated differently than the records that follow. As a result, the traditional program normally reads and processes the first record in an initialization module. Using this thinking, you may want to use a structure chart like the one shown in figure 3-10. Here, using a common read module, you can read and process the first record in module 000, then process subsequent records via module 300. In fact, other systems of structured programming recommend just this approach.

To me, however, this approach is illogical. And it is a throwback to traditional thinking. When you use the structure shown in figure 3-10, module 300 depends upon the processing done in module 000. As a result, these modules aren't properly independent; they must be closely coordinated. Furthermore, why should this program require a read module as a subordinate to the top-level module when

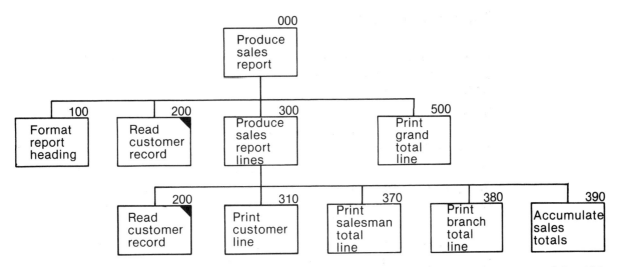

Figure 3-10   An unacceptable structure for the report-preparation program because modules 000 and 300 aren't independent of each other

other programs don't? This is procedural, not functional, thinking. In my opinion, then, the structure shown in figure 3-10 is unacceptable.

The COBOL Code

If you look at the COBOL listing, you can see that only two of the modules in this program are at all complicated. These are modules 200 and 220. Module 200 is fairly complicated because it is the primary control module of the program. Module 220 is fairly complicated because it provides for printing branch and salesman data in only the first line of each branch or salesman group. Once you understand these modules, it should be easy for you to understand the other modules of the program.

000-PRODUCE-SALES-REPORT   This illustrates the simple coding structure that most top-level modules should have. It calls module 100; it calls module 200 until all customer-master records have been read; and it calls module 400. In a production program, it might also send a message to the system operator indicating that the program ran to completion, but this depends on your installation standards.

200-PRODUCE-SALES-REPORT-LINES   This module illustrates the use of a first-record switch so the first record in a file can be processed differently from the subsequent records. As I mentioned in the discussion of the structure chart for this program, I think this is a better way of handling the first record than processing it in the top-level module as would be done using the structure in figure 3-10.

To make the code as readable as possible, the programmer wrote this module using one nested IF statement. But, of course, this module could be coded in many different ways. In any event, I'd like you to notice how easy it is to follow the code even though four levels of nesting are used. To understand the code in this module, you should realize that the salesman key consists of salesman number within branch number because the same salesman number can be used in more than one branch.

You should also notice that this module follows the principle of moving control code up the line into the control module itself. In this case, all control-field changes are coded in this module, even though some could be moved down-the-line into modules 290 and 300. By coding this module in this way, the subordinate modules are completely independent. And it's easy to understand the logic of this module.

You may have noticed that the code in this module doesn't provide for an out-of-sequence condition. However, this could easily be added to this module. By moving Y into TRAN-EOF-SW when an out-of-sequence record is read, you could pass control back to the top-level module, end the program, and send an appropriate error message to the operator. If the system sorts the records just before this report-preparation program is executed, however, I don't feel that this out-of-sequence testing is necessary.

210-READ-CUSTOMER-RECORD   This module reads one record and, when the end-of-file condition is reached, moves Y to the end-of-file switch.

220-PRINT-CUSTOMER-LINE   This module illustrates the extended meaning I allow for the verb *print*. Besides printing the customer line, this module (1) calls a read module to get a related salesman record and (2) computes two of the fields that must be printed.

The first sentence of this module is a nested IF statement that moves the appropriate values into the branch number, salesman number, and salesman name fields of the report. The logic is relatively complex because these fields are only supposed to be printed in the first line of a group. For instance, the branch number is only supposed to print in the first customer line for a branch. And the salesman number and name are only supposed to print in the first customer line for a salesman. As you can see, then, this nested IF statement duplicates some of the logic of module 200 in order to get this printing right.

Although module 200 could have set switches that module 220 could have used to tell when to print the branch number, salesman number, and salesman name fields, the programmer wrote the program this way because it led to more readable code. In general, you should only pass switch values from a called module to a calling module. To reverse this direction means that the called module isn't properly independent.

240-PRINT-REPORT-LINE   This module is the top module in the general print routine. It tests to see whether or not page overflow should take place, and, if it should, it calls module 250. After page overflow takes place and the page heading is printed, the next report line is moved into the output area for the print file and the line is printed by module 270. This should explain why modules 220, 290, and 300 move the lines to be printed into a work area called NEXT-REPORT-LINE rather than the output area for the print file. At the time that module 240 is called, you don't know whether heading lines will be printed next or whether report lines will be printed.

280-ACCUMULATE-SALES-TOTALS   This module accumulates the totals for each salesman, for each branch, and for the entire company. It does so by adding each of the values in two input fields to three total fields. As we see it, this is the most straightforward way to accumulate these totals. Then, the related total fields need only to be reset to zero after they are printed.

Another way to accumulate these values is to only accumulate the salesman totals in this module. Then, after a salesman total has been printed, the salesman totals must be added to the branch totals. And after a branch total has been printed, the branch totals must be added to the grand totals. Although this way of accumulating totals means that the object program will execute fewer add instructions, it also means the print modules will have to include the code for rolling over the totals from one level to the next. As a result, we prefer the code shown in the model program because it makes the program easier to read and understand.

One caution here is to resist the temptation to put a short module like this in line; that is, you shouldn't put this code in the calling module. As long as this code represents a legitimate function (as the code in this module does), it should remain independent. Remember, there is always the possibility that the report or the computations will be expanded, so keeping this module separate provides for easy program maintenance.

290-PRINT-SALESMAN-TOTAL-LINE   This module also illustrates the extended meaning of the verb *print*. Here, the print module computes two of the fields that must be printed and resets the salesman totals to zero. If you want to roll the salesman totals over to the branch totals rather than accumulate branch totals as done in module 280, you would add the salesman totals to the branch totals in this module before resetting the salesman totals to zero.

300-PRINT-BRANCH-TOTAL-LINE   This module also illustrates the extended meaning of the verb *print*. Here, the print module computes two of the fields that must be printed and resets the branch totals to zero. If you want to roll the branch totals over to the grand totals rather than accumulate the grand totals as done in module 280, you would add the branch totals to the grand totals in this module before resetting the branch totals to zero.

400-PRINT-GRAND-TOTAL-LINE   This module also illustrates the extended meaning of the verb *print*. Here, the print module computes two of the fields that must be printed

The sequential update or
file-maintenance program

General information

In most installations, sequential update and file-maintenance programs are the workhorses. They are used to keep a wide variety of files up-to-date. In general, a sequential update or file-maintenance program reads a sequential file of transactions and a sequential file of master records. The output of the program is a new master file that is up-to-date.

Although some people use the terms *update* and *maintain* as general verbs that mean to "keep the records in a file up-to-date," we think it's best to give these verbs more specific meanings. With that intent, we use the term *update* when a program changes the records in a file based on operational data such as sales, hours worked, or receipts to inventory. If, for example, a program modifies the fields in the records of an inventory master file based on the data in a transaction file of receipts to inventory, the program is an *update program.*

In contrast, a *file-maintenance program* processes transactions that contain maintenance data rather than operational data. As a result, a file-maintenance program may add records to a file, delete records from a file, or change records in a file. When records are changed, the fields are usually set to the values given in the transaction record. This contrasts the changes done in an update program in which the values in the master fields are usually increased or decreased by the values in the transaction record.

Whether a program updates records or maintains them, there is a basic program logic that underlies a sequential program like this. It is based on a comparision of the *control fields* in the master and transaction records that are read. In a program that updates or maintains an inventory master file, for example, the control field is the inventory item number or code. In order for the program to work, both files must be in sequence by the control field because a sequential update or file-maintenance program will read all input files in sequence.

As the program reads the records in the input files, if the control field of a transaction record and the control field of a master record are equal, it means that the transaction record should be either a deletion or a change record, and processing continues accordingly. Similarly, if the control field of the transaction record is less than that of the master record, it means that the transaction didn't have a matching master record, so the transaction should represent an addition record which should be added to the master file. Finally, if the control field of the transaction record is greater than that of the master record, it means that there aren't any transactions for the master record.

In contrast to a random update or maintenance program, a sequential program forces procedural thinking like this upon you. And to a large extent, this thinking goes back to the days of computing when most files were kept on magnetic tapes rather than on direct-access devices. That's why it's usually more difficult to develop a sequential update or maintenance program than it is to develop a random program for the same purpose. Instead of concentrating on the functions that the program requires, you have to be aware that the files are being read one record at a time and that you can't get a master record back once you've written it.

**The basic structure
of a sequential update or file-maintenance program**

Figure 3-11 presents the basic structure for a sequential update program. As you can see, the level-2 modules read a transaction record, get a master record, apply the transaction record to the master record with equal control field, and print a transaction as invalid if no master record has an equal control field.

In this case, *apply* means to update the matching master record in internal storage, but *not* to actually write the updated master record on the new master file. The new master record isn't written until a transaction with a higher control field than that of the master record is read. Then, the get-master-record module calls the write-master-record module so the updated master record is actually written on the master file.

One of the key modules in this basic structure is the get-master-record module. It is called until the control field of the current master record is either equal to that in the transaction record or greater than that in the transaction record. If the master and transaction are equal, the update-master-record module calls the apply-valid-transaction module to update the

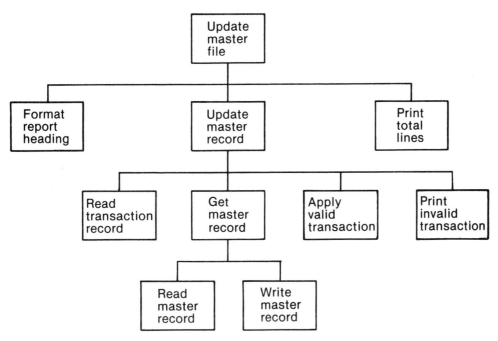

Figure 3-11   The basic structure of a sequential update program

master record. Otherwise, it calls the print-invalid-transaction module to print the transaction on the invalid-transaction listing so the invalid transactions can be corrected and reentered into the system.

Although a sequential file-maintenance program is similar to a sequential update program, it must provide for additions and deletions as well as for changed records. As a result, the basic structure of a sequential file-maintenance program is a bit more complicated than the structure of an update program. This is illustrated by the file-maintenance structure shown in figure 3-12. Here, the process-transaction-record module calls modules for applying additions, applying changes, applying deletions, and printing invalid transactions. You will see this structure illustrated in the model program for sequential file maintenance.

Although we recommend the structures shown in figure 3-11 and 3-12, you should realize that update and maintenance programs can be developed quite effectively using other structures. As a result, we will present some alternative structures when we discuss the structure of the model file-maintenance program. Keep in mind, though, that the structures we just presented are the most effective ones we've ever used. And they can easily be adapted for use in most sequential update and maintenance programs.

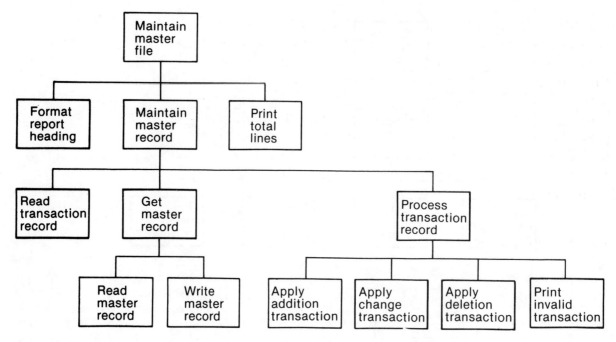

Figure 3-12   The basic structure of a sequential file-maintenance program

I/O requirements

In many cases, an update or maintenance program will have to process transactions from more than one file. For instance, a program might update an inventory master file based on the data in three input files: a file of inventory receipts, a file of inventory issues, and a file of miscellaneous adjustments. This doesn't have much effect on the structure of a program, however, because you treat all of the transaction files as a single transaction file. Then, as long as you always are working on the transaction with the lowest control-field value, the effect is the same as if you read one record at a time from a single transaction file. Needless to say, all of the transaction files processed by a sequential update or maintenance program must be in the same sequence based on the same control field.

In terms of master files, a sequential update or maintenance program should always have one input master file and one output master file. Then, the input file is called the *old master file*, and the output file is called the *new master file*.

As you will see in the model program, some update or maintenance programs write a file of invalid, or error, transactions. By the same token, some write a file of valid transactions that will be used to update other master files in a later step in the system.

Since all input files must be in sequence based on a control field, some update or maintenance programs sort the transaction file before they process it. And some programs that process multiple transaction files, first merge the transaction files into a single transaction file. In either case, the program uses the SORT or MERGE statement to call the system's sort/merge program. Incidentally, on many systems, it's faster to sort two or more input files together so they become a single file than it is to merge the input files into a single file.

Printing requirements

An update or maintenance program usually requires a listing of the invalid, or error, transactions; that is, the ones that couldn't be processed properly. In addition, a program may require a listing of the processed transactions; it depends on the system's audit trail requirements. At the least, however, an update or maintenance program should print totals showing how many records the program added to the file, deleted from the file, and changed in the file, and how many transactions were invalid.

Combining program functions

Many update or maintenance programs do some editing of the transaction records. And some do complete editing of the transaction records. To show how this changes the basic structure of an update program, figure 3-13 presents a modified version of the chart in figure 3-11. In this case, the update-master-record module calls the get-valid-transaction module until it gets a valid transaction or there are no more transaction records. Then, it processes the valid transaction using the same structure as in figure 3-11.

Similarly, figure 3-14 presents a structure chart for an edit-and-maintenance program. This is a modified version of the chart in figure 3-12. Again, the primary level-1 module calls the get-valid-transaction module until it gets a valid transaction record or until there are no more transaction records. Then, it processes the valid transaction using the same basic structure as in figure 3-12.

Although most update and maintenance programs prepare reports, they are usually just simple listings such as update or error listings. These listings are used as part of the audit trail and for error correction. Because they are simple,

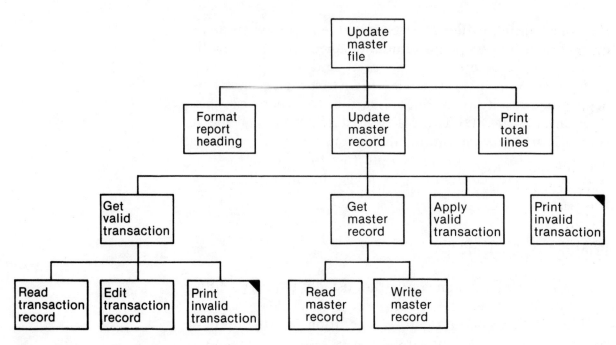

Figure 3-13   The basic structure of a sequential edit-and-update program

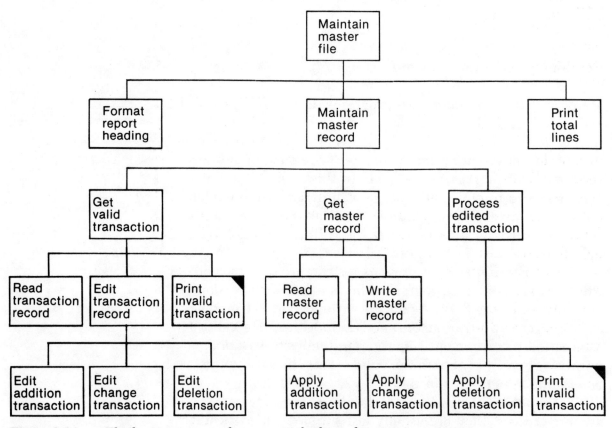

Figure 3-14   The basic structure of a sequential edit-and-maintain program

they don't usually add much to the structural complexity of
an update or maintenance program.

The model program
for sequential file-maintenance

The file-maintenance program in this book is designed to
show you some of the typical requirements of a program like
this. Because it uses the basic file-maintenance structure
shown in figure 3-12, you shouldn't have much trouble
adapting its structure and code to other update or file-
maintenance programs.

The program specifications

The sequential file-maintenance program in this book maintains a sequential inventory master file stored on tape or disk.
The transaction file for the program contains three types of
records: addition records, change records, and deletion
records. If a change or deletion record is unmatched in the
master file, it indicates a transaction error. And if an addition
record is matched, it indicates a transaction error. These error
records are to be written on a file of error transactions. As the
program maintains the master records, it must prepare a
maintenance listing that shows the changes that have been
made to the master file.

The transaction records are actually in sequence by
transaction code within item number. Since the transaction
codes are 1 for a deletion, 2 for an addition, and 3 for a
change, a deletion will always come before an addition for a
record and an addition will always come before any changes
for a record. As a result, it is possible to delete a master
record, add a new record with the same item number to the
file, and then change this new master record based on one or
more change transactions.

Although this program is realistic in that it provides for
all file-maintenance possibilities, the record layouts themselves
are unrealistic. In actual practice, an inventory master record
has many more fields than are shown in the record layout.
Similarly, the change and addition records would normally
contain more fields. In designing this problem, however, I
wanted to emphasize the logical requirements of the program,
not the number of input and output fields.

The specifications state that the transaction records have been sorted and edited before the file-maintenance run. As a result, the program doesn't have to sequence-check the transaction records, and it doesn't have to check for error conditions that should have been caught in the editing run.

The structure chart

As I mentioned earlier, it's difficult to design a sequential update or file-maintenance program because you have to be concerned with the procedure that reads the records in each input file in sequence and writes the new master records in sequence. As a result, I'm not at all sure that we have the perfect design for this type of program. I'm not even sure that there is a perfect design. All I can say is that we considered many options before we settled on the design for the model program. And we like this design better than any of the alternatives that we came up with. If you check the structure chart for this model program, you can see that it uses the basic structure shown in figure 3-12.

Although a file-maintenance program can be designed in many different ways, I think the best thing to do is to find a structure that you like, settle on it, and use it as a model for all of the file-maintenance programs that you write. And you should do the same thing for a sequential update program. Once you have a good model, it can save you many hours of development time. In fact, you can usually use the modules in the top three or four levels of the program in all the file-maintenance and update programs you develop. The primary changes from one program to the next will be in the work modules, not the control modules, and these changes are usually routine.

If you study the structure chart for the model program, you can see that module 370 appears in three places. As a result, the structure chart could be simplified somewhat by structuring the process-inventory-transaction leg of the program as in figure 3-15. To us, however, it's logical to call the print-maintenance-line leg of the program from each of the three apply-transaction modules. So there's little to be gained by this structural change.

To give you some perspective on alternate designs, look at the structure chart in figure 3-16. This is actually the structure chart that we published in our first book on structured programming as a "model" solution. If you study it, though, you can see some shortcomings that make it unacceptable. In particular, the shaded modules represent traditional

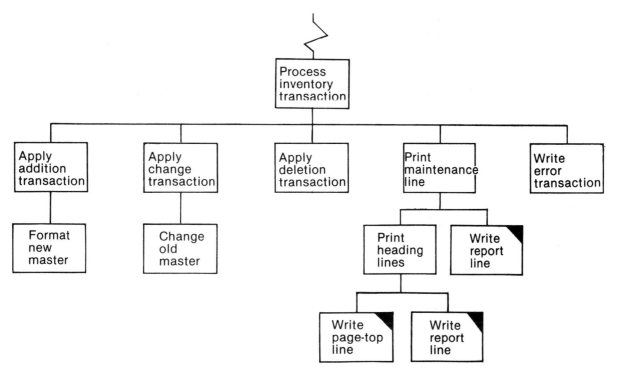

Figure 3-15　Another acceptable structure for the process-inventory-transaction leg of the sequential file-maintenance program

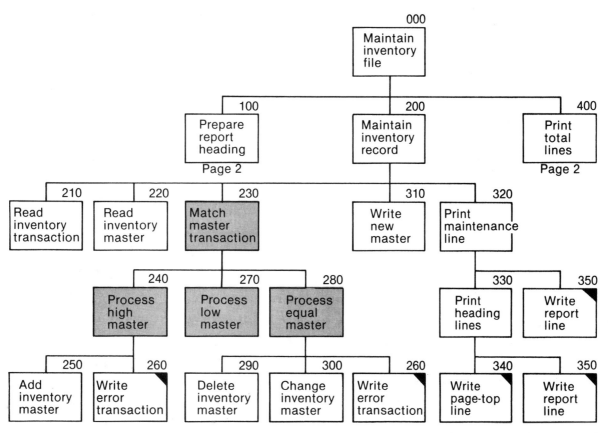

Figure 3-16　An unacceptable structure for the sequential file-maintenance program that illustrates procedural thinking

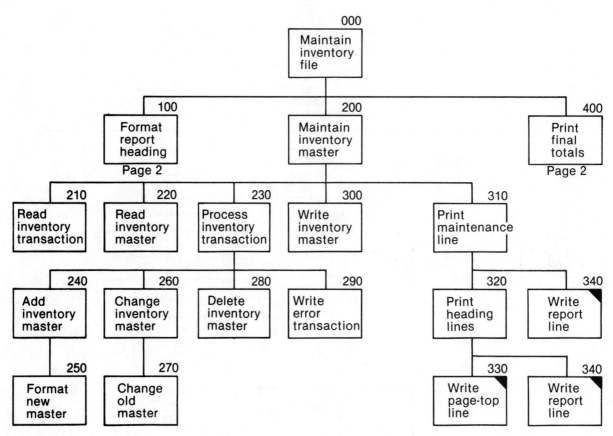

Figure 3-17 Another acceptable structure for the sequential file-maintenance program

procedural thinking; modules like "match master tran" and "process equal master" do *not* represent program functions. In fact, dozens of our customers wrote in to complain about this program design and the lack of readability in the resulting code.

Once we realized the limitations of the structure in figure 3-16, we used the structure in figure 3-17 for sequential file-maintenance programs. Although this structure was logical enough, it still left something to be desired. In particular, the code in module 200 was difficult to read and understand because it depended a lot on the passing of switch values so module 200 could tell when to read an old master or transaction record or when to write a new master record or print a maintenance line. In fact, much of this code was procedural, rather than functional, just as the code for the design in figure 3-16 was. When we realized this, we decided to rethink our model solution and we ended up with the basic design in figure 3-12.

On the positive side, though, you should realize that the designs in figures 3-16 and 3-17 do work. Once you understand the code in the critical modules, it's easy to understand the rest of the program. In the program in figure 3-17, for example, only modules 200 and 230 present any development difficulties; the rest of the program is quite straightforward. So once you test and debug these modules, it's easy to develop and modify the rest of the program.

With this as background, we feel that the structure chart for the model program is as workable as any other that we've seen. Using this basic design, you can develop a sequential file-maintenance program with relative ease. And the resulting COBOL code should be quite readable.

The COBOL code

If you check the COBOL code for this program, you can see that it is quite straightforward. Only the code for module 320 presents any difficulties. As a result, you should be able to use this code as the basis for writing many of the modules in your own file-maintenance programs.

000-MAINTAIN-INVENTORY-FILE   Note in this module that the primary level-1 module, module 300, is performed until ALL-RECORDS-PROCESSED. This is a condition that means that all of the records in both the transaction and the master file have been read and processed. This switch is turned on in module 300 when the control fields in both the master and the transaction records are equal to HIGH-VALUE.

300-MAINTAIN-INVENTORY-RECORD   This module starts by performing the module that reads a transaction record. Next, it performs the get-inventory-master module until the item number in the inventory master record isn't less than the item number in the maintenance transaction. That means the item number in the inventory master is either equal to or greater than the item number in the transaction. Then if both the transaction and master control fields are equal to HIGH-VALUE, the module turns the ALL-RECORDS-PROCESSED switch on. Otherwise, it processes the inventory transaction.

310-READ-INVENTORY-TRANSACTION   Unlike the previous model programs, this program doesn't turn an end-of-file switch on when the end-of-file condition for the transaction file is detected. Instead, it moves HIGH-VALUE into the transaction control field, which forces a greater-than comparison when the transaction control field is compared to the master control field in module 300. In general, you should define all control fields in an update or file-maintenance program as alphanumeric (PIC X). Then you should move HIGH-VALUE (not nines) into the master control field when the end of the file is reached and you want to force a greater-than comparison.

320-GET-INVENTORY-MASTER   This is the most complicated module in the program because it must determine when to write another record on the new master file and when to read another record from the old master. And this isn't always easy.

For instance, since the program specifications say that the program must provide for change transactions for a master record that has just been added to the file, the program can't write an addition record to the new master file until it's sure that there are no change records for it. So most of the code in this module is logic designed to make sure that master records are read and written at the right time.

Although the model program requires that the transaction file be sorted by transaction code, there are other possible combinations of additions, deletions, and changes that a program like this might have to provide for. For instance, some maintenance specifications state that a program must be able to delete master records that have just been added to the file. As written, however, the model program will handle any logical combination of transactions that you will ever encounter including deletions after additions.

The logic of this module is handled by one nested IF statement that starts by reading one transaction record if this is the first time the module is being executed (FIRST-EXECUTION). If it's not, the next IF statement handles writing and reading of the master records during the subsequent executions of this module. The IF portion of this IF statement handles reading and writing if the last master record hasn't been deleted (NOT MASTER-DELETED). The ELSE portion of this IF statement handles writing and reading if the last master record has been deleted; in this case, the program doesn't write the deleted master record. In other words, the IF and the ELSE portions of the second IF statement in this module are the same except that the ELSE portion doesn't write the deleted master record on the new master file and it turns the master-deleted switch off.

The code that decides whether to read an old master follows:

```
IF MASTER-HELD-FOR-ADDITION
     MOVE HELD-MASTER-RECORD
          TO INVENTORY-MASTER-RECORD
     MOVE "N" TO MASTER-HELD-FOR-ADDITION-SW
ELSE
     PERFORM 330-READ-INVENTORY-MASTER
```

In other words, if the last item processed was an addition, the program doesn't need to read the next master record. It simply moves the master record that was held while the addition record was being processed into the master record area. In module 420, you can see how the master record that was read prior to an addition transaction is moved into the HELD-MASTER-RECORD area of storage in the first place. On the other hand, if a master record wasn't held for addition, this module calls module 330 to read the next inventory master.

As you can see, this module is complex only because the program provides for additions to and deletions from the master file. Otherwise, it would simply write a new master and read an old master each time it is executed (after its first execution). As a result, this type of module in an update program or in a maintenance program that only provides for changes is quite straightforward.

330-READ-INVENTORY-MASTER   As in module 310, this read module doesn't use an end-of-file switch. Instead, it moves HIGH-VALUE into the master control field to force a greater-than comparison in module 300.

350-PROCESS-INVENTORY-TRAN   This module determines what type of transaction is being processed (deletion, addition, or change) and calls the appropriate module based on this determination. Note, however, that it only calls one of the "apply transaction" modules if the transaction is valid. If the transaction isn't valid, this module calls module 410 to write an error transaction on the error file.

360-APPLY-DELETION-TRANSACTION   When you delete a record in a sequential file-maintenance program, you don't really do anything. You just don't write it on the new master file. As a result, this module simply turns the MASTER-DELETED-SW on so module 320 won't write the old master record on the new master file. Then, this module moves an appropriate message to the maintenance line, adds 1 to the deletion count, and calls module 370 to print a line on the maintenance listing.

420-APPLY-ADDITION-TRANSACTION   This module starts by moving the last master record to the HELD-MASTER-RECORD area unless the last master record was deleted. Then, it calls module 430 to format the new master record in the old master record area. In other words, the added master record will now be treated as if it had just been read from the old master file. After that the module moves a message to the maintenance line, adds 1 to the addition count, and calls module 370 to print the maintenance line.

430-FORMAT-ADDITION-RECORD   This module formats an addition record that will be written on the new master file. It moves fields from the transaction record to the master record area and initializes fields to zeros. In an actual production program, a module like this might contain dozens of MOVE statements.

440-APPLY-CHANGE-TRANSACTION   This module starts by calling module 450 to change the required fields in the master record. Then, it moves a message to the maintenance line, adds 1 to the change count, and calls module 370 to print the maintenance line.

450-CHANGE-OLD-MASTER-RECORD   In this program, if a field in the transaction record for a change record is blank, the program assumes that the corresponding field in the master record is supposed to be left unchanged. Otherwise, it moves the transaction field into the corresponding field of the master record. In this module, then, each field in the transaction record is checked to see whether it contains blanks. If it doesn't, the field is moved to the master record.

The random update or file-maintenance program

General information

In a random update or file-maintenance program, the master records are read and written in a random, rather than a sequential, order. These programs are practical when the activity of the master file is low or when the master file isn't kept in sequence due to other system considerations.

In this book, we distinguish between update and file-maintenance programs, although many people don't make this distinction. We use the term *update* when a program changes the records in a file based on operational data such as sales, hours worked, or receipts to inventory. We use the term *file maintenance* when the transactions contain maintenance rather than operational data. This is explained in more detail in the analysis of the sequential update or file-maintenance program.

In actual practice, most files that can be accessed on a random basis are stored in some sort of indexed file organization. In this case, the records can be accessed sequentially as well as randomly. But if the activity for an indexed file is low, it is usually more efficient to update or maintain the file on a random, rather than a sequential, basis.

For some types of file organization, a deleted record isn't actually removed from the file; instead, a deletion code is moved into its first storage position indicating that the record is no longer active. For instance, HIGH-VALUE can be moved into the first byte of a record to indicate that it is deleted. Then, all programs that process the file must ignore any records with the deletion code. When you use COBOL compilers that support the 1974 or later standards for relative or indexed files, however, the DELETE verb logically removes a record from a file so you don't have to use this extra logic for the delete function.

Whether a master file has indexed organization or some other organization that allows random processing, there is an underlying logic to a random update or maintenance program. The general procedure is to get a valid transaction and to randomly access and read the master record with the same control-field number (or *key*). If the transaction is an addition record and a matching master record can be found, it indicates an error condition (a *duplicate*). If the transaction is a change or a deletion record and a matching master record *can't* be found, it also indicates an error condition.

When compared to a sequential update or maintenance program, a random program seems more logical. When you want to add a record to a file, for example, you first check to make sure that a record with the same key isn't already on the file. If it isn't, you add the record to the file. Similarly, if you want to delete or change a record in a file, you read the master record with the same key and you delete or change the record. It's that straightforward.

The basic structure
of a random update or file-maintenance program

Figure 3-18 presents the basic structure that we recommend for a random update program. As you can see, the four level-2 modules: (1) get a valid transaction, (2) apply the valid transaction to the master record with the same key, (3) write the valid transaction on the valid-transaction file (if this is required by the specifications), and (4) rewrite the updated master record on the master file.

In the get-valid-transaction leg, the program reads a record, edits it, and, if the transaction is invalid, prints a line on the invalid-transaction listing. As part of the editing, the program reads a master record with the same key as the transaction to make sure there is one. As a result, the program doesn't have to read the master record in one of the other legs of the program.

To apply the valid transaction to a master record, the program updates the fields in the master record. For object-program efficiency, though, the program shouldn't rewrite the master record onto the master file until all transactions for that master record have been processed (this assumes that the transaction records are in sequence by master-record key). As a result, the read-master-record module shouldn't be called unless the key in a transaction record is different than the key of the preceding transaction record. You'll see this illustrated in the model program for a random update.

If you don't care about object-program efficiency, you can simplify the logic of an update program by rewriting an

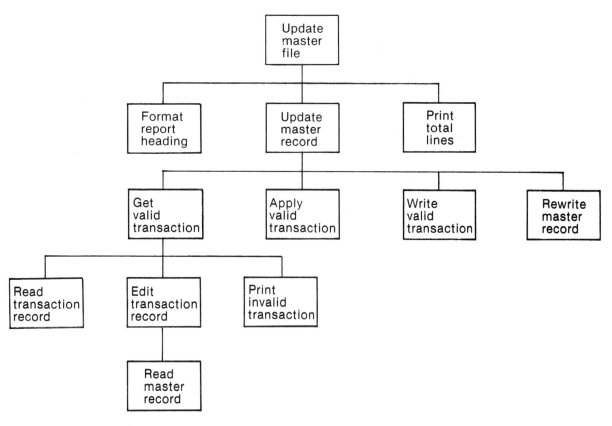

Figure 3-18   The basic structure of a random update program

updated record on the master file each time a transaction is
processed. In this case, the rewrite-master-record module is
subordinate to the apply-valid-transaction module in the
structure chart. In many update programs, however, several
transactions are likely to apply to a single master record so
this can seriously affect the number of I/O operations
required by the program.

Although a random maintenance program is similar to a
random update program, it must provide for additions and
deletions as well as for changes. As a result, the basic
structure of a random file-maintenance program is more
complicated than the structure of an update program. This is
illustrated by the file-maintenance structure shown in figure
3-19. Here, the process-valid-transaction module calls modules
for adding, changing and deleting master records. In a
program like this, however, object-program efficiency usually
isn't a concern so the program can write or rewrite the
affected master record on the master file each time a
transaction is processed.

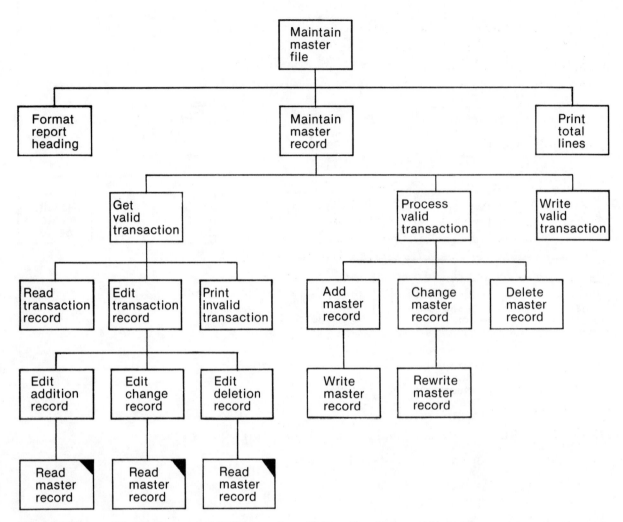

Figure 3-19   The basic structure of a random file-maintenance program

Although we recommend the structures shown in figure 3-18 and 3-19, you should realize that update and maintenance programs can be developed quite effectively using other structures. For instance, figure 3-20 presents another acceptable structure for a random file-maintenance program. In this case, the get-valid-transaction leg doesn't read the master record with the same key so it can't know for sure whether the transaction is valid. As a result, the program has to call the print-invalid-transaction module from two different modules. Also, since the span of control of the maintain-master-record module is 7, it is going to be more complicated than the one required by the design in figure 3-19. Nevertheless, you still end up with an effective program.

As we see it, then, the important thing is that you settle on a standard design for random update and file-maintenance programs. Unless you develop better designs of your own, though, we recommend the structures in figures 3-18 and 3-19. They will help you develop programs that are both readable and maintainable. And you'll be able to adapt them to most random update and maintenance programs.

I/O requirements

In some cases, an update program will update more than one master file. For instance, a program might update both a customer and a salesman master file based on sales transactions. This doesn't have much effect on the structure of an update program, however. It just means an extra read module, an extra update module, and an extra rewrite module for each extra master file. Since the transaction file can only be in the key-sequence of one of the master files, you won't have to be concerned about object-program efficiency when you code the modules for the extra master files.

As the structure charts in figures 3-18 and 3-19 indicate, many update and maintenance programs write a file of valid transactions that can be used to update other master files in a later step in the system. By the same token, some update or maintenance programs write an error file of invalid transactions. This file can then be used to print an invalid-transaction listing.

Since a key-sequenced transaction file can improve the object-program efficiency of a program, some update or maintenance programs sort the transaction file before they process it. Then, the program only has to read and write a master record once for all of the transactions that affect it. Because maintenance programs generally process only one transaction record for each master record, sorting usually isn't required in a file-maintenance program.

Printing requirements

An update or maintenance program usually requires a listing of the invalid, or error, transactions; that is, the ones that couldn't be processed properly. In addition, a program may require a listing of the processed transactions; it depends on the audit trail requirements. At the least, however, an update or maintenance program should print totals showing how many records the program added to the file, deleted from the file, and changed in the file, and how many transactions were invalid.

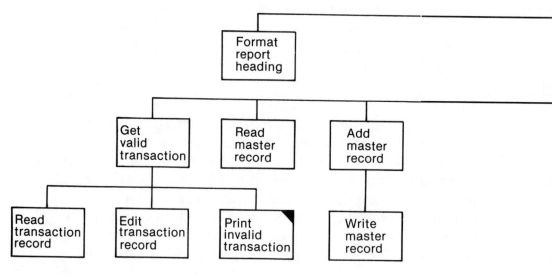

Figure 3-20 Another acceptable structure for a random file-maintenance program

Combining program functions

As you can tell from the structure charts in this section, many update or maintenance programs do some editing of the transaction records. So it's not uncommon to combine an edit function with an update function. In the chart in figure 3-18, for example, the edit-transaction-record module could be the top module for an editing leg that edits all of the fields in the record.

Although most update and maintenance programs prepare reports, they are usually just simple listings such as update or error listings. These listings are used primarily for audit trail and error correction. Because they are simple, they don't usually add much to the structural complexity of an update or maintenance program.

The model random update program

The random update program in this book is designed to show you some of the typical requirements of a program like this. Because it uses the basic update structure shown in figure 3-18, you shouldn't have much trouble adapting its structure

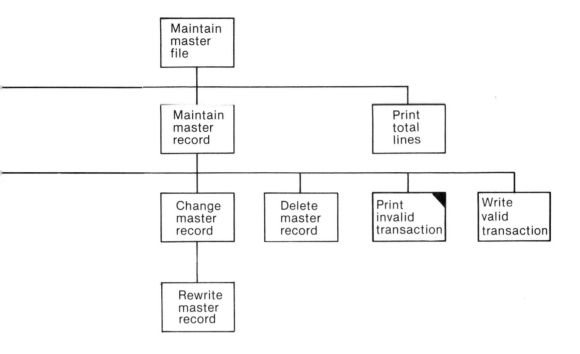

and code to other update programs. However, it uses this
structure as the output procedure of a SORT statement, so the
model program will also show you how to combine a random
update function with a sort of the transaction file.

The program specifications

The random update program in this book updates an
inventory master file based on only one type of transaction:
receipts to inventory. Since a random update only operates on
the master records affected by the transactions, this is
acceptable in terms of efficiency. In fact, it's not uncommon
for a random update program to process only one type of
transaction, one of low volume, while a sequential update
program for the same file processes the high-volume types of
transactions. Since a sequential update program operates on
all of the records in a master file, processing receipt records
alone probably wouldn't be practical for sequential files.

  As you can see, the record layouts for this program are
unrealistic. In actual practice, an inventory master record
would contain many more fields, and a receipt record would
contain more fields and would be used to update more than

one field in the master record. As before, however, I want you to concentrate on the logic of the program. And whether your program updates one field or dozens of fields, the structure and logic of the program are the same.

Because the input transaction file is in random order and the valid-transaction output file must be in item-number sequence, a sort is required within this program. Since sorted transactions can improve the efficiency of a random update on an indexed file, this sort should be done before the update portion of the program. Then, the program can be coded so it only reads and rewrites a master record once, no matter how many transactions are applied to it.

The structure chart

If you check the structure chart for the model program, you can see that it uses the basic structure shown in figure 3-18. However, the sort requirement causes another level of structure to be placed above the basic update structure. Thus, module 300 in the structure chart for the model program corresponds to the top-level module of figure 3-18. Module 300 is actually the start of the output procedure for the SORT statement in the model program, so it becomes the top-level module for the processing done by the program after the sorting is done.

Although a random update program can be designed in many different ways, I think the best thing to do is to find a structure that you like, settle on it, and use it as a model for all of the update programs that you write. And you should do the same thing for a random file-maintenance program. Once you have a good model, it can save you many hours of development time. In fact, you can usually use the modules in the top three or four levels of the program in all the update and file-maintenance programs you develop. The primary changes from one program to the next will be in the work modules, not the control modules, and these changes are usually routine.

With this as background, we feel that the structure chart for the model program is as workable as any other that we've seen. And it leads to COBOL code that is quite readable.

The COBOL code

If you review the COBOL code for this program, you can see that it is quite straightforward. When you use an internal sort, you have to use some code that we wouldn't recommend otherwise. But once you get used to it, it presents few problems. Other than this, the only code that isn't easy to follow is the code in modules 600 and 630 that relates to object-program efficiency.

000-UPDATE-INVENTORY-FILE   This top-level module contains the SORT statement because the transaction file is to be sorted before the master file is updated. On an IBM mainframe, if the sort fails, the SORT-RETURN code is set to a value other than zero. Then, this module displays a message indicating that the sort failed. After the sort completes, all of the processing is done in the output procedure of the SORT statement, so the top-level module of the update portion of the program is module 300.

300-PROCESS-SORTED-TRAN-FILE   This module, which is the start of the output procedure for the SORT statement, performs module 400 to format the report heading. Next, it performs module 600 until all transaction records have been processed. Then, it performs module 800 to print the totals on the invalid-transaction listing. Because all of the remaining modules in this program are part of the output procedure of the SORT statement, the fourth statement in this module branches to 300-EXIT, which is the last paragraph in the output-procedure section.

600-PROCESS-SORTED-TRAN-RECORD   This module turns the valid-transaction switch off and then performs module 610 until it gets a valid transaction or there are no more transaction records. If a valid transaction is read, this module checks for the first-record condition since special processing must be performed for the first valid transaction. Then, the module calls module 690 to apply the transaction to the master record and module 700 to write the valid transaction on the valid-transaction file.

Note, however, that this module doesn't actually rewrite a master record on the file unless there are no more records for the master (RT-ITEM-NUMBER NOT EQUAL TO OLD-ITEM-NUMBER). Then, it calls module 710 to rewrite the updated master record on the master file. And it moves the next master to be processed to the appropriate area in working storage. Needless to say, if the program specifications didn't require this concern for object program efficiency, this code could be simplified. As the program is, a master record will only be read and written once, no matter how many transactions apply to it.

610-GET-RECEIPT-TRANSACTION   This module calls module 620, which returns the next transaction from the sort. Then, this module calls module 630, which edits the transaction record. If the transaction is invalid, this module calls module 650, which prints a line on the invalid-transaction listing.

620-RETURN-SORTED-TRANSACTION   This module contains the RETURN statement that will return the sorted records from the sort file so they can be processed by the update portion of the program. In other words, the RETURN statement is logically equivalent to a READ statement. COBOL requires that this statement be in an output-procedure section, so this program must be divided into two sections: one for all paragraphs preceding module 300, and one for all paragraphs thereafter.

630-EDIT-TRANSACTION-FIELDS   This module starts by checking to see whether the transaction has a different key than the last transaction. If it doesn't, it means that the transaction applies to the same master record as the last valid transaction so the master record doesn't have to be read. In this case, this module doesn't call module 640.

If the module does have to read a master record, the item number field is considered valid if the master record is found. Otherwise, this module moves a message to the error-code field in an invalid-transaction line and sets the valid-transaction switch off. Then, no other field edits are performed.

If the item number field is valid, this module continues by editing the other fields in the transaction record. If any of them are invalid, this module moves the appropriate error message to the invalid-transaction line and sets the valid-transaction switch off.

If the program specifications for an update or maintenance program don't call for field editing, this module only has to check the key field to make sure that the record is valid. This doesn't change the structure of the program, however. It just means that this module is shorter and simpler.

640-READ-INVENTORY-MASTER   This module tries to read the master record that has the same key number as the transaction record. If there is no such record, this module moves N to the master-found switch. This code assumes that you are using a compiler that logically removes a record from a file when you delete it.

If you are using a compiler or a file organization that makes you put deletion codes in records that are deleted, this module must be a bit more extensive. If a master record with the same key as the transaction is found, the module must check to see whether the delete switch is on (usually, this is the first field in the master record). If it is, it means that the master is no longer active, so it's the same as if no master were found. In either of these two cases, N must be moved to the master-found switch and a line must be printed on the invalid-transaction listing.

690-APPLY-VALID-TRANSACTION   This module is unrealistic since only one field in the master record is updated. As I have mentioned, several fields are normally changed in an actual update program. And sometimes dozens of fields are changed in a single record during the execution of an update program. But even if this module does consist of only one statement, you should resist the temptation to code it in line since it represents a complete function.

Section 4

Interactive program analyses

This section presents general information about the interactive programs in section 6 of this handbook. Then, it presents analyses of these interactive programs.

The model programs represent solutions for the same interactive programming problem, but they show how the solutions are implemented on three different types of computer systems. The first program shows a solution using Microsoft COBOL on an IBM PC. The second program shows a solution using Wang VS COBOL on a Wang VS system. The third program shows a solution using CICS on an IBM 4300 running under DOS/VSE.

The programming problem for these interactive programs is simply to maintain a file of name-and-address records on an interactive basis. As simple as this problem is, however, it shows you the basic structure of any interactive program. Once you understand how this structure is implemented on your system, you can combine interactive entry with any of the batch functions presented in section 3 of this book.

General information
about interactive programs

An interactive program is one that interacts with the user of the program. On most systems, of course, this interaction is done by way of a computer terminal. The program displays messages, data, and questions on the screen of the terminal; the computer user sends commands, data, and responses back to the program by entering them on the keyboard of the terminal.

Because the "conversation" between the computer and the computer user can be extensive, interactive programs are often extensive. In addition, interactive programs often combine the entry of data with other functions such as preparing reports and updating or maintaining files. As a result, it's more difficult to describe the essential qualities of an interactive program than it is to describe those of a batch program.

The functions of an interactive program

In general, an interactive program (1) receives data from an entry operator or computer user, (2) edits it to make sure it is valid, and (3) either processes it or saves it for batch processing by a subsequent program. As a result, most interactive programs are at least entry-and-edit programs. As a result, they have many of the characteristics of a batch edit program.

After a valid transaction or file of transactions has been accepted by an interactive program, the program can update or maintain one or more files based on the transactions. For instance, it is common for an interactive program to update all related master files after each valid transaction has been accepted for processing. Thus, an interactive order-entry program may update the inventory file, the accounts receivable file, the customer file, and the salesman commission file. A program like this may also create a file of valid transactions for use in backup procedures or as an audit trail.

In contrast, some interactive programs don't update any files. Instead, they write the valid transactions onto a transaction file for batch processing later on. In many cases, this is more efficient than interactive updating because the transactions can be sorted into efficient processing sequences before they are processed. Similarly, some interactive programs update some files, those that must be kept up-to-date at all times, but they also create transaction files that can be used to update less critical files on a batch basis later on.

An interactive program can prepare one or more reports. However, the reports are normally prepared on a batch basis after the interactive portion of the program gets the user's specifications for the reports. For instance, one of our accounting programs first finds out how the user wants the accounting data summarized; it does this on an interactive basis. Once it has the user's specifications, it prepares the requested report on a batch basis.

In a *menu program*, the computer user selects one of the options displayed in a *menu* on the screen of the terminal. Then, the interactive program calls the program that the user requested. As a result, a menu program is usually a short program that is almost trivial. So once you've written one menu program, you should have no trouble writing other menu programs. In fact, many interactive systems provide menu generators so you don't even have to code these programs. As a result, we'll make no effort to discuss the characteristics of a menu program in this handbook.

The screen flow of interactive programs

Screen flow refers to the movement from one screen format to another within an interactive program. In figure 4-1, for example, you can see a screen flow diagram for a typical one-screen program. Here, the user enters data into the only screen of the program. If the editing routines find the data to be valid, the transaction is processed; otherwise, the operator must modify the data until it is accepted as valid. After a transaction has been processed, the program clears the screen and the work fields so the operator can enter the next transaction on the screen.

Although one-screen programs are common, there is a problem with them. In brief, they don't give the entry operators a chance to sight-verify the data they have entered. As a result, the accuracy of the data depends entirely on how good the editing routines for the entries are. But this usually means that some invalid data will be accepted by the system. It also means that an operator can be frustrated when he releases a transaction by accident, it is accepted as valid by

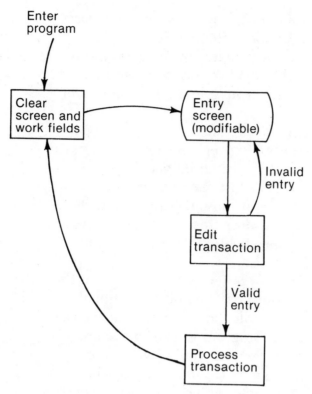

Enter
program

Clear
screen and
work fields

Entry
screen
(modifiable)

Invalid
entry

Edit
transaction

Valid
entry

Process
transaction

Figure 4-1   A screen flow diagram for a single entry-screen program without sight verification

the editing routines, and the operator can't get it back to correct it. This is a particular problem when the data is entered by non-technical personnel in the user department rather than by trained data entry operators.

Whenever possible, then, a program should give the operators a chance to sight-verify the data they have entered. In general, this requires one verification screen for each entry screen used by the program. In figure 4-2, for example, you can see the entry and verification screens used by an order-entry program. In the top portion of this figure, you can see the entry screen that lets the operator enter customer number, purchase order number, and the item number and quantity for each of the items ordered by a customer. As you can imagine, it's possible for these entries to pass the editing routines of a program and still be incorrect.

But in the bottom portion of this figure, you can see a verification screen for these entries. Before displaying this screen, the program looks up the related records and gets the data needed to expand the operator's entries. As a result, the operator can see more completely the effect of the entries he has made. By sight verifying this data, the operator can make sure the data is correct. Then, when he indicates that the data is acceptable, the transaction is processed.

Layout of entry screen

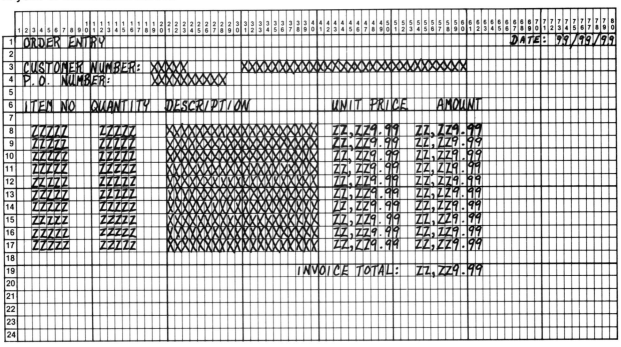

Layout of verification screen

Figure 4-2 Screen layouts for the entry and verification screens of an order entry program

Interactive program analyses **145**

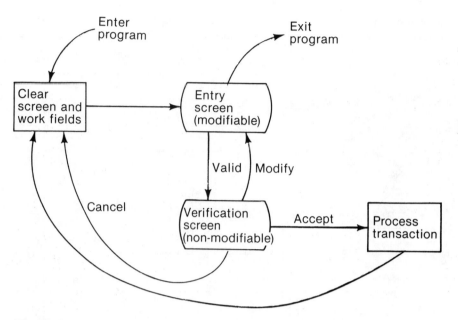

Figure 4-3   A screen flow diagram for a single entry-screen program with verification

In any event, if you write an interactive program that provides for sight verification of the entries for a single screen, the screen flow will be something like that shown in figure 4-3. This doesn't show when the editing will take place, but you should realize that editing is done each time the operator releases data for processing. Then, if the editing routines detect errors, the program returns the operator to the entry screen with an appropriate error message. But if no errors are detected, the program sends the verification screen to the operator. Then, if the operator accepts it, the program processes the transaction. Otherwise, based on the operator's response, the program either gives the operator a chance to modify the data in the screen by returning him to the entry screen. Or, the program clears the screen and work fields and returns the operator to the entry screen so he can start over.

If you write a program with more than one entry screen and you want to allow for sight verification by the operator, you must provide one verification screen for each entry screen. In addition, if you want to give the operator a chance to go back to an earlier screen after entering the data in all of the screens, you must provide a final verification screen. This

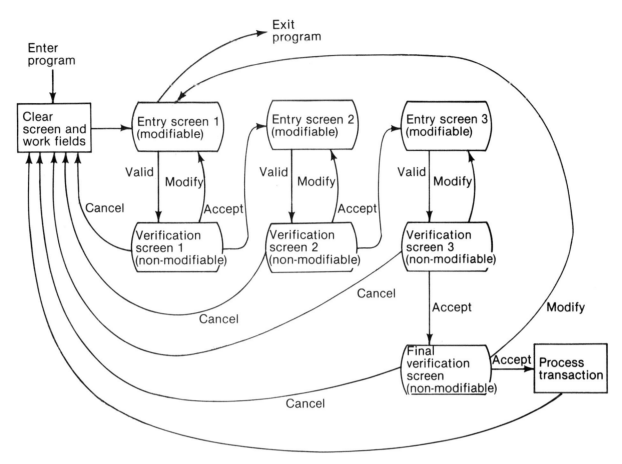

Figure 4-4   A screen flow diagram that provides for complete verification of a transaction that requires three entry screens

is illustrated by the screen flow diagram in figure 4-4 which provides for three entry screens. If the operator decides on the final verification screen that he wants to modify something he entered, the program returns to screen 1 so the operator can review his entries from the start and correct whatever needs to be corrected.

When you provide for sight verification by the operator, your system becomes easier to use. Or, to use the current jargon, it becomes more "user friendly." One of the most frustrating entry problems is to enter data that you know is incorrect and not be given the chance to correct it by the program. So we recommend that you provide for sight verification whenever it is practical.

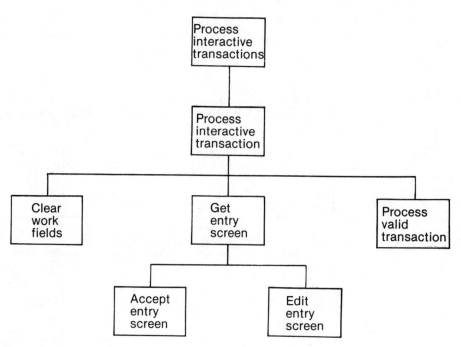

Figure 4-5   The basic structure of a single entry-screen program without verification

The basic structure of an interactive program

In general, interactive programs are less limited than batch programs. As a result, it's more difficult to give the basic structure of an interactive program than it is to give one for a batch program. Nevertheless, there is a structure that is common to most interactive programs. By showing you a few examples of structures for interactive programs, I think you'll discover this basic structure for yourself. Then, you can modify it to suit the interactive programs you are developing.

Figure 4-5 gives the basic structure for a program that uses a single entry-screen without verification. This type of program is often used by trained entry operators on large systems. If you compare this with the screen flow diagram in figure 4-1, you can see the relationship between screen flow and program structure. After the program gets a valid transaction, it processes it. This processing can be as simple as writing the record on a transaction file for later batch processing. Or it can be as complicated as updating or maintaining all related files as well as preparing print lines for one or more reports based on the transaction. As a result, the process-valid-transaction module could be the top-level module for extensive processing functions.

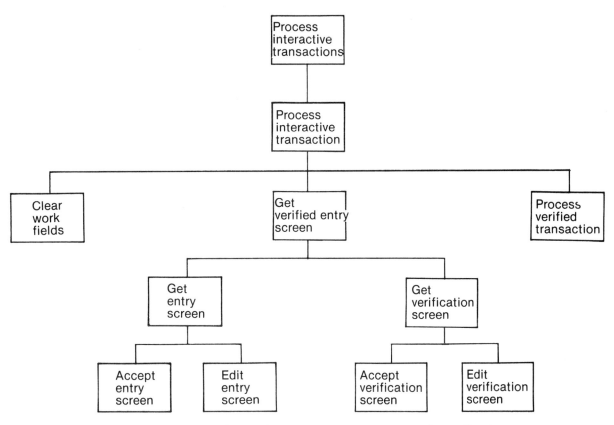

Figure 4-6 The basic structure of a single entry-screen program with verification

Figure 4-6 gives the basic structure for a single entry screen program with verification, and figure 4-7 gives the basic structure for a three entry-screen program with verification. Both of these programs process only one kind of transaction, but the program charted in figure 4-7 requires three entry screens to get all of the data in one transaction. After this program gets verified data from the three entry screens, it offers a final verification screen to the computer user.

When an interactive program processes more than one type of transaction, it's common for it first to find out what kind of transaction the operator is going to enter. If, for example, an operator is entering receipts to inventory and inventory scrap vouchers in an inventory application, the program should find out what type of transaction the operator wants to enter. Then, it should display a screen that is appropriate for the transaction type.

The basic structure for a program that processes two transactions is shown in figure 4-8. After the program finds

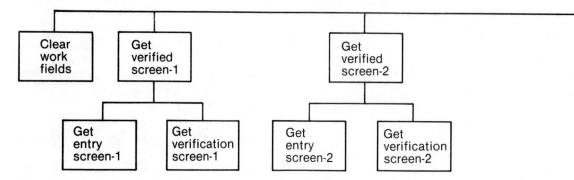

Figure 4-7   The basic structure of a three entry-screen program with complete verification that processes only one type of transaction

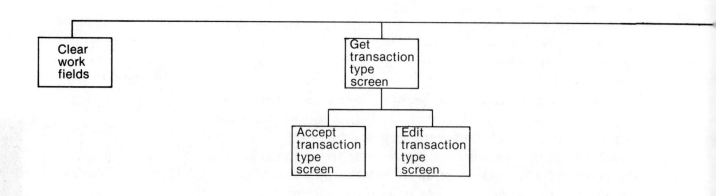

Figure 4-8   The basic structure of a program that processes two types of transactions with complete verification

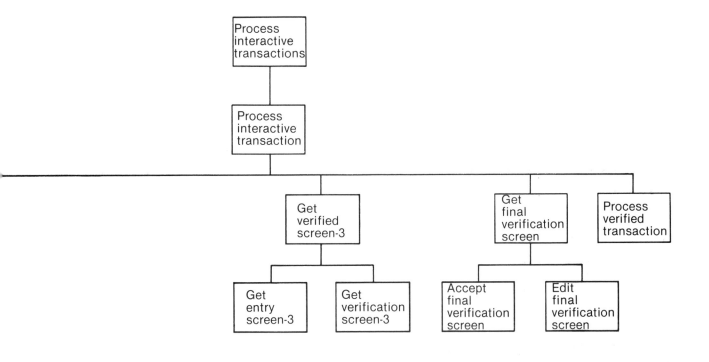

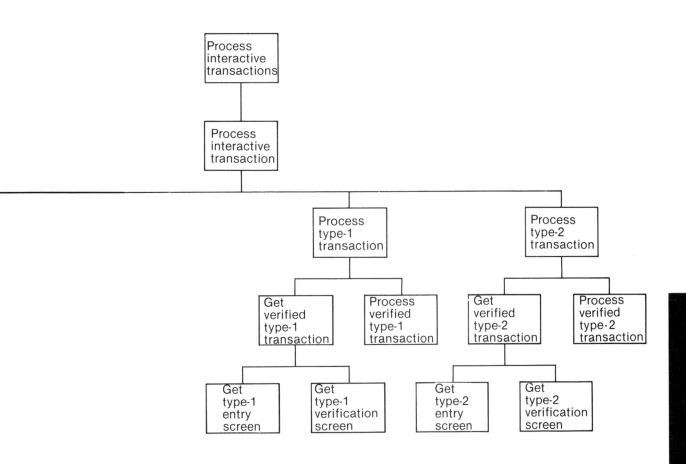

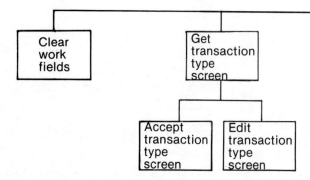

Figure 4-9   A second structure for a program that processes two types of transactions with complete verification...one that leads to less readable code.

out what type of transaction the operator is going to enter by getting the transaction-type screen, the program calls the appropriate processing module. This module in turn gets the verified data for the transaction and processes it. Needless to say, you can expand this basic structure to process many different transaction types.

Figure 4-9 presents another structure chart for a program that processes two types of transactions. But this structure puts the emphasis on screen handling rather than transaction processing. Although this structure is logical and it can work well for some programs, it can also lead to code that is difficult to read in the primary level-1 module. When in doubt, then, we recommend the basic structure in figure 4-8 when you are writing a program that processes more than one transaction type.

The basic specifications of the model programs

The three interactive programs in this book are all solutions for the same basic program specifications. These specifications

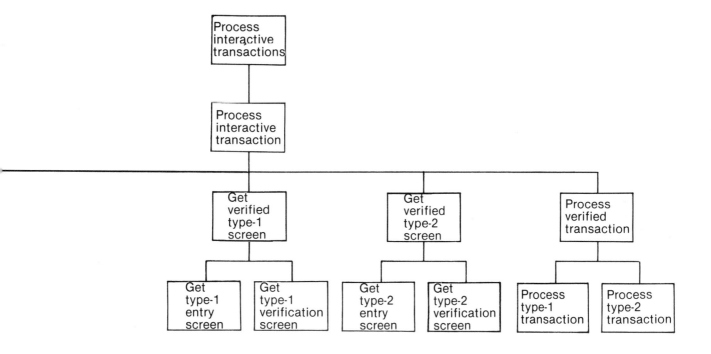

are for a simple interactive program that maintains a customer master file. Its screen flow is diagrammed in figure 4-10.

To start, the program gets an action code (or transaction-type code) from the action screen, but it also gets a customer code. The action can be to add a record to the customer file, to delete a record from the file, or to change a record in the file. Then, if the combination of the customer code and action code are valid, the program continues with the next screen.

If the transaction is a change or an addition, the program gets the data from the customer-entry screen. This screen allows the operator to change data taken from a master record that already exists or to enter data for the new record that is to be added to the file. After the programs gets valid data from this screen, it gets the data from a transaction-verification screen. This data tells the program whether the operator wants to accept the transaction, modify the transaction using the customer-entry screen, or to cancel the transaction altogether and start again with the action screen.

If the transaction is a deletion, the program skips the customer-entry screen. Instead, it gets the data from the

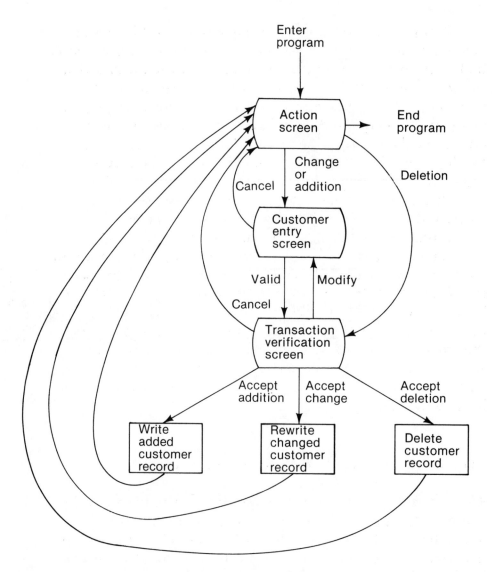

Figure 4-10   A general screen flow diagram for the model interactive program

transaction-verification screen. Then, the operator can tell the
program whether he wants to accept the deletion transaction
or cancel it. In other words, the operator has only two choices
for a deletion (accept or cancel), but he has three choices for
a change or an addition (accept, modify, or cancel).

If you've written programs like this before, you know
that you won't always let the operator enter the desired
customer code for a new customer (an addition). Instead,
you'll let the computer system assign the next available code
to the addition record. In this case, however, we're assuming
that the user wants to assign mnemonic codes for his
customers. Thus, DELTA might be the customer code for
Delta Lithograph Company and IBM might be the code for
International Business Machines. That way, if the number of
customers in the file is relatively low, the user can remember
most of the codes of his key customers.

Similarly, if the transactions for a program like this are entered in batches by transaction type, you probably wouldn't make the operator enter the action code for each transaction. Instead, you would have the operator enter the action code only once for each batch of transactions. If, for example, the operator was going to enter a batch of additions, he would only enter the action code for additions at the start of the batch. Then, the program would only ask for the customer codes and field entries for the addition records until all of them had been processed. At that time, the operator would indicate that he wanted to enter a different type of transaction and the program would respond accordingly.

You can see, then, that the screen layouts and screen flow for a program like this depend to a large extent on the user's specifications. If the user is going to enter the transactions in large batches sorted by transaction type, you can improve upon the screen flow specified for the model programs. On the other hand, if only a few transactions are going to be entered at a time and they aren't going to be sorted by transaction type, the screen flow for the model program will be quite efficient.

The three systems used for the model programs

Although this program is simple, it illustrates the basic design and code for an effective interactive program. It also illustrates the differences in design and code forced upon the developer by the compiler or system he's using. That's why this handbook presents three programs for these program specifications.

The first program is a *field-oriented* program. It is written for the IBM PC using Microsoft COBOL. It accepts data entered by the user one field at a time. If a field is invalid, a message is sent to the operator indicating that he must enter the field again. In this program, all screen-handling functions are provided for by the COBOL compiler using extensions to the 1974 COBOL standards.

The second program is a *screen-oriented* program. It is written for the Wang VS system using Wang's VS COBOL. It accepts a full screen of data at one time. The program then edits all of the fields of the screen. If one or more fields is invalid, a message is sent to the operator indicating the problem with the first error field and all error fields are highlighted. In this program too, all screen-handling functions are provided by the COBOL compiler using extensions to the 1974 COBOL standards.

The third program is a screen-oriented program like the Wang VS program. But it is written using CICS on an IBM mainframe. As a result, its screen-handling functions are provided by CICS, not by the COBOL compiler. In this system, the programmer writes CICS commands within the COBOL program for all screen-handling functions and for all file-handling functions. In addition, the programmer defines the screens of the program by writing an assembler-language program. In other words, the screens are defined outside of the COBOL program. As a result, this program differs significantly from both the Microsoft COBOL and the Wang VS COBOL programs.

We decided to use these systems because they represent the development practices common to the vast majority of modern computer systems. As a result, if you're not using one of these systems, one of them should be enough like your system so its model program will be useful to you. Then, you can use this model program as a basis for developing your own models.

The model program
using Microsoft COBOL on an IBM PC

The program specifications

If you look at the program overview, the screen flow diagram, and the screen layouts for this program, you should be able to understand what the program is supposed to do. If the operator presses function key 10 (F10) on the action screen, the program ends. Otherwise, the program moves from one screen to another as shown by the screen flow diagram. When a transaction is accepted by the operator on the transaction-verification screen, the program maintains the appropriate record in the master file. Note on the layout for the transaction-verification screen that the message in line 24 for a deletion transaction is somewhat different than the message for an addition or change transaction.

When you review the screen-handling code in this program, you can see that it doesn't really accept the data from all of the fields in a screen at one time. Instead, one ACCEPT statement gets one field of data. Nevertheless, you should think in terms of screens rather than fields when you design a program.

When you use Microsoft COBOL, you can code a program so it accepts one field or one full screen of data at a time. Although we recommend that you code most programs as screen-oriented programs, you will sometimes want to code a program on a field-oriented basis. So this program illustrates the design and coding techniques for field-oriented programs.

Although the IBM PC has ten function keys, it is difficult to use them effectively via Microsoft COBOL. That's why only one function key is used. As you can see in the layout for the customer-entry screen and the transaction-verification screen, function key 10 will cancel an entry altogether and give the operator a chance to start over.

The structure chart

If you look at the structure chart for this program, you can see that it has the same basic structure as the chart in figure 4-8. At level 1, module 100 displays the screen constants.

These are the first and sixth lines of a screen, which are the same on all three of the screen layouts. After the program has processed all of the transactions entered by the operator by repeatedly executing module 200, it executes module 900, which clears the screen so none of its data will show on the screen when the next program starts its execution.

When the primary level-1 module, module 200, calls module 300, it gets an action screen. For the entries in this screen to be valid, the action code must be consistent with the customer code. If, for example, the operator indicates an addition, the program must *not* be able to find a record in the customer file that has the customer code entered by the operator. Similarly, if the operator indicates a change or deletion, the program must be able to find a customer record that has the customer code entered by the operator. In any event, module 200 calls module 300, which gets an action screen until it is valid or the operator presses function key 10, which means that the program should end.

After module 200 gets a valid action screen, it calls module 400 for an addition transaction, 700 for a change transaction, and 800 for a deletion transaction. These modules in turn get a transaction from the operator until it has been accepted and processed or until it has been cancelled.

At level 3 and below, this program uses more modules than either of the other interactive programs uses because this program accepts and edits the entries one field at a time. For instance, module 330 accepts the action code and module 340 edits it. Similarly, modules 430, 460, 490, 520, and 550 each get only one field. So each of these modules calls one module to accept the field and another module to edit the field. Whenever one of the edit modules in the program detects an invalid field, it calls module 350, a common module that displays an error message so the operator can reenter the field.

The get-valid-action-screen leg of the program has an extra level of subordination in it because the action code and the customer code must be consistent in order for either entry to be valid. When the programmer discovered this during coding, she added module 315 to the program and moved modules 320 through 380 down one level in the structure chart. If you study the code for these modules, you will see why that was necessary.

Because the verification of a deletion is done somewhat differently than that for a change or an addition, the process-customer-deletion leg of this program doesn't use module 580 to get a transaction-verification screen. Instead, it uses module 820 to get a deletion-verification screen. You should realize, however, that this is the same as the transaction-verification screen but it doesn't offer the choice of modifying the transaction. Although you could code module 580 and its subordinates so they would handle all three types of transactions, the use of new modules for verifying deletions simplifies the COBOL code. As you can see in the programs for the other systems, though, how you handle this depends a lot on the COBOL compiler and computer system you're using.

The COBOL code

As simple as the program specifications are, this COBOL program requires 524 lines of code. So you can see that a program that requires the entry of many fields can easily be thousands of lines long. On the other hand, most of the modules in this program are short and the logic is straightforward so this program is easy to read and understand. Using similar coding techniques, you can write lengthy interactive programs that are easy to read and maintain.

In the descriptions that follow, I will try to ignore the compiler-dependent code and emphasize the control code. So even if you aren't familiar with Microsoft COBOL, I think you'll be able to figure out what the code accomplishes.

000-MAINTAIN-CUSTOMER-FILE This is a straightforward module that calls module 100, calls module 200 until the operator indicates that the program should end, and calls module 900 to clear the screen for the next program. Then, this module uses the CHAIN command to return control of the system to a menu program so the user can select the next program he wants to use.

100-DISPLAY-SCREEN-CONSTANTS This module clears the screen and displays the screen constants that will be used throughout the program in the first line of the screen.

200-MAINTAIN-CUSTOMER-RECORD This module starts by clearing the customer key field and action field and calling module 300 to get a valid action screen. Then, if the operator hasn't indicated that the program should end, it calls modules 400, 700, or 800 to process the type of transaction that the operator is going to enter. It calls these modules until they are accepted and processed by the operator or until they are cancelled.

300-GET-VALID-ACTION-SCREEN   This module calls module 310 to format the action screen. Then, it calls module 315 to get the action screen entries until they are valid. For them to be valid, the action code and the customer code must be consistent or the operator must have indicated that the program should end (pressing function key 10).

315-GET-ACTION-ENTRIES   This module calls module 320 to get an action code until the code is valid. Next, it calls module 360 to get a customer code until the code is valid. Then, it calls module 390 to edit the customer code with the action code to be sure that the two are consistent. If they aren't consistent, control passes back to module 300 and module 315 is executed again starting with the entry of the action code.

320-GET-ACTION-CODE   This module calls module 330 to accept the action code. Then, it calls module 340 to edit the action code. This is the basic coding structure for a module that gets the data for a single field. A module like this is normally performed until the data for the field is valid.

330-ACCEPT-ACTION-CODE   This module accepts the entry for a one-character action code. It also sets the END-PROGRAM-SW if the operator has pressed function key 10. It illustrates the basic coding structure of all the accept modules in this program.

340-EDIT-ACTION-CODE   This module edits the action code to make sure it is either an A, C, or D. If it isn't, it is considered invalid and the module moves N to the VALID-ENTRY-SW. It also moves an appropriate message to the SCREEN-ERROR-MESSAGE field and calls module 350 to display the message. It illustrates the basic coding structure of most of the edit modules in this program.

350-DISPLAY-ERROR-MESSAGE   This is a common module that is used to display all of the editing error messages in line 23 of the entry screens.

360-GET-CUSTOMER-CODE   Since this module gets data for only one field, this module calls module 370 to accept the data for that field. Then, it calls module 380 to edit the data for that field.

390-EDIT-ACTION-ENTRIES   This module checks to be
sure that the customer code entered by the operator is
consistent with the action code. It does this by calling module
395 to read the customer record and comparing the results of
the read with the action code entered by the operator. If the
results are invalid, it moves an error message to the SCREEN-
ERROR-MESSAGE field and displays the message by calling
module 350.

400-PROCESS-CUSTOMER-ADDITION   This module
calls module 410 to format the customer-entry screen. Then,
it calls module 420 to get the customer entries for the
addition. Unless the operator cancels the transaction, this
module calls module 580 to get the operator's verification
response after he sight-verifies the entries he's made. Last, if
the operator accepts the entries, this module calls module 610
to write the new customer record on the file. This is the basic
coding structure used in the process-change module too.

420-GET-VALID-CUSTOMER-DATA   This module calls
one module for each of the fields that the operator enters for
a master record. The modules are called until valid data is
entered for the field or until the operator cancels the
transaction. If the operator cancels, no other field-entry
modules are called by this module.

430-GET-CUSTOMER-NAME   This module shows the
basic structure for any module in this program that gets data
for a field. First, it calls a module to accept the field. Second,
it calls a module to edit the field. But if the operator has
indicated that the entries should be cancelled by pressing
function key 10, the edit module isn't called.

440-ACCEPT-CUSTOMER-NAME   This is a typical
module that accepts a field using Microsoft COBOL. The
second ACCEPT statement activates the F10 condition code if
the operator has pressed function key 10.

580-GET-TRAN-VERIFICATION   This module simply
calls module 590 to accept the verification response. Then, it
calls module 600 to edit the response.

610-WRITE-CUSTOMER-RECORD   This module writes
a new customer record on the customer master file. If the

INVALID KEY clause is executed, it usually means that a customer record with the new customer code already exists. And that, of course, is a programming error. As a result, the message that is displayed by this module is for the programming staff, not for the user. It should never be displayed once the program is put into operation. This same type of message is displayed by modules 710 and 850.

800-PROCESS-CUSTOMER-DELETION   This module calls module 810 to format the deletion-verification screen. Then, it calls module 820 to get verification of the deletion transaction. Although this program could have used one verification module to verify all types of transaction, the code is simplified by using a separate module for deletion verification. If the transaction is accepted, this module calls module 850 to delete the record from the file.

810-FORMAT-DELETION-SCREEN   This module displays the contents of the record to be deleted, a prompt for the entry of the verification flag, and an operator message. The message indicates to the operator that he has only two choices: accept the deletion or cancel the transaction. In contrast, the verification screen for additions and changes offers three choices: accept, modify, or cancel.

900-CLEAR-SCREEN   This module clears the entire screen so the system is ready for the next program. After this module is executed, control returns to module 000 and the program ends.

The model program
using VS COBOL on a Wang VS system

The program specifications

If you look at the program overview, the screen flow diagram, and the screen layouts for this program, you should be able to understand what the program is supposed to do. If the operator uses program function key 16 (PF16) on the action screen, the program ends. Otherwise, the program moves from one screen to another as shown by the screen flow diagram. When a transaction is accepted by the operator on the transaction-verification screen, the program maintains the appropriate record in the customer file.

Because a Wang terminal has 16 program function keys (PF keys) and because Wang COBOL makes it easy to use these keys, the program specifications provide for the use of these keys. This makes this program easier to use than the same program in Microsoft COBOL. To indicate whether a record is to be added, changed, or deleted on the action screen, for example, the operator presses PF1 for an addition, PF2 for a change, and PF3 for a deletion. On the verification screen, the operator presses PF1 to accept a transaction, PF4 to modify it, and PF16 to cancel it.

The structure chart

If you look at the structure chart for this program, you can see that it has a structure that is similar to the basic interactive structure shown in figure 4-8. At level 1, module 100 sets the field attributes that will be used by the program. Then, module 200 is the primary module that will be repeatedly executed while the program is in operation. This module controls the execution of the modules that get verified transactions and process them.

For each transaction, module 200 calls module 300 until it gets a valid action screen. Then, depending on the transaction type, module 200 calls module 400, 500, or 600. These modules get the required entries until the transaction has been accepted and processed or until the transaction has been cancelled.

Because Wang VS COBOL accepts and displays full screens of data, this program requires fewer modules than a program that accepts one field at a time. For instance, module 420 accepts a full screen of data and module 430 edits it. These are the primary entry and edit modules of this program. In contrast, module 310 only gets the data for one field and the entry of one PF key because that's all it needs to get. And module 440 only gets the entry of one PF key.

After the addition, change, and deletion legs of the program get a verified transaction, they write, rewrite, or delete the customer record on the customer file. For instance, module 450 writes a new record on the customer file. And module 620 deletes a customer record.

Because the Wang VS system is a multiterminal system, this program is written so more than one user can use the customer file at the same time. In this case, the danger is that two users might by chance operate on the same record at the same time. And this could lead to faulty results. To prevent this, module 330 of the program specifies WITH HOLD on the READ statement for the customer record that is about to be changed. This is Wang COBOL language that means that no other program can modify the record until the program that is holding it releases it. A program can release a held record in several ways: by executing *any* WRITE, REWRITE, or DELETE statement; by executing a READ WITH HOLD on *any* file; or by executing a CLOSE on the file that contains the record being held. Needless to say, any multiterminal system must provide a facility like this if files are to be shared by its users.

You may have noticed that the structure chart for this program differs from the basic structure chart in figure 4-8. Specifically, the module that verifies the customer data is subordinate to the module that gets the customer data rather than being on the same level. This structure is acceptable because verifying the customer data can logically be thought of as part of the process of getting the customer data. And, on the Wang VS system, the coding can be simplified somewhat by using this structure.

The COBOL code

As simple as the program specifications are, this COBOL program requires 662 lines of code. So you can see that a program that requires the entry of many fields can easily be thousands of lines long. On the other hand, most of the modules in this program are short and the logic is straightforward so this program is easy to read and understand. Using similar coding techniques, you can write lengthy interactive programs that are easy to read and maintain.

You might notice in this program that VS COBOL requires a SELECT statement for the terminal screen. Also, that you use the DISPLAY AND READ statement in the Procedure Division to display data on a screen and to get the data from the screen. You should also notice that you define the screens used by the program in the Working-Storage Section of the Data Division. In contrast, you define a screen outside of the COBOL program when you use CICS on an IBM mainframe.

One of the cumbersome aspects of the Wang compiler is its facilities for changing the attributes of a field on a screen. For instance, changing a field from normal intensity to bright intensity, requires a statement like

```
MOVE FAC-BRT-PRO-ALL TO FAC OF TVS-CODE.
```

This statement changes the field attribute character of the customer-code field in the transaction-verification screen. And similar statements are required to move the cursor from one screen location to another. Because you want to be able to change these attributes in order to highlight a field that is in error and to move the cursor to it, you must use code like this if you want to make your programs easy to use. Unfortunately, this attribute-handling code isn't very readable. And a typical interactive program requires dozens of lines just for changing these attributes.

In the descriptions that follow, I will try to ignore the compiler-dependent Wang code and emphasize the control code. So even if you aren't familiar with Wang COBOL, I think you'll be able to figure out what the code accomplishes.

000-MAINTAIN-CUSTOMER-FILE   Because this is a multi-user system, this module opens the customer master file as SHARED. This means that more than one user can access the records in it. Then, this module calls module 100 to set the field attributes used by the program, after which it calls module 200 until the operator indicates that the program should end.

After all transactions are processed, this program issues the STOP RUN statement. On the Wang system, this means that the program that called this program will be loaded and

Interactive program analyses

executed. In this case, it means that the system will probably return to a maintenance menu.

100-SET-FIELD-ATTRIBUTES   This module sets up the constant field-attribute characters that will be used by the screens of this program. It also initializes the screen-order area so the keyboard is unlocked and the alarm doesn't sound when a screen is displayed.

200-MAINTAIN-CUSTOMER-RECORD   This module initializes the position of the cursor on the screen and sets two fields to spaces before it gets into its control logic. Then, it calls module 300 until it gets a valid action entry or until the operator indicates that the program should end. If the entries are valid, this module calls module 400, 500, or 600 depending on the type of transaction being processed.

300-GET-ACTION-ENTRY   This module calls module 310 to get the data in the action screen. Then, it calls module 320 to edit the data.

310-ACCEPT-ACTION-ENTRY   This module illustrates the VS COBOL code for accepting a screen and using PF keys. Notice that before the screen is displayed the screen-order area is moved to the order area of the action screen. The screen-order area defines certain attributes of the screen, such as cursor position. This allows for the screen attributes to be changed from one display to the next.

320-EDIT-ACTION-ENTRY   When the program accepts the action screen, it gets the entry for the customer code as well as the PF key entry that indicates the action to be taken. Then, when this module is executed, it edits the customer code to make sure that it isn't blank. If it isn't, this module checks to make sure that the customer code is consistent with the action. To do this, this module calls module 330 to read a customer record with the customer code entered by the operator. If the record is found and the action code is addition, it indicates that either the customer code or the action or both are invalid. Similarly, if the record isn't found and the action is change or deletion, it indicates invalid entries.

When this module detects invalid data, it moves a field attribute character to the customer-code field that makes it blink. It also turns the beeper on and sets up an error message that identifies the entry problem for the operator. Then, the beeper will sound, the field will blink, and the message will be displayed the next time module 310 is executed.

330-READ-CUSTOMER-RECORD   This module tries to read a record with the customer code entered by the operator. If the record isn't found, the record-found switch is turned off.

400-PROCESS-CUSTOMER-ADDITION   This module sets up the attributes and work fields for the customer-entry screen. Next, it calls module 410 to get the data from this screen until it is valid or the operator cancels the transaction. Then, if the operator hasn't cancelled the transaction, the program calls module 450 to write the customer record on the master file.

410-GET-CUSTOMER-DATA   This module calls module 420 to get the data from a customer-entry screen. Then, if the operator hasn't cancelled the transaction, it calls module 430 to edit the data. Finally, if the entries are valid, it calls module 440 to verify the data.

420-ACCEPT-CUSTOMER-DATA   This module gets the data from a customer-entry screen.

430-EDIT-CUSTOMER-DATA   This module edits all of the fields accepted from the customer-entry screen. To edit the state and zip code fields, it calls two subprograms, STATEDIT and ZIPEDIT. If a field is in error, the program moves field attribute characters to it that cause it to blink. Since a screen has only one cursor, the cursor will end up on the last error field that is edited. That's why this module edits the fields from the bottom of the screen to the top. Then, the cursor ends up on the first field in error.

This module also moves an error message into line 23 of the screen for each field in error. So, again, only the last error message will actually be in this field when the editing is done. But, because the fields are edited from the bottom of the screen to the top, the message will apply to the first field in error.

If you ignore the compiler-dependent code, this module represents a basic structure that you should use for full-screen edit modules. If you want your programs to be easy to use, the edit modules should make sure that at least (1) an error message is displayed for the first field in error, (2) all error fields are highlighted, and (3) the cursor is positioned at the first field in error. In addition, this program sounds the beeper to alert the user to an error.

440-VERIFY-CUSTOMER-DATA   This module allows the operator to verify the customer data entered for an addition or change transaction. Although the same screen is displayed for a deletion transaction, different PF keys are activated and a different message is displayed so a separate module is called for this function.

450-WRITE-CUSTOMER-RECORD   This module writes a customer record on the customer master file. If the INVALID KEY clause is executed, it usually means that a customer record with the same key already exists. And that of course is a programming error. As a result, the message that is displayed by this module is for the programming staff, not for the user. It should never be displayed once the program is put into operation. This same type of message is displayed by modules 510 and 620.

500-PROCESS-CUSTOMER-CHANGE   This module is analagous to module 400 so it should be easy to follow.

600-PROCESS-CUSTOMER-DELETION   This module is analagous to module 400. However, since no data is required for a deletion transaction, this module doesn't have to call module 410 to get the customer-entry screen.

The model program
using CICS on an IBM Mainframe

The program specifications

If you look at the program overview, the screen flow
diagram, and the screen layouts for this program, you should
be able to understand what the program is supposed to do. If
the operator uses the CLEAR key on the action screen, the
program ends. Otherwise, the program moves from one
screen to another as shown by the screen flow diagram. When
a transaction is accepted by the operator on the transaction-
verification screen, the program maintains the appropriate
record in the customer file.

Because a CICS terminal has a number of program
function keys (PF keys) and other attention identifier keys
(AID keys), the program specifications provide for the use of
these keys. To indicate whether a record is to be added,
changed, or deleted on the action screen, for example, the
operator presses PF1 for an addition, PF2 for a change, and
PF3 for a deletion. On the verification screen, the operator
presses PF1 to accept a transaction, PF4 to modify it, and
CLEAR to cancel it.

The structure chart

If you look at the structure chart for this program, you can
see that it provides for the pseudo-conversational
programming that is essential to CICS object-program
efficiency. As a result, it has little relationship to the basic
structure of figure 4-8. In this case, the design as well as the
code is significantly affected by the characteristics of the
development language.

As you can see, though, the structure chart for this
program follows our CICS design standards. At level 1, you
will find one module for each of the screens used by the
program. You will also find a module that is used to start the
terminal session. This module is numbered so it comes last in
the program, because this improves the program's run-time
efficiency.

At levels 2 and 3, there is one module for each CICS screen-handling or file-handling command. For instance, module 1100 will issue a CICS command that receives one action screen. And module 1210 will issue a CICS command that reads one customer record. Remember that in a CICS program, all I/O operations must be done using CICS commands rather than COBOL statements.

The mapset listings

If you check the assembler-language mapset listing, you can see that the programmer coded only one parameter per line. This makes the listing more readable than it would be if more than one parameter were coded per line.

The symbolic mapset created by the programmer

If you compare the symbolic mapset created by the programmer with the symbolic mapset generated by BMS, you can see why we recommend creating your own mapsets. The use of the programmer's symbolic mapset in the COBOL program will lead to code that is much more readable than it would be if the BMS generated mapset were used.

The COBOL code

When you review the COBOL code, you can see that each module of the program is coded as a COBOL section. This is consistent with our CICS standards.

If you are familiar with CICS commands, you probably realize that this code is about as readable as CICS code can be. If you aren't familiar with CICS, you can quickly see how cumbersome it is to code when using CICS. In fact, you can't even tell what the program is doing without the mapset listings. And even though you define screens outside of the COBOL program when you use CICS, this simple program still requires 829 lines of code.

The communication area in the Data Division defines fields that will be passed from one execution of the program to the next. Because this is a pseudo-conversational program, the program will terminate each time a screen is sent to the terminal. Then, when the operator presses an AID key that indicates the screen's data is ready to be sent to the program, the program is restarted. As a result, the top-level module must be able to tell which level-1 module to execute each time it is restarted. And it does this by evaluating the data in the communication area. Since the program must also know what type of transaction is being processed, an action flag is included in the communication area.

In the descriptions that follow, I will assume that you're familiar with CICS code so I will emphasize the control code and the coding structures used. If you aren't familiar with CICS, you'll probably have considerable difficulty understanding what the code accomplishes. But that simply highlights the relative difficulty of CICS programming when compared with programming in Microsoft COBOL or Wang VS COBOL.

0000-MAINTAIN-CUSTOMER-FILE   This top-level module determines which module to call each time the program is restarted. If the session is just starting, it calls module 8000. Otherwise, it calls either module 1000, 2000, or 3000 to process a screen. After these modules have been executed, if the operator has indicated that the session should be ended, the program transfers control to another CICS program (MNT2000, a menu program). Otherwise, the program ends with an appropriate transaction ID so this program will be restarted the next time the terminal is ready to send its data.

8000-START-TERMINAL-SESSION   Even though this module is numbered 8000, it is the one that is called at the start of a session. Its function is to send the first action screen to the terminal by calling module 1400.

1000-PROCESS-ACTION-SCREEN   This module starts by clearing the action field and calling module 1100 to receive an action screen. When it receives it, if an invalid key was pressed, module 1400 is called to send the action screen back to the terminal for a valid key. Otherwise, if the session isn't ended, it calls module 1200 to edit the data in the screen. If the data is valid and the transaction is an addition or change, it calls module 1300 to send the customer entry screen to the terminal. If the transaction is a deletion, it calls module 1500 to send the transaction-verification screen to the terminal. If the data isn't valid, it calls module 1400 to send the action screen back to the terminal for a valid combination of entries.

1100-RECEIVE-ACTION-SCREEN   This module consists of seven paragraphs. The first paragraph issues the HANDLE AID and the RECEIVE MAP commands of CICS. The next five paragraphs handle the AID keys: one for the CLEAR key; one each for the three PF keys used by this screen; and one for any other AID keys that the operator may have used. The seventh paragraph is simply an EXIT paragraph so control will always be returned to the calling module.

1200-EDIT-ACTION-ENTRY   When the program receives the action screen, it gets the entry for the customer code as well as the PF key entry that indicates the action to be taken. Then, when this edit module is executed, it edits the customer code to make sure that it isn't blank. If it isn't, this module checks to make sure that the customer code is consistent with the action to be taken. To do this, this module calls module 1210 to read a customer record with the customer code entered by the operator. If the record is found and the action is addition, it indicates that either the customer code or the action or both are invalid. Similarly, if the record isn't found and the action is change or deletion, it indicates an invalid entry.

When this module detects invalid data, it sets up the symbolic map so the customer code is bright. It also sets up an error message that identifies the entry problem for the operator. Then, when module 1400 sends the action screen back to the terminal, the operator will be able to correct his error.

1210-READ-CUSTOMER-RECORD   This module provides for a CICS file-handling command that will try to read the master record with the same key as the one entered by the operator. It is coded as a COBOL section consisting of three paragraphs. The first paragraph issues the CICS commands. The second paragraph handles the not-found condition of a random read statement. The last paragraph is an EXIT paragraph that is used to make sure that control will always be returned to the calling module.

1300-SEND-CUSTOMER-SCREEN   This module consists of one CICS command that sends the customer-entry screen to the terminal. It illustrates the recommended coding style for any send-screen module.

1400-SEND-ACTION-SCREEN   This module is analagous to module 1300, but it sends an action screen instead of a customer-entry screen.

1500-SEND-VERIFY-SCREEN   This module is analagous to module 1300, but it sends a transaction-verification screen rather than an action screen and the cursor option is omitted so the cursor will be placed in the home position.

2000-PROCESS-CUSTOMER-SCREEN   This module starts by calling module 2100 to receive the data from a customer-entry screen. When it receives it, if an invalid key was pressed, module 1300 is called to send the customer-entry screen back to the terminal for a valid key. If the clear key is pressed, the transaction is cancelled and module 1400 is called to send the action screen back to the terminal to begin a new transaction. Otherwise, it calls module 2200 to edit the data. If the data is valid, it calls module 1500 to send the transaction-verification screen to the terminal. Otherwise, it calls module 1300 to send the customer-entry screen back to the terminal so the operator can correct his entry errors.

2200-EDIT-CUSTOMER-DATA   This module shows the basic coding structure that an edit module should have. When it detects an invalid field, it sets up the symbolic map so the cursor will be located on the error field, the field in error will be bright, and an appropriate error message will be displayed when the customer-entry screen is sent back to the terminal. Since the screen can only display one message at a time and since the cursor can only be in one place at a time, this module edits the fields from the bottom of the screen to the top. Then, the cursor will be placed at the first error field in the screen and the error message will also relate to this field.

3000-PROCESS-VERIFY-SCREEN   This module starts by calling module 3100 to receive the data from a transaction-verification screen. Then, if the entry is valid and the transaction isn't to be cancelled or modified, module 3200, 3300, or 3400 is called to process the transaction, depending on the type of transaction. After it calls one of these modules, it calls module 1400 to send the action screen back to the terminal so the operator can start another transaction. Module 1400 is also called if the transaction is cancelled. But, if the entry is to be modified, module 1300 is called to send the customer-entry screen back to the terminal so the operator can modify the transaction. Finally, if the entry isn't valid, module 1500 is called to send the verify screen back to the terminal so the operator can enter a valid verification response.

3100-RECEIVE-VERIFY-SCREEN   This module consists of six paragraphs. The first paragraph issues the HANDLE AID and the RECEIVE MAP commands of CICS. The next four paragraphs handle the AID keys: one for the CLEAR key; one each for the two PF keys used by this screen; and one for any other AID keys that the operator may have used. The sixth paragraph is simply an EXIT paragraph so control will always be returned to the calling module.

3200-ADD-CUSTOMER-MASTER   This module adds a record to a master file by calling module 3210 to write the record on the file.

3300-CHANGE-CUSTOMER-MASTER   This module calls module 3310 to read the related master record with the intent to update it. This reads the master record and protects it so no other program can modify it until this program releases it. Then, this module releases the record by calling module 3320 to rewrite the updated record on the file.

3310-READ-CUSTOMER-FOR-UPDATE   This module executes the CICS read-for-update command. If the record isn't found, the second paragraph in this COBOL section moves an error message to the screen that will be sent back to the terminal. In this case, however, a not-found condition indicates a programming error, because the program is supposed to have already read the record with the current key. So the operator should never see the error message for the not-found condition.

3320-REWRITE-CUSTOMER-RECORD   This module rewrites an updated record on the master file. After it has been executed, the record is released for use by other programs in the system.

3400-DELETE-CUSTOMER-MASTER   This module starts by calling module 3310 to read a record with the intent to update it. In this case, however, the program intends to delete it, but in terms of program logic, that's the same thing. Then, the program deletes the record by calling module 3410.

Section 5

Batch
model programs

This section presents four batch programs that are intended to be models for the development of other batch programs. The programs in sequence are (1) an edit program, (2) a report-preparation (or extract) program, (3) a sequential file-maintenance program, and (4) a random update program.

Although the trend in the data processing industry is to develop more interactive systems and fewer batch systems, batch programs will continue to be used for many years to come for at least two reasons. First, some applications are still impractical as interactive applications. Second, most interactive systems include some batch programs. In any event, once you understand the programs for these batch functions, you will be better able to understand interactive programs that provide for these functions.

The batch programs were developed on an IBM 4300 running under DOS/VSE using the VS COBOL compiler at the 1974 level of COBOL standards. As a result, the code is applicable to any 1974 ANS COBOL compiler.

Although we feel that these programs are written to the highest standards of professional excellence, we realize that some of the design and coding practices that we have used are debatable. What we recommend, then, is that you only use these programs as development models until you are able to develop better models of your own.

Model program 1

The edit program

| Program: | INV2100 EDIT INVENTORY TRANSACTIONS | Page: | 1 |

| Designer: | Anne Prince | Date: | 08-17-84 |

Input/output specifications

File	Description	Use
INVTRAN	Inventory transaction file	Input
PARTNUM	Part number file	Input
VINVTRAN	Valid inventory transaction file	Output
IINVTLST	Print file: Invalid inventory transaction listing	Output

Process specifications

This program edits a file of transaction records consisting of two record types: sales transactions and return transactions. Although the formats for these records are similar, they are not exactly alike.

For efficiency, since the company has less than 100 inventory items, load a part-number table at the start of the program that can be used to check for valid part numbers throughout the program. The part numbers can be read from the part-number file. The records in this file are in order of transaction frequency; the first part number has the most activity, the last part number has the least.

Print the output listing in the same order that the transactions are read. And print the editing totals on a separate page on the invalid transaction listing.

The records in the valid transaction file have the same format as the records in the input transaction file.

Process specifications

> **The basic processing requirements follow:**
>
> Load the part-number table.
>
> Do until the end of the inventory transaction file:
>
> 1. Read an inventory transaction record.
>
> 2. Edit the transaction fields.
>
> 3. If the transaction is invalid, print a line on the invalid transaction listing.
>
> 4. If the transaction is valid, write a record to the valid transaction file.
>
> After all transactions have been processed, print the total page.

Program:	INV2100 EDIT INVENTORY TRANSACTIONS	Page:	3
Designer:	Anne Prince	Date:	08-17-84

Process specifications

```
Editing rules for a sales transaction:

ITR-UPDATE-CODE              Must be "C"
ITR-TRAN-CODE                Must be 1
ITR-REF-NO                   No restrictions
ITR-REF-DATE                 Use DATEDIT subprogram; must be a valid
                             date in the form MMDDYY
ITR-BRANCH-NO                Numeric, greater than zero, and less than
                             25
ITR-SALESMAN-NO              Numeric and greater than zero
ITR-CUSTOMER-NO              Numeric and greater than zero
ITR-QUANTITY                 Numeric and greater than zero
ITR-PART-NO                  Must match with a number in the
                             part-number table that is loaded at the
                             start of the program
ITR-RETURN-CODE              Not used


Editing rules for a return transaction:

ITR-UPDATE-CODE              Must be "C"
ITR-TRAN-CODE                Must be 2
ITR-REF-NO                   No restrictions
ITR-REF-DATE                 Use DATEDIT subprogram; must be a valid
                             date in the form MMDDYY
ITR-BRANCH-NO                Not used
ITR-SALESMAN-NO              Not used
ITR-CUSTOMER-NO              Numeric and greater than zero
ITR-QUANTITY                 Numeric and greater than zero
ITR-PART-NO                  Must match with a number in the
                             part-number table that is loaded at the
                             start of the program
ITR-RETURN-CODE              Alphabetic
```

```
        BKEND    C.PARTNUM

    *
     01   PART-NUMBER-RECORD.
    *
          05   PNR-PART-NO                 PIC X(5).
          05   PNR-PART-DESCRIPTION        PIC X(20).

        BKEND
```

```
        BKEND    C.INVTRAN

    *
     01   INVENTORY-TRANSACTION-RECORD.
    *
          05   ITR-TYPE-CODE.
               10   ITR-UPDATE-CODE        PIC X.
               10   ITR-TRAN-CODE          PIC X.
          05   ITR-REF-NO                  PIC X(10).
          05   ITR-REF-DATE                PIC X(6).
          05   ITR-BRANCH-NO               PIC XX.
          05   ITR-SALESMAN-NO             PIC XXX.
          05   ITR-CUSTOMER-NO             PIC X(5).
          05   ITR-QUANTITY                PIC X(5).
          05   ITR-PART-NO                 PIC X(5).
          05   ITR-RETURN-CODE             PIC X(4).

        BKEND
```

Document name Invalid Sales and Return Listing **Date** 8-17-84

Program name INV2 00   **Designer** Anne Prince

Record Name		
Heading-Line-1	1	DATE: 99/99/99 PAGE: ZZ9
Heading-Line-2	2	TIME: 99:99 XX INV2100
Heading-Line-3	3	INVALID SALES AND RETURN TRANSACTIONS MIKE MURACH & ASSOCIATES, INC.
	4	
Heading-Line-4	5	TRAN UPDATE REFERENCE BRANCH SALESMAN CUSTOMER PART RETURN
Heading-Line-5	6	CODE CODE NUMBER DATE NUMBER NUMBER NUMBER QUANTITY NUMBER CODE
	7	
Invalid-Transaction-Line	8	XX* XX* XXXXXXX* XX/XX/XX* XX* XXX* XXXX* XXXX* XXX* X*
	9	XX* XX* XXXXXXX* XX/XX/XX* XX* XXX* XXXX* XXXX* XXX* X*
	10	XX
	11	
	12	
	13	
	14	
Error-Code-Line	15	
	16	* INDICATES ERROR FIELDS
	17	
	18	
	19	
Total-page:	20	
	21	
Heading-Line-1	22	DATE: 99/99/99 PAGE: ZZ9
Heading-Line-2	23	TIME: 99:99 XX INV2100
	24	
Summary-Heading	25	SUMMARY FOR SALES AND RETURN EDITING RUN MIKE MURACH & ASSOCIATES, INC.
	26	
Total-Line	27	VALID SALES ZZ,ZZ9-
	28	RETURNS ZZ,ZZ9-
	29	TOTAL ZZ,ZZ9-*
	30	
	31	INVALID SALES ZZ,ZZ9-
	32	RETURNS ZZ,ZZ9-
	33	TOTAL ZZ,ZZ9-*
	34	
	35	INVALID TRAN CODES ZZ,ZZ9-*
	36	
	37	TRANSACTIONS PROCESSED ZZ,ZZ9-* X
	38	
	39	
	40	
	41	
	42	
	43	
	44	
	45	
	46	
	47	
	48	
	49	
	50	

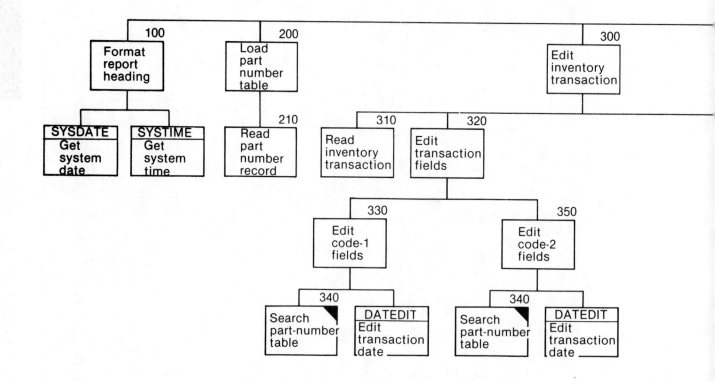

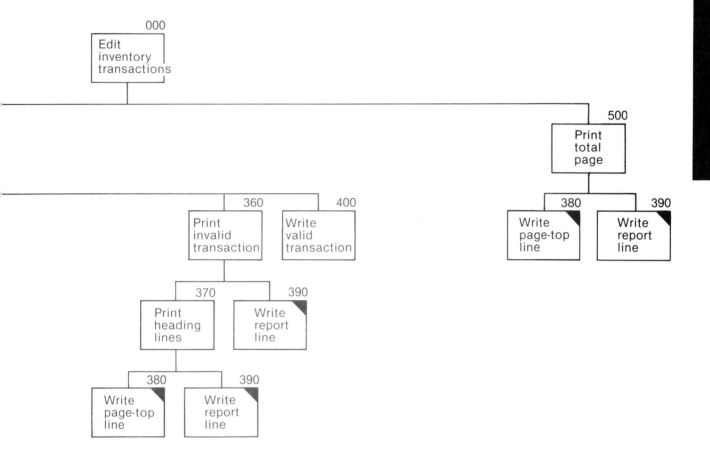

```
   CBL APOST,LANGLVL(1),LIB
00001     000100 IDENTIFICATION DIVISION.
00002     000200*
00003     000300 PROGRAM-ID.          INV2100.
00004     000400*AUTHOR.              ANNE PRINCE.
00005     000500*INSTALLATION.        MMA.
00006     000600*DATE.                SEPTEMBER 10, 1984.
00007     000700*
00008     000800 ENVIRONMENT DIVISION.
00009     000900*
00010     001000 CONFIGURATION SECTION.
00011     001100*
00012     001200 SOURCE-COMPUTER.     IBM-370.
00013     001300 OBJECT-COMPUTER.     IBM-370.
00014     001400*
00015     001500 INPUT-OUTPUT SECTION.
00016     001600*
00017     001700 FILE-CONTROL.
00018     001800*
00019     001900     SELECT PARTNUM   ASSIGN TO SYS005-AS-PARTNUM.
00020     002000     SELECT INVTRAN   ASSIGN TO SYS008-AS-INVTRAN.
00021     002100     SELECT VINVTRN   ASSIGN TO SYS007-AS-VINVTRN.
00022     002200     SELECT IINVTLST  ASSIGN TO SYS006-UR-1403-S.
00023     002300*
00024     002400 DATA DIVISION.
00025     002500*
00026     002600 FILE SECTION.
00027     002700*
00028     002800 FD   PARTNUM
00029     002900      LABEL RECORDS ARE STANDARD
00030     003000      RECORD CONTAINS 25 CHARACTERS.
00031     003100*
00032     003200 COPY PARTNUM.
00033 C         *
00034 C            01  PART-NUMBER-RECORD.
00035 C         *
00036 C                05  PNR-PART-NO            PIC X(5).
00037 C                05  PNR-PART-DESCRIPTION   PIC X(20).
00038     003300*
00039     003400 FD   INVTRAN
00040     003500      LABEL RECORDS ARE STANDARD
00041     003600      RECORD CONTAINS 42 CHARACTERS.
00042     003700*
00043     003800 01   INVENTORY-TRANSACTION        PIC X(42).
00044     003900*
00045     004000 FD   VINVTRN
00046     004100      LABEL RECORDS ARE STANDARD
00047     004200      RECORD CONTAINS 42 CHARACTERS.
00048     004300*
00049     004400 01   VALID-INVENTORY-TRANSACTION     PIC X(42).
00050     004500*
00051     004600 FD   IINVTLST
00052     004700      LABEL RECORDS ARE OMITTED
00053     004800      RECORD CONTAINS 132 CHARACTERS.
00054     004900*
00055     005000 01   PRINT-AREA      PIC X(132).
00056     005100*
00057     005200 WORKING-STORAGE SECTION.
00058     005300*
00059     005400 01   SWITCHES.
00060     005500*
00061     005600     05  PART-NUMBER-EOF-SW      PIC X     VALUE 'N'.
00062     005700         88  PART-NUMBER-EOF                VALUE 'Y'.
00063     005800     05  TRAN-EOF-SW             PIC X     VALUE 'N'.
00064     005900         88  TRAN-EOF                       VALUE 'Y'.
00065     006000     05  VALID-TRAN-SW           PIC X.
00066     006100         88  VALID-TRAN                     VALUE 'Y'.
```

```
00067    006200       05   PART-NUMBER-FOUND-SW        PIC X.
00068    006300            88   PART-NUMBER-FOUND                      VALUE 'Y'.
00069    006400       05   VALID-DATE-SW               PIC X.
00070    006500            88   VALID-DATE                             VALUE 'Y'.
00071    006600�
00072    006700 01   COUNT-FIELDS                      COMP-3.
00073    006800✳
00074    006900       05   TRANS-PROCESSED-COUNT       PIC S9(5)     VALUE ZERO.
00075    007000       05   INVALID-TRAN-CODE-COUNT     PIC S9(5)     VALUE ZERO.
00076    007100       05   INVALID-SALES-COUNT         PIC S9(5)     VALUE ZERO.
00077    007200       05   VALID-SALES-COUNT           PIC S9(5)     VALUE ZERO.
00078    007300       05   INVALID-RETURN-COUNT        PIC S9(5)     VALUE ZERO.
00079    007400       05   VALID-RETURN-COUNT          PIC S9(5)     VALUE ZERO.
00080    007500       05   INVALID-COUNT               PIC S9(5)     VALUE ZERO.
00081    007600       05   VALID-COUNT                 PIC S9(5)     VALUE ZERO.
00082    007700✳
00083    007800 01   PRINT-FIELDS.
00084    007900✳
00085    008000       05   SPACE-CONTROL   PIC S9                      COMP  SYNC.
00086    008100       05   LINE-COUNT      PIC S999     VALUE +999     COMP  SYNC.
00087    008200       05   LINES-ON-PAGE   PIC S999     VALUE +57      COMP  SYNC.
00088    008300       05   PAGE-COUNT      PIC S999     VALUE ZERO     COMP-3.
00089    008400✳
00090    008500 01   DATE-FIELDS.
00091    008600✳
00092    008700       05   TODAYS-DATE     PIC 9(6).
00093    008800✳
00094    008900 01   PART-NUMBER-TABLE.
00095    009000✳
00096    009100       05   PN-TABLE-ENTRY       OCCURS 100 TIMES
00097    009200                                 INDEXED BY PN-TABLE-INDEX
00098    009300                                 PIC X(5).
00099    009400       05   PN-ENTRY-COUNT       INDEX.
00100    009500✳
00101    009600 01   MISCELLANEOUS-FIELDS.
00102    009700✳
00103    009800       05   ERROR-INDICATOR     PIC X    VALUE '*'.
00104    009900✳
00105    010000 COPY INVTRAN.
00106 C        ✳
00107 C        01   INVENTORY-TRANSACTION-RECORD.
00108 C        ✳
00109 C             05   ITR-TYPE-CODE.
00110 C                  10   ITR-UPDATE-CODE      PIC X.
00111 C                  10   ITR-TRAN-CODE        PIC X.
00112 C             05   ITR-REF-NO               PIC X(10).
00113 C             05   ITR-REF-DATE             PIC X(6).
00114 C             05   ITR-BRANCH-NO            PIC XX.
00115 C             05   ITR-SALESMAN-NO          PIC XXX.
00116 C             05   ITR-CUSTOMER-NO          PIC X(5).
00117 C             05   ITR-QUANTITY             PIC X(5).
00118 C             05   ITR-PART-NO              PIC X(5).
00119 C             05   ITR-RETURN-CODE          PIC X(4).
00120    010100✳
00121    010200 01   COMPANY-NAME.
00122    010300✳
00123    010400       05   FILLER   PIC X(10)   VALUE SPACE.
00124    010500       05   FILLER   PIC X(20)   VALUE 'MIKE MURACH & ASSOCI'.
00125    010600       05   FILLER   PIC X(20)   VALUE 'ATES, INC.' .
00126    010700✳
00127    010800 01   REPORT-TITLE.
00128    010900✳
00129    011000       05   FILLER   PIC X(11)   VALUE SPACE.
00130    011100       05   FILLER   PIC X(20)   VALUE 'INVALID SALES AND RE'.
00131    011200       05   FILLER   PIC X(29)   VALUE 'TURN TRANSACTIONS'.
00132    011300✳
```

```
00133    011400 COPY RPTHDG14.
00134 C       ≠
00135 C          01   HEADING-LINE-1.
00136 C       ≠
00137 C             05   FILLER                    PIC X(7)     VALUE 'DATE:'.
00138 C             05   HDG1-DATE                 PIC 99/99/99.
00139 C             05   FILLER                    PIC X(26)    VALUE SPACE.
00140 C             05   HDG1-COMPANY-NAME         PIC X(50).
00141 C             05   FILLER                    PIC X(31)    VALUE SPACE.
00142 C             05   FILLER                    PIC X(6)     VALUE 'PAGE:'.
00143 C             05   HDG1-PAGE-NUMBER          PIC ZZ9.
00144 C       ≠
00145 C          01   HEADING-LINE-2.
00146 C       ≠
00147 C             05   HDG2-TIME-DATA.
00148 C                10   FILLER                 PIC X(7)     VALUE 'TIME:'.
00149 C                10   HDG2-HOURS             PIC XX.
00150 C                10   FILLER                 PIC X        VALUE ':'.
00151 C                10   HDG2-MINUTES           PIC XX.
00152 C                10   FILLER                 PIC X        VALUE SPACE.
00153 C                10   HDG2-TIME-SUFFIX       PIC X(8).
00154 C             05   FILLER                    PIC X(101)   VALUE SPACE.
00155 C             05   HDG2-REPORT-NUMBER        PIC X(10).
00156 C       ≠
00157 C          01   HEADING-LINE-3.
00158 C       ≠
00159 C             05   FILLER                    PIC X(36)    VALUE SPACE.
00160 C             05   HDG3-REPORT-TITLE         PIC X(60).
00161    011500≠
00162    011600 01   HEADING-LINE-4.
00163    011700≠
00164    011800    05   FILLER    PIC X(20)    VALUE 'TRAN    UPDATE    REFE'.
00165    011900    05   FILLER    PIC X(20)    VALUE 'RENCE                 '.
00166    012000    05   FILLER    PIC X(20)    VALUE 'BRANCH    SALESMAN    '.
00167    012100    05   FILLER    PIC X(20)    VALUE 'CUSTOMER              '.
00168    012200    05   FILLER    PIC X(20)    VALUE '    PART      RETURN   '.
00169    012300    05   FILLER    PIC X(20)    VALUE '                      '.
00170    012400    05   FILLER    PIC X(12)    VALUE '            '.
00171    012500≠
00172    012600 01   HEADING-LINE-5.
00173    012700≠
00174    012800    05   FILLER    PIC X(20)    VALUE 'CODE      CODE     NUM'.
00175    012900    05   FILLER    PIC X(20)    VALUE 'BER       DATE        '.
00176    013000    05   FILLER    PIC X(20)    VALUE 'NUMBER     NUMBER     '.
00177    013100    05   FILLER    PIC X(20)    VALUE ' NUMBER     QUANTITY  '.
00178    013200    05   FILLER    PIC X(20)    VALUE '  NUMBER     CODE     '.
00179    013300    05   FILLER    PIC X(20)    VALUE '                      '.
00180    013400    05   FILLER    PIC X(12)    VALUE '            '.
00181    013500≠
00182    013600 01   INVALID-TRANSACTION-LINE.
00183    013700≠
00184    013800    05   ITL-TRAN-CODE-ERR     PIC X.
00185    013900    05   ITL-TRAN-CODE         PIC X.
00186    014000    05   FILLER                PIC X(6).
00187    014100    05   ITL-UPDATE-CODE-ERR   PIC X.
00188    014200    05   ITL-UPDATE-CODE       PIC X.
00189    014300    05   FILLER                PIC X(5).
00190    014400    05   ITL-REF-NO-ERR        PIC X.
00191    014500    05   ITL-REF-NO            PIC X(10).
00192    014600    05   FILLER                PIC XX.
00193    014700    05   ITL-REF-DATE-ERR      PIC X.
00194    014800    05   ITL-REF-DATE          PIC XX/XX/XX.
00195    014900    05   FILLER                PIC X(4).
00196    015000    05   ITL-BRANCH-NO-ERR     PIC X.
00197    015100    05   ITL-BRANCH-NO         PIC XX.
00198    015200    05   FILLER                PIC X(6).
00199    015300    05   ITL-SALESMAN-NO-ERR   PIC X.
```

```
00200   015400     05   ITL-SALESMAN-NO      PIC XXX.
00201   015500     05   FILLER               PIC X(6).
00202   015600     05   ITL-CUSTOMER-NO-ERR  PIC X.
00203   015700     05   ITL-CUSTOMER-NO      PIC X(5).
00204   015800     05   FILLER               PIC X(7).
00205   015900     05   ITL-QUANTITY-ERR     PIC X.
00206   016000     05   ITL-QUANTITY         PIC X(5).
00207   016100     05   FILLER               PIC XX.
00208   016200     05   ITL-PART-NUMBER-ERR  PIC X.
00209   016300     05   ITL-PART-NUMBER      PIC X(5).
00210   016400     05   FILLER               PIC X(5).
00211   016500     05   ITL-RETURN-CODE-ERR  PIC X.
00212   016600     05   ITL-RETURN-CODE      PIC X(4).
00213   016700     05   FILLER               PIC X(42).
00214   016800*
00215   016900 01  ERROR-CODE-LINE.
00216   017000*
00217   017100     05   FILLER      PIC X(132)  VALUE '* INDICATES ERROR FIELDS'.
00218   017200*
00219   017300 01  SUMMARY-HEADING.
00220   017400*
00221   017500     05   FILLER      PIC X(20)   VALUE 'SUMMARY FOR SALES AN'.
00222   017600     05   FILLER      PIC X(112)  VALUE 'D RETURN EDITING RUN'.
00223   017700*
00224   017800 01  TOTAL-LINE.
00225   017900*
00226   018000     05   TL-HEADING   PIC X(22).
00227   018100     05   FILLER       PIC XX.
00228   018200     05   TL-COUNT     PIC ZZ,ZZ9.
00229   018300     05   FILLER       PIC X.
00230   018400     05   TL-AST-1     PIC X.
00231   018500     05   FILLER       PIC X.
00232   018600     05   TL-AST-2     PIC X.
00233   018700     05   FILLER       PIC X(98)   VALUE SPACE.
00234   018800*
00235   018900 PROCEDURE DIVISION.
00236   019000*
00237   019100 000-EDIT-INVENTORY-TRANS.
00238   019200*
00239   019300     OPEN INPUT   PARTNUM
00240   019400                  INVTRAN
00241   019500          OUTPUT VINVTRN
00242   019600                 IINVTLST.
00243   019700     PERFORM 100-FORMAT-REPORT-HEADING.
00244   019800     PERFORM 200-LOAD-PART-NUMBER-TABLE
00245   019900          VARYING PN-TABLE-INDEX FROM 1 BY 1
00246   020000          UNTIL PART-NUMBER-EOF.
00247   020100     PERFORM 300-EDIT-INVENTORY-TRAN
00248   020200          UNTIL TRAN-EOF.
00249   020300     PERFORM 500-PRINT-TOTAL-PAGE.
00250   020400     CLOSE PARTNUM
00251   020500           INVTRAN
00252   020600           VINVTRN
00253   020700           IINVTLST.
00254   020800     STOP RUN.
00255   020900*
00256   021000 100-FORMAT-REPORT-HEADING.
00257   021100*
00258   021200     CALL 'SYSDATE' USING TODAYS-DATE.
00259   021300     MOVE TODAYS-DATE    TO HDG1-DATE.
00260   021400     MOVE COMPANY-NAME   TO HDG1-COMPANY-NAME.
00261   021500     CALL 'SYSTIME' USING  HDG2-TIME-DATA.
00262   021600     MOVE 'INV2100'     TO HDG2-REPORT-NUMBER.
00263   021700     MOVE REPORT-TITLE  TO HDG3-REPORT-TITLE.
00264   021800*
00265   021900 200-LOAD-PART-NUMBER-TABLE.
00266   022000*
```

```
00267    022100    PERFORM 210-READ-PART-NUMBER-RECORD.
00268    022200    IF NOT PART-NUMBER-EOF
00269    022300        MOVE PNR-PART-NO TO PN-TABLE-ENTRY (PN-TABLE-INDEX)
00270    022400    ELSE
00271    022500        SET PN-TABLE-INDEX DOWN BY 1
00272    022600        SET PN-ENTRY-COUNT TO PN-TABLE-INDEX.
00273    022700*
00274    022800 210-READ-PART-NUMBER-RECORD.
00275    022900*
00276    023000    READ PARTNUM
00277    023100        AT END
00278    023200            MOVE 'Y' TO PART-NUMBER-EOF-SW.
00279    023300*
00280    023400 300-EDIT-INVENTORY-TRAN.
00281    023500*
00282    023600    PERFORM 310-READ-INVENTORY-TRAN.
00283    023700    IF NOT TRAN-EOF
00284    023800        PERFORM 320-EDIT-TRANSACTION-FIELDS
00285    023900        IF NOT VALID-TRAN
00286    024000            PERFORM 360-PRINT-INVALID-TRANSACTION
00287    024100        ELSE
00288    024200            PERFORM 400-WRITE-VALID-TRANSACTION.
00289    024300*
00290    024400 310-READ-INVENTORY-TRAN.
00291    024500*
00292    024600    READ INVTRAN INTO INVENTORY-TRANSACTION-RECORD
00293    024700        AT END
00294    024800            MOVE 'Y' TO TRAN-EOF-SW.
00295    024900    IF NOT TRAN-EOF
00296    025000        ADD 1 TO TRANS-PROCESSED-COUNT.
00297    025100*
00298    025200 320-EDIT-TRANSACTION-FIELDS.
00299    025300*
00300    025400    MOVE 'Y'  TO VALID-TRAN-SW.
00301    025500    MOVE SPACE TO INVALID-TRANSACTION-LINE.
00302    025600    IF ITR-TRAN-CODE = 1
00303    025700        PERFORM 330-EDIT-CODE-1-FIELDS
00304    025800    ELSE IF ITR-TRAN-CODE = 2
00305    025900        PERFORM 350-EDIT-CODE-2-FIELDS
00306    026000    ELSE
00307    026100        MOVE ERROR-INDICATOR TO ITL-TRAN-CODE-ERR
00308    026200        MOVE 'N'              TO VALID-TRAN-SW
00309    026300        ADD 1                 TO INVALID-TRAN-CODE-COUNT.
00310    026400*
00311    026500 330-EDIT-CODE-1-FIELDS.
00312    026600*
00313    026700    IF ITR-UPDATE-CODE NOT = 'C'
00314    026800        MOVE 'N'              TO VALID-TRAN-SW
00315    026900        MOVE ERROR-INDICATOR TO ITL-UPDATE-CODE-ERR.
00316    027000    CALL 'DATEDIT' USING ITR-REF-DATE, VALID-DATE-SW.
00317    027100    IF NOT VALID-DATE
00318    027200        MOVE 'N'              TO VALID-TRAN-SW
00319    027300        MOVE ERROR-INDICATOR TO ITL-REF-DATE-ERR.
00320    027400    IF      ITR-BRANCH-NO NOT NUMERIC
00321    027500        OR ITR-BRANCH-NO NOT GREATER ZERO
00322    027600        OR ITR-BRANCH-NO NOT LESS 25
00323    027700        MOVE 'N'              TO VALID-TRAN-SW
00324    027800        MOVE ERROR-INDICATOR TO ITL-BRANCH-NO-ERR.
00325    027900    IF      ITR-SALESMAN-NO NOT NUMERIC
00326    028000        OR ITR-SALESMAN-NO NOT GREATER ZERO
00327    028100        MOVE 'N'              TO VALID-TRAN-SW
00328    028200        MOVE ERROR-INDICATOR TO ITL-SALESMAN-NO-ERR.
00329    028300    IF      ITR-CUSTOMER-NO NOT NUMERIC
00330    028400        OR ITR-CUSTOMER-NO NOT GREATER ZERO
00331    028500        MOVE 'N'              TO VALID-TRAN-SW
00332    028600        MOVE ERROR-INDICATOR TO ITL-CUSTOMER-NO-ERR.
00333    028700    IF      ITR-QUANTITY NOT NUMERIC
```

```
00334    028800                    OR ITR-QUANTITY NOT GREATER ZERO
00335    028900              MOVE 'N'                 TO VALID-TRAN-SW
00336    029000              MOVE ERROR-INDICATOR TO ITL-QUANTITY-ERR.
00337    029100         PERFORM 340-SEARCH-PART-NUMBER-TABLE.
00338    029200         IF NOT PART-NUMBER-FOUND
00339    029300              MOVE 'N'                 TO VALID-TRAN-SW
00340    029400              MOVE ERROR-INDICATOR TO ITL-PART-NUMBER-ERR.
00341    029500         IF NOT VALID-TRAN
00342    029600              ADD 1 TO INVALID-SALES-COUNT
00343    029700         ELSE
00344    029800              ADD 1 TO VALID-SALES-COUNT.
00345    029900*
00346    030000 340-SEARCH-PART-NUMBER-TABLE.
00347    030100*
00348    030200         SET PN-TABLE-INDEX TO 1.
00349    030300         SEARCH PN-TABLE-ENTRY
00350    030400              AT END
00351    030500                   MOVE 'N' TO PART-NUMBER-FOUND-SW
00352    030600              WHEN ITR-PART-NO = PN-TABLE-ENTRY (PN-TABLE-INDEX)
00353    030700                   MOVE 'Y' TO PART-NUMBER-FOUND-SW
00354    030800              WHEN PN-TABLE-INDEX GREATER PN-ENTRY-COUNT
00355    030900                   MOVE 'N' TO PART-NUMBER-FOUND-SW.
00356    031000*
00357    031100 350-EDIT-CODE-2-FIELDS.
00358    031200*
00359    031300         IF ITR-UPDATE-CODE NOT = 'C'
00360    031400              MOVE 'N'                 TO VALID-TRAN-SW
00361    031500              MOVE ERROR-INDICATOR TO ITL-UPDATE-CODE-ERR.
00362    031600         CALL 'DATEDIT' USING ITR-REF-DATE, VALID-DATE-SW.
00363    031700         IF NOT VALID-DATE
00364    031800              MOVE 'N'                 TO VALID-TRAN-SW
00365    031900              MOVE ERROR-INDICATOR TO ITL-REF-DATE-ERR.
00366    032000         IF         ITR-CUSTOMER-NO NOT NUMERIC
00367    032100              OR ITR-CUSTOMER-NO NOT GREATER ZERO
00368    032200              MOVE 'N'                 TO VALID-TRAN-SW
00369    032300              MOVE ERROR-INDICATOR TO ITL-CUSTOMER-NO-ERR.
00370    032400         IF         ITR-QUANTITY NOT NUMERIC
00371    032500              OR ITR-QUANTITY NOT GREATER ZERO
00372    032600              MOVE 'N'                 TO VALID-TRAN-SW
00373    032700              MOVE ERROR-INDICATOR TO ITL-QUANTITY-ERR.
00374    032800         PERFORM 340-SEARCH-PART-NUMBER-TABLE.
00375    032900         IF NOT PART-NUMBER-FOUND
00376    033000              MOVE 'N'                 TO VALID-TRAN-SW
00377    033100              MOVE ERROR-INDICATOR TO ITL-PART-NUMBER-ERR.
00378    033200         IF         ITR-RETURN-CODE NOT ALPHABETIC
00379    033300              OR ITR-RETURN-CODE = SPACE
00380    033400              MOVE 'N'                 TO VALID-TRAN-SW
00381    033500              MOVE ERROR-INDICATOR TO ITL-RETURN-CODE-ERR.
00382    033600         IF NOT VALID-TRAN
00383    033700              ADD 1 TO INVALID-RETURN-COUNT
00384    033800         ELSE
00385    033900              ADD 1 TO VALID-RETURN-COUNT.
00386    034000*
00387    034100 360-PRINT-INVALID-TRANSACTION.
00388    034200*
00389    034300         IF LINE-COUNT GREATER LINES-ON-PAGE
00390    034400              PERFORM 370-PRINT-HEADING-LINES.
00391    034500         MOVE ITR-TRAN-CODE           TO ITL-TRAN-CODE.
00392    034600         MOVE ITR-UPDATE-CODE         TO ITL-UPDATE-CODE.
00393    034700         MOVE ITR-REF-NO              TO ITL-REF-NO.
00394    034800         MOVE ITR-REF-DATE            TO ITL-REF-DATE.
00395    034900         MOVE ITR-BRANCH-NO           TO ITL-BRANCH-NO.
00396    035000         MOVE ITR-SALESMAN-NO         TO ITL-SALESMAN-NO.
00397    035100         MOVE ITR-CUSTOMER-NO         TO ITL-CUSTOMER-NO.
00398    035200         MOVE ITR-QUANTITY            TO ITL-QUANTITY.
00399    035300         MOVE ITR-PART-NO             TO ITL-PART-NUMBER.
00400    035400         MOVE ITR-RETURN-CODE         TO ITL-RETURN-CODE.
```

```
00401   035500      MOVE INVALID-TRANSACTION-LINE TO PRINT-AREA.
00402   035600      PERFORM 390-WRITE-REPORT-LINE.
00403   035700      MOVE 1                        TO SPACE-CONTROL.
00404   035800*
00405   035900 370-PRINT-HEADING-LINES.
00406   036000*
00407   036100      ADD 1              TO PAGE-COUNT.
00408   036200      MOVE PAGE-COUNT       TO HDG1-PAGE-NUMBER.
00409   036300      MOVE HEADING-LINE-1 TO PRINT-AREA.
00410   036400      PERFORM 380-WRITE-PAGE-TOP-LINE.
00411   036500      MOVE HEADING-LINE-2 TO PRINT-AREA.
00412   036600      MOVE 1              TO SPACE-CONTROL.
00413   036700      PERFORM 390-WRITE-REPORT-LINE.
00414   036800      MOVE HEADING-LINE-3 TO PRINT-AREA.
00415   036900      PERFORM 390-WRITE-REPORT-LINE.
00416   037000      MOVE HEADING-LINE-4 TO PRINT-AREA.
00417   037100      MOVE 2              TO SPACE-CONTROL.
00418   037200      PERFORM 390-WRITE-REPORT-LINE.
00419   037300      MOVE HEADING-LINE-5 TO PRINT-AREA.
00420   037400      MOVE 1              TO SPACE-CONTROL.
00421   037500      PERFORM 390-WRITE-REPORT-LINE.
00422   037600      MOVE 2              TO SPACE-CONTROL.
00423   037700*
00424   037800 380-WRITE-PAGE-TOP-LINE.
00425   037900*
00426   038000      WRITE PRINT-AREA
00427   038100          AFTER ADVANCING PAGE.
00428   038200      MOVE 1 TO LINE-COUNT.
00429   038300*
00430   038400 390-WRITE-REPORT-LINE.
00431   038500*
00432   038600      WRITE PRINT-AREA
00433   038700          AFTER ADVANCING SPACE-CONTROL LINES.
00434   038800      ADD SPACE-CONTROL TO LINE-COUNT.
00435   038900*
00436   039000 400-WRITE-VALID-TRANSACTION.
00437   039100*
00438   039200      WRITE VALID-INVENTORY-TRANSACTION
00439   039300          FROM INVENTORY-TRANSACTION-RECORD.
00440   039400*
00441   039500 500-PRINT-TOTAL-PAGE.
00442   039600*
00443   039700      ADD 1               TO PAGE-COUNT.
00444   039800      MOVE PAGE-COUNT       TO HDG1-PAGE-NUMBER.
00445   039900      MOVE HEADING-LINE-1  TO PRINT-AREA.
00446   040000      PERFORM 380-WRITE-PAGE-TOP-LINE.
00447   040100      MOVE HEADING-LINE-2  TO PRINT-AREA.
00448   040200      MOVE 1               TO SPACE-CONTROL.
00449   040300      PERFORM 390-WRITE-REPORT-LINE.
00450   040400      MOVE SUMMARY-HEADING TO PRINT-AREA.
00451   040500      MOVE 3               TO SPACE-CONTROL.
00452   040600      PERFORM 390-WRITE-REPORT-LINE.
00453   040700      MOVE SPACE TO TOTAL-LINE.
00454   040800      COMPUTE VALID-COUNT = VALID-SALES-COUNT
00455   040900                        + VALID-RETURN-COUNT.
00456   041000      COMPUTE INVALID-COUNT = INVALID-SALES-COUNT
00457   041100                        + INVALID-RETURN-COUNT.
00458   041200      MOVE 'VALID    SALES'        TO TL-HEADING.
00459   041300      MOVE VALID-SALES-COUNT       TO TL-COUNT.
00460   041400      MOVE TOTAL-LINE              TO PRINT-AREA.
00461   041500      PERFORM 390-WRITE-REPORT-LINE.
00462   041600      MOVE SPACE                   TO TOTAL-LINE.
00463   041700      MOVE '       RETURNS'        TO TL-HEADING.
00464   041800      MOVE VALID-RETURN-COUNT      TO TL-COUNT.
00465   041900      MOVE TOTAL-LINE              TO PRINT-AREA.
00466   042000      MOVE 1                       TO SPACE-CONTROL.
00467   042100      PERFORM 390-WRITE-REPORT-LINE.
```

```
00468    042200        MOVE SPACE                      TO TOTAL-LINE.
00469    042300        MOVE '           TOTAL'         TO TL-HEADING.
00470    042400        MOVE VALID-COUNT                TO TL-COUNT.
00471    042500        MOVE '*'                        TO TL-AST-1.
00472    042600        MOVE TOTAL-LINE                 TO PRINT-AREA.
00473    042700        PERFORM 390-WRITE-REPORT-LINE.
00474    042800        MOVE SPACE                      TO TOTAL-LINE.
00475    042900        MOVE 'INVALID SALES'            TO TL-HEADING.
00476    043000        MOVE INVALID-SALES-COUNT        TO TL-COUNT.
00477    043100        MOVE TOTAL-LINE                 TO PRINT-AREA.
00478    043200        MOVE 2                          TO SPACE-CONTROL.
00479    043300        PERFORM 390-WRITE-REPORT-LINE.
00480    043400        MOVE SPACE                      TO TOTAL-LINE.
00481    043500        MOVE '         RETURNS'         TO TL-HEADING.
00482    043600        MOVE INVALID-RETURN-COUNT       TO TL-COUNT.
00483    043700        MOVE TOTAL-LINE                 TO PRINT-AREA.
00484    043800        MOVE 1                          TO SPACE-CONTROL.
00485    043900        PERFORM 390-WRITE-REPORT-LINE.
00486    044000        MOVE SPACE                      TO TOTAL-LINE.
00487    044100        MOVE '           TOTAL'         TO TL-HEADING.
00488    044200        MOVE INVALID-COUNT              TO TL-COUNT.
00489    044300        MOVE '*'                        TO TL-AST-1.
00490    044400        MOVE TOTAL-LINE                 TO PRINT-AREA.
00491    044500        PERFORM 390-WRITE-REPORT-LINE.
00492    044600        MOVE SPACE                      TO TOTAL-LINE.
00493    044700        MOVE 'INVALID TRAN CODES'       TO TL-HEADING.
00494    044800        MOVE INVALID-TRAN-CODE-COUNT    TO TL-COUNT.
00495    044900        MOVE '*'                        TO TL-AST-1.
00496    045000        MOVE TOTAL-LINE                 TO PRINT-AREA.
00497    045100        MOVE 2                          TO SPACE-CONTROL.
00498    045200        PERFORM 390-WRITE-REPORT-LINE.
00499    045300        MOVE SPACE                      TO TOTAL-LINE.
00500    045400        MOVE 'TRANSACTIONS PROCESSED'   TO TL-HEADING.
00501    045500        MOVE TRANS-PROCESSED-COUNT      TO TL-COUNT.
00502    045600        MOVE '*'                        TO TL-AST-1.
00503    045700        MOVE '*'                        TO TL-AST-2.
00504    045800        MOVE TOTAL-LINE                 TO PRINT-AREA.
00505    045900        PERFORM 390-WRITE-REPORT-LINE.
```

DATE: 10/25/84
TIME: 2:27 PM

MIKE MURACH & ASSOCIATES, INC.

INVALID SALES AND RETURN TRANSACTIONS

TRAN CODE	UPDATE CODE	REFERENCE NUMBER	DATE	BRANCH NUMBER	SALESMAN NUMBER	CUSTOMER NUMBER	QUANTITY	PART NUMBER	RETURN CODE
1	C	90347	≠31/01/83	12	039	03095	00003	10	
2	C	892847K	≠02/31/84			02907	00003	3	AJK
2	C	829347	04/10/84			90837	00021	14	≠
2	C	9283478	04/18/84			00028	00001	12	≠1
1	C	82984	04/24/84	12	028	03734	00001	≠37	AMP
≠	C	921834	04/28/84	15	392	03824	00003	14	
1	C	028947	04/28/84	≠38	398	39027	00013	21	
1	≠D	923847	05/02/84	10	021	00145	00005	2	
1	C	9238	05/05/84	13	293	09382	≠R42	10	
1	C	28394L3	05/10/84	06	298	≠W394	00003	19	
2	C	02848	05/10/84			≠00000	00002	14	DHG
2	C	IE92847	05/13/84			09283	≠Q9230	18	BJA
2	C	2908347	05/13/84			98347	00002	≠28	AMP
1	C	934781	05/20/84	≠A4	892	39827	≠00000	4	
2	C	92374	05/24/84			02983	00001	21	CGC
1	C	928304	05/25/84	02	≠413	92837	00001	17	
1	C	0234978	05/25/84	14	≠000	38754	00003	7	
2	≠X	8239487	05/28/84	02	938	00390	00002	21	
2	≠X	298347	≠05/38/84		023	≠023JR	≠00000	≠QW	JC
1	C	8993847	06/01/84	03	023	00874	≠00000	14	≠3
1	C	3892413	06/02/84	05	398	≠00000	00007	11	
2	C	924789	06/03/82			≠U39	00001	19	CRL
1	≠V	928347	≠13/24/84	≠29	≠A29	≠W9300	≠	≠38	
1	C	02347K	≠52/22/84	≠00	029	01938	00003	20	

DATE: 10/25/84
TIME: 2:27 PM

MIKE MURACH & ASSOCIATES, INC.

SUMMARY FOR SALES AND RETURN EDITING RUN

```
VALID     SALES                   2
          RETURNS                 1
               TOTAL              3 *

INVALID   SALES                  13
          RETURNS                10
               TOTAL             23 *

INVALID TRAN CODES                1 *

TRANSACTIONS PROCESSED           27 * * *
```

Model program 2

The report-preparation program

Program:	MKTG1200 Produce Sales Report	Page:	1
Designer:	Anne Prince	Date:	08-24-84

Input/output specifications

File	Description	Use
CUSTMST	Customer master file	Input
SALESMN	Salesman master file	Input
SALESRPT	Print file: Sales report	Output

Process specifications

The customer master file is in sequence by customer number within salesman number within branch number. This file should be read sequentially, and one line should be printed for each record in the file.

The year-to-date sales for the current and previous year are contained in each customer record, and the change amount and change percent are calculated from these values.

The salesman master file is indexed by salesman number within branch number. This file should be read randomly by the program, and the salesman records should be used to get the salesmen's names for the sales report.

Totals should be printed for each salesman and branch. At the end of the report, a grand total of all sales should be printed.

Process specifications

The basic processing requirements follow.

Do until the end of the customer master file:

1. Read a customer record.

2. If the salesman key in a customer record is different than the one in the previous customer record, calculate the salesman change amount and change percent and print a salesman total line. Then, reset the salesman totals to zero and read the salesman master file.

3. If the branch number in the customer record is different than the one in the previous customer record, calculate the branch change amount and change percent and print a branch total line. Then, reset the branch totals to zero.

4. Calculate the customer change amount and change percent and print a customer sales line.

5. Add the customer sales totals to the salesman, branch, and grand totals.

After all customers have been processed, calculate the total change amount and change percent and print a grand total line.

```
BKEND    C.CUSTMAST

✿
 01   CUSTOMER-MASTER-RECORD.
✿
      05   CM-CUSTOMER-KEY.
           10   CM-SALESMAN-KEY.
                15   CM-BRANCH-NUMBER      PIC XX.
                15   CM-SALESMAN-NUMBER    PIC XX.
           10   CM-CUSTOMER-NUMBER         PIC X(5).
      05   CM-CUSTOMER-NAME                PIC X(25).
      05   CM-SALES-THIS-YTD               PIC S9(5)V99   COMP-3.
      05   CM-SALES-LAST-YTD               PIC S9(5)V99   COMP-3.

      BKEND
```

```
      BKEND    C.SALESMAN

 ✻
  01   SALESMAN-MASTER-RECORD.
 ✻
     05   SM-SALESMAN-KEY.
          10   SM-BRANCH-NUMBER      PIC XX.
          10   SM-SALESMAN-NUMBER    PIC XX.
     05   SM-SALESMAN-NAME           PIC X(25).

     BKEND
```

Document name **Year-To-Date Sales Report**   Date **8-23-84**

Program name **MKTG1200**   Designer **Anne Prince**

Record Name		
Heading-Line-1	DATE: 99/99/99	PAGE: ZZ9
Heading-Line-2	TIME: 99:99 XX	MKTG1200
Heading-Line-3		
	YEAR-TO-DATE SALES REPORT	
Heading-Line-4	BRANCH SALESMAN SALESMAN CUSTOMER CUSTOMER	SALES SALES CHANGE CHANGE
Heading-Line-5	NO NO NAME NO NAME	THIS YTD LAST YTD AMOUNT CHANGE
Customer-Line	XX XX X ZZZZ9 X ZZ,ZZ9.99 ZZ,ZZ9.99 ZZ,ZZ9.99- ZZZ9-	
Salesman-Total-Line	SALESMAN TOTALS: Z,ZZZ,ZZ9.99- Z,ZZZ,ZZ9.99- Z,ZZZ,ZZ9.99- ZZZ9-	
Branch-Total-Line	XX X ZZZZ9 X BRANCH TOTALS: Z,ZZZ,ZZ9.99 Z,ZZZ,ZZ9.99 Z,ZZZ,ZZ9.99- ZZZ9-	
	SALESMAN TOTALS: Z,ZZZ,ZZ9.99- Z,ZZZ,ZZ9.99- Z,ZZZ,ZZ9.99- ZZZ9-	
	BRANCH TOTALS: Z,ZZZ,ZZ9.99- Z,ZZZ,ZZ9.99- Z,ZZZ,ZZ9.99- ZZZ9-	
Grand-Total-Line	GRAND TOTALS: ZZZ,ZZZ,ZZ9.99- ZZZ,ZZZ,ZZ9.99- ZZZ,ZZZ,ZZ9.99- ZZZ9-	

MIKE MURACH & ASSOCIATES, INC.

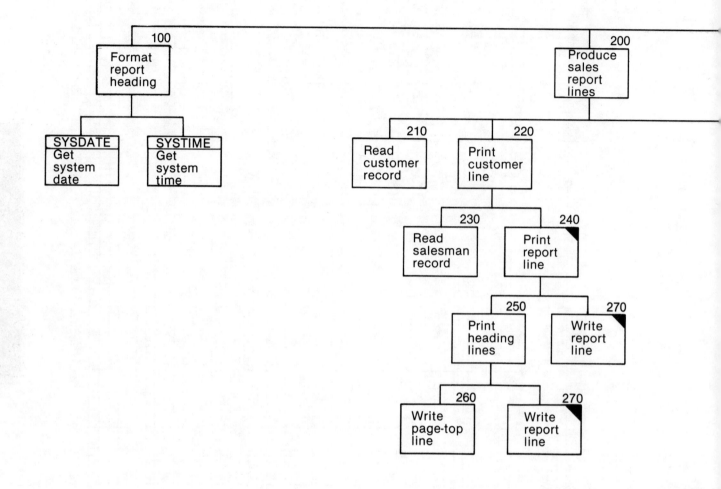

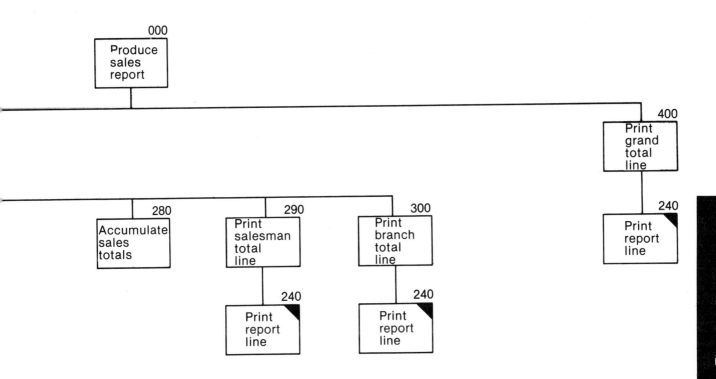

000
Produce
sales
report

400
Print
grand
total
line

280
Accumulate
sales
totals

290
Print
salesman
total
line

300
Print
branch
total
line

240
Print
report
line

240
Print
report
line

240
Print
report
line

240
Print
report
line

The report-
preparation program

```
CBL APOST,LANGLVL(1),CLIST,LIB
00001     000100 IDENTIFICATION DIVISION.
00002     000200✳
00003     000300 PROGRAM-ID.      MKTG1200.
00004     000400✳AUTHOR.          ANNE PRINCE.
00005     000500✳INSTALLATION.    MMA.
00006     000600✳DATE.            SEPTEMBER 10, 1984.
00007     000700✳
00008     000800 ENVIRONMENT DIVISION.
00009     000900✳
00010     001000 CONFIGURATION SECTION.
00011     001100✳
00012     001200 SOURCE-COMPUTER.     IBM-370.
00013     001300 OBJECT-COMPUTER.     IBM-370.
00014     001400✳
00015     001500 INPUT-OUTPUT SECTION.
00016     001600✳
00017     001700 FILE-CONTROL.
00018     001800     SELECT CUSTMST   ASSIGN TO SYS005-AS-CUSTMST.
00019     001900     SELECT SALESMN   ASSIGN TO SYS008-SALESMN
00020     002000                      ORGANIZATION IS INDEXED
00021     002100                      ACCESS IS RANDOM
00022     002200                      RECORD KEY IS SM-SALESMAN-KEY.
00023     002300     SELECT SALESRPT ASSIGN TO SYS006-UR-1403-S.
00024     002400✳
00025     002500 DATA DIVISION.
00026     002600✳
00027     002700 FILE SECTION.
00028     002800✳
00029     002900 FD   CUSTMST
00030     003000     LABEL RECORDS ARE STANDARD
00031     003100     RECORD CONTAINS 42 CHARACTERS.
00032     003200✳
00033     003300 COPY CUSTMAST.
00034 C        ✳
00035 C            01   CUSTOMER-MASTER-RECORD.
00036 C        ✳
00037 C            05   CM-CUSTOMER-KEY.
00038 C                10   CM-SALESMAN-KEY.
00039 C                    15   CM-BRANCH-NUMBER      PIC XX.
00040 C                    15   CM-SALESMAN-NUMBER    PIC XX.
00041 C                10   CM-CUSTOMER-NUMBER    PIC X(5).
00042 C            05   CM-CUSTOMER-NAME          PIC X(25).
00043 C            05   CM-SALES-THIS-YTD         PIC S9(5)V99   COMP-3.
00044 C            05   CM-SALES-LAST-YTD         PIC S9(5)V99   COMP-3.
00045     003400✳
00046     003500 FD   SALESMN
00047     003600     LABEL RECORDS ARE STANDARD
00048     003700     RECORD CONTAINS 29 CHARACTERS.
00049     003800✳
00050     003900 COPY SALESMAN.
00051 C        ✳
00052 C            01   SALESMAN-MASTER-RECORD.
00053 C        ✳
00054 C            05   SM-SALESMAN-KEY.
00055 C                10   SM-BRANCH-NUMBER     PIC XX.
00056 C                10   SM-SALESMAN-NUMBER   PIC XX.
00057 C            05   SM-SALESMAN-NAME         PIC X(25).
00058     004000✳
00059     004100 FD   SALESRPT
00060     004200     LABEL RECORDS ARE OMITTED
00061     004300     RECORD CONTAINS 132 CHARACTERS.
00062     004400✳
00063     004500 01   PRINT-AREA.
00064     004600✳
00065     004700     05   PRINT-LINE  PIC X(132).
00066     004800✳
```

```
00067     004900 WORKING-STORAGE SECTION.
00068     005000*
00069     005100 01  SWITCHES.
00070     005200*
00071     005300     05  FIRST-RECORD-SW PIC X      VALUE 'Y'.
00072     005400         88  FIRST-RECORD           VALUE 'Y'.
00073     005500     05  CUSTOMER-EOF-SW PIC X      VALUE 'N'.
00074     005600         88  CUSTOMER-EOF           VALUE 'Y'.
00075     005700     05  RECORD-FOUND-SW PIC X      VALUE 'Y'.
00076     005800         88  RECORD-FOUND           VALUE 'Y'.
00077     005900*
00078     006000 01  CONTROL-FIELDS.
00079     006100*
00080     006200     05  OLD-SALESMAN-KEY.
00081     006300         10  OLD-BRANCH-NUMBER    PIC 99.
00082     006400         10  OLD-SALESMAN-NUMBER PIC 99.
00083     006500*
00084     006600 01  WORK-FIELDS             COMP-3.
00085     006700*
00086     006800     05  CHANGE-AMOUNT    PIC S9(7)V99     VALUE ZERO.
00087     006900     05  CHANGE-PERCENT   PIC S9(3)V99     VALUE ZERO.
00088     007000*
00089     007100 01  PRINT-FIELDS.
00090     007200*
00091     007300     05  SPACE-CONTROL    PIC S9                   COMP  SYNC.
00092     007400     05  LINE-COUNT       PIC S999    VALUE +999  COMP  SYNC.
00093     007500     05  LINES-ON-PAGE    PIC S999    VALUE +53   COMP  SYNC.
00094     007600     05  PAGE-COUNT       PIC S999    VALUE ZERO  COMP-3.
00095     007700*
00096     007800 01  TOTAL-FIELDS                    COMP-3.
00097     007900*
00098     008000     05  SALESMAN-TOTAL-THIS-YTD PIC S9(7)V99     VALUE ZERO.
00099     008100     05  SALESMAN-TOTAL-LAST-YTD PIC S9(7)V99     VALUE ZERO.
00100     008200     05  BRANCH-TOTAL-THIS-YTD   PIC S9(7)V99     VALUE ZERO.
00101     008300     05  BRANCH-TOTAL-LAST-YTD   PIC S9(7)V99     VALUE ZERO.
00102     008400     05  TOTAL-SALES-THIS-YTD    PIC S9(9)V99     VALUE ZERO.
00103     008500     05  TOTAL-SALES-LAST-YTD    PIC S9(9)V99     VALUE ZERO.
00104     008600*
00105     008700 01  DATE-FIELDS.
00106     008800*
00107     008900     05  TODAYS-DATE      PIC 9(6).
00108     009000*
00109     009100 01  NEXT-REPORT-LINE     PIC X(132).
00110     009200*
00111     009300 01  COMPANY-NAME.
00112     009400*
00113     009500     05  FILLER        PIC X(10)  VALUE SPACE.
00114     009600     05  FILLER        PIC X(20)  VALUE 'MIKE MURACH & ASSOCI'.
00115     009700     05  FILLER        PIC X(20)  VALUE 'ATES, INC.          '.
00116     009800*
00117     009900 01  REPORT-TITLE.
00118     010000*
00119     010100     05  FILLER        PIC X(17)  VALUE SPACE.
00120     010200     05  FILLER        PIC X(20)  VALUE 'YEAR-TO-DATE SALES R'.
00121     010300     05  FILLER        PIC X(23)  VALUE 'EPORT'.
00122     010400*
00123     010500 COPY RPTHDG14.
00124 C      *
00125 C          01  HEADING-LINE-1.
00126 C      *
00127 C              05  FILLER             PIC X(7)    VALUE 'DATE:'.
00128 C              05  HDG1-DATE          PIC 99/99/99.
00129 C              05  FILLER             PIC X(26)   VALUE SPACE.
00130 C              05  HDG1-COMPANY-NAME  PIC X(50).
00131 C              05  FILLER             PIC X(31)   VALUE SPACE.
00132 C              05  FILLER             PIC X(6)    VALUE 'PAGE:'.
00133 C              05  HDG1-PAGE-NUMBER   PIC ZZ9.
```

```
00134 C          ✣
00135 C               01   HEADING-LINE-2.
00136 C          ✣
00137 C                    05   HDG2-TIME-DATA.
00138 C                         10   FILLER              PIC X(7)     VALUE 'TIME:'.
00139 C                         10   HDG2-HOURS          PIC XX.
00140 C                         10   FILLER              PIC X        VALUE ':'.
00141 C                         10   HDG2-MINUTES        PIC XX.
00142 C                         10   FILLER              PIC X        VALUE SPACE.
00143 C                         10   HDG2-TIME-SUFFIX    PIC X(8).
00144 C                    05   FILLER                   PIC X(101)   VALUE SPACE.
00145 C                    05   HDG2-REPORT-NUMBER       PIC X(10).
00146 C          ✣
00147 C               01   HEADING-LINE-3.
00148 C          ✣
00149 C                    05   FILLER                   PIC X(36)    VALUE SPACE.
00150 C                    05   HDG3-REPORT-TITLE        PIC X(60).
00151   010600✣
00152   010700 01   HEADING-LINE-4.
00153   010800✣
00154   010900      05   FILLER      PIC X(20)    VALUE 'BRANCH    SALESMAN  SA'.
00155   011000      05   FILLER      PIC X(20)    VALUE 'LESMAN                '.
00156   011100      05   FILLER      PIC X(20)    VALUE '      CUSTOMER   CUSTO'.
00157   011200      05   FILLER      PIC X(20)    VALUE 'MER                   '.
00158   011300      05   FILLER      PIC X(20)    VALUE '          SALES       '.
00159   011400      05   FILLER      PIC X(20)    VALUE '    SALES          CH'.
00160   011500      05   FILLER      PIC X(12)    VALUE 'ANGE   CHANGE'.
00161   011600✣
00162   011700 01   HEADING-LINE-5.
00163   011800✣
00164   011900      05   FILLER      PIC X(20)    VALUE '  NO          NO      NA'.
00165   012000      05   FILLER      PIC X(20)    VALUE 'ME                    '.
00166   012100      05   FILLER      PIC X(20)    VALUE '          NO     NAME '.
00167   012200      05   FILLER      PIC X(20)    VALUE '                      '.
00168   012300      05   FILLER      PIC X(20)    VALUE '         THIS YTD     '.
00169   012400      05   FILLER      PIC X(20)    VALUE ' LAST YTD          AM'.
00170   012500      05   FILLER      PIC X(20)    VALUE 'OUNT      %'.
00171   012600✣
00172   012700 01   CUSTOMER-LINE.
00173   012800✣
00174   012900      05   FILLER              PIC XX       VALUE SPACE.
00175   013000      05   CL-BRANCH-NO        PIC XX.
00176   013100      05   FILLER              PIC X(7)     VALUE SPACE.
00177   013200      05   CL-SALESMAN-NO      PIC XX.
00178   013300      05   FILLER              PIC X(5)     VALUE SPACE.
00179   013400      05   CL-SALESMAN-NAME    PIC X(25).
00180   013500      05   FILLER              PIC X(4)     VALUE SPACE.
00181   013600      05   CL-CUSTOMER-NO      PIC ZZZZ9.
00182   013700      05   FILLER              PIC XXX      VALUE SPACE.
00183   013800      05   CL-CUSTOMER-NAME    PIC X(25).
00184   013900      05   FILLER              PIC X(5)     VALUE SPACE.
00185   014000      05   CL-SALES-THIS-YTD   PIC ZZ,ZZ9.99-.
00186   014100      05   FILLER              PIC X(5)     VALUE SPACE.
00187   014200      05   CL-SALES-LAST-YTD   PIC ZZ,ZZ9.99-.
00188   014300      05   FILLER              PIC X(5)     VALUE SPACE.
00189   014400      05   CL-CHANGE-AMOUNT    PIC ZZ,ZZ9.99-.
00190   014500      05   FILLER              PIC X        VALUE SPACE.
00191   014600      05   CL-CHANGE-PERCENT   PIC ZZZ9-.
00192   014700      05   CL-CHANGE-PERCENT-R REDEFINES CL-CHANGE-PERCENT
00193   014800                               PIC X(5).
00194   014900✣
00195   015000 01   SALESMAN-TOTAL-LINE.
00196   015100✣
00197   015200      05   FILLER              PIC X(63)    VALUE SPACE.
00198   015300      05   FILLER              PIC X(19)    VALUE 'SALESMAN TOTALS:'.
00199   015400      05   SL-SALES-THIS-YTD   PIC Z,ZZZ,ZZ9.99-.
00200   015500      05   FILLER              PIC XX       VALUE SPACE.
```

```
00201   015600   05    SL-SALES-LAST-YTD         PIC Z,ZZZ,ZZ9.99-.
00202   015700   05    FILLER                    PIC XX        VALUE SPACE.
00203   015800   05    SL-CHANGE-AMOUNT          PIC Z,ZZZ,ZZ9.99-.
00204   015900   05    FILLER                    PIC X         VALUE SPACE.
00205   016000   05    SL-CHANGE-PERCENT         PIC ZZZ9-.
00206   016100   05    SL-CHANGE-PERCENT-R       REDEFINES SL-CHANGE-PERCENT
00207   016200                                   PIC X(5).
00208   016300*
00209   016400 01  BRANCH-TOTAL-LINE.
00210   016500*
00211   016600   05    FILLER                    PIC X(65)     VALUE SPACE.
00212   016700   05    FILLER                    PIC X(17)     VALUE 'BRANCH TOTALS:'.
00213   016800   05    BL-SALES-THIS-YTD         PIC Z,ZZZ,ZZ9.99-.
00214   016900   05    FILLER                    PIC XX        VALUE SPACE.
00215   017000   05    BL-SALES-LAST-YTD         PIC Z,ZZZ,ZZ9.99-.
00216   017100   05    FILLER                    PIC XX        VALUE SPACE.
00217   017200   05    BL-CHANGE-AMOUNT          PIC Z,ZZZ,ZZ9.99-.
00218   017300   05    FILLER                    PIC X         VALUE SPACE.
00219   017400   05    BL-CHANGE-PERCENT         PIC ZZZ9-.
00220   017500   05    BL-CHANGE-PERCENT-R       REDEFINES BL-CHANGE-PERCENT
00221   017600                                   PIC X(5).
00222   017700*
00223   017800 01  GRAND-TOTAL-LINE.
00224   017900*
00225   018000   05    FILLER                    PIC X(66)     VALUE SPACE.
00226   018100   05    FILLER                    PIC X(14)     VALUE 'GRAND TOTALS:'.
00227   018200   05    GTL-SALES-THIS-YTD        PIC ZZZ,ZZZ,ZZ9.99-.
00228   018300   05    GTL-SALES-LAST-YTD        PIC ZZZ,ZZZ,ZZ9.99-.
00229   018400   05    GTL-CHANGE-AMOUNT         PIC ZZZ,ZZZ,ZZ9.99-.
00230   018500   05    FILLER                    PIC X         VALUE SPACE.
00231   018600   05    GTL-CHANGE-PERCENT        PIC ZZZ9-.
00232   018700   05    GTL-CHANGE-PERCENT-R      REDEFINES GTL-CHANGE-PERCENT
00233   018800                                   PIC X(5).
00234   018900*
00235   019000 PROCEDURE DIVISION.
00236   019100*
00237   019200 000-PRODUCE-SALES-REPORT.
00238   019300*
00239   019400        OPEN INPUT   CUSTMST
00240   019500                     SALESMN
00241   019600             OUTPUT SALESRPT.
00242   019700        PERFORM 100-FORMAT-REPORT-HEADING.
00243   019800        PERFORM 200-PRODUCE-SALES-REPORT-LINES
00244   019900            UNTIL CUSTOMER-EOF.
00245   020000        PERFORM 400-PRINT-GRAND-TOTAL-LINE.
00246   020100        CLOSE CUSTMST
00247   020200              SALESMN
00248   020300              SALESRPT.
00249   020400        STOP RUN.
00250   020500*
00251   020600 100-FORMAT-REPORT-HEADING.
00252   020700*
00253   020800        CALL 'SYSDATE' USING TODAYS-DATE.
00254   020900        MOVE TODAYS-DATE   TO HDG1-DATE.
00255   021000        MOVE COMPANY-NAME TO HDG1-COMPANY-NAME.
00256   021100        CALL 'SYSTIME' USING HDG2-TIME-DATA.
00257   021200        MOVE 'MKTG1200'   TO HDG2-REPORT-NUMBER.
00258   021300        MOVE REPORT-TITLE TO HDG3-REPORT-TITLE.
00259   021400*
00260   021500 200-PRODUCE-SALES-REPORT-LINES.
00261   021600*
00262   021700        PERFORM 210-READ-CUSTOMER-RECORD.
00263   021800        IF NOT CUSTOMER-EOF
00264   021900            IF FIRST-RECORD
00265   022000                PERFORM 220-PRINT-CUSTOMER-LINE
00266   022100                PERFORM 280-ACCUMULATE-SALES-TOTALS
00267   022200                MOVE CM-SALESMAN-KEY TO OLD-SALESMAN-KEY
```

The report-
preparation program

```
00268   022300                    MOVE 'N'                    TO FIRST-RECORD-SW
00269   022400              ELSE
00270   022500                IF CM-SALESMAN-KEY NOT GREATER OLD-SALESMAN-KEY
00271   022600                    PERFORM 220-PRINT-CUSTOMER-LINE
00272   022700                    PERFORM 280-ACCUMULATE-SALES-TOTALS
00273   022800                ELSE
00274   022900                    IF CM-BRANCH-NUMBER GREATER OLD-BRANCH-NUMBER
00275   023000                        PERFORM 290-PRINT-SALESMAN-TOTAL-LINE
00276   023100                        PERFORM 300-PRINT-BRANCH-TOTAL-LINE
00277   023200                        PERFORM 220-PRINT-CUSTOMER-LINE
00278   023300                        PERFORM 280-ACCUMULATE-SALES-TOTALS
00279   023400                        MOVE CM-SALESMAN-KEY TO OLD-SALESMAN-KEY
00280   023500                    ELSE
00281   023600                        PERFORM 290-PRINT-SALESMAN-TOTAL-LINE
00282   023700                        PERFORM 220-PRINT-CUSTOMER-LINE
00283   023800                        PERFORM 280-ACCUMULATE-SALES-TOTALS
00284   023900                        MOVE CM-SALESMAN-NUMBER
00285   024000                            TO OLD-SALESMAN-NUMBER
00286   024100              ELSE
00287   024200                  PERFORM 290-PRINT-SALESMAN-TOTAL-LINE
00288   024300                  PERFORM 300-PRINT-BRANCH-TOTAL-LINE.
00289   024400*
00290   024500 210-READ-CUSTOMER-RECORD.
00291   024600*
00292   024700      READ CUSTMST
00293   024800          AT END
00294   024900              MOVE 'Y' TO CUSTOMER-EOF-SW.
00295   025000*
00296   025100 220-PRINT-CUSTOMER-LINE.
00297   025200*
00298   025300      IF FIRST-RECORD
00299   025400          MOVE CM-BRANCH-NUMBER     TO CL-BRANCH-NO
00300   025500          MOVE CM-SALESMAN-NUMBER TO CL-SALESMAN-NO
00301   025600          MOVE CM-SALESMAN-KEY      TO SM-SALESMAN-KEY
00302   025700          MOVE 'Y'                  TO RECORD-FOUND-SW
00303   025800          PERFORM 230-READ-SALESMAN-RECORD
00304   025900          IF RECORD-FOUND
00305   026000              MOVE SM-SALESMAN-NAME TO CL-SALESMAN-NAME
00306   026100          ELSE
00307   026200              MOVE 'SALESMAN RECORD NOT FOUND'
00308   026300                  TO CL-SALESMAN-NAME
00309   026400          ELSE
00310   026500          IF CM-SALESMAN-KEY GREATER OLD-SALESMAN-KEY
00311   026600            IF CM-BRANCH-NUMBER GREATER OLD-BRANCH-NUMBER
00312   026700                MOVE CM-BRANCH-NUMBER     TO CL-BRANCH-NO
00313   026800                MOVE CM-SALESMAN-NUMBER TO CL-SALESMAN-NO
00314   026900                MOVE CM-SALESMAN-KEY      TO SM-SALESMAN-KEY
00315   027000                MOVE 'Y'                  TO RECORD-FOUND-SW
00316   027100                PERFORM 230-READ-SALESMAN-RECORD
00317   027200                IF RECORD-FOUND
00318   027300                    MOVE SM-SALESMAN-NAME TO CL-SALESMAN-NAME
00319   027400                ELSE
00320   027500                    MOVE 'SALESMAN RECORD NOT FOUND'
00321   027600                        TO CL-SALESMAN-NAME
00322   027700            ELSE
00323   027800                MOVE SPACE                TO CL-BRANCH-NO
00324   027900                MOVE CM-SALESMAN-NUMBER TO CL-SALESMAN-NO
00325   028000                MOVE CM-SALESMAN-KEY      TO SM-SALESMAN-KEY
00326   028100                MOVE 'Y'                  TO RECORD-FOUND-SW
00327   028200                PERFORM 230-READ-SALESMAN-RECORD
00328   028300                IF RECORD-FOUND
00329   028400                    MOVE SM-SALESMAN-NAME TO CL-SALESMAN-NAME
00330   028500                ELSE
00331   028600                    MOVE 'SALESMAN RECORD NOT FOUND'
00332   028700                        TO CL-SALESMAN-NAME
00333   028800          ELSE
00334   028900              MOVE SPACE TO CL-SALESMAN-NAME
```

```
00335   029000                              CL-SALESMAN-NO
00336   029100                              CL-BRANCH-NO.
00337   029200        MOVE CM-CUSTOMER-NUMBER TO CL-CUSTOMER-NO.
00338   029300        MOVE CM-CUSTOMER-NAME   TO CL-CUSTOMER-NAME.
00339   029400        MOVE CM-SALES-THIS-YTD  TO CL-SALES-THIS-YTD.
00340   029500        MOVE CM-SALES-LAST-YTD  TO CL-SALES-LAST-YTD.
00341   029600        COMPUTE CHANGE-AMOUNT = CM-SALES-THIS-YTD
00342   029700                             - CM-SALES-LAST-YTD.
00343   029800        MOVE CHANGE-AMOUNT TO CL-CHANGE-AMOUNT.
00344   029900        IF CM-SALES-LAST-YTD NOT EQUAL ZERO
00345   030000            COMPUTE CHANGE-PERCENT ROUNDED = CHANGE-AMOUNT
00346   030100                                         / CM-SALES-LAST-YTD
00347   030200                                         * 100
00348   030300            MOVE CHANGE-PERCENT TO CL-CHANGE-PERCENT
00349   030400        ELSE
00350   030500            MOVE 'N/A' TO CL-CHANGE-PERCENT-R.
00351   030600        MOVE CUSTOMER-LINE TO NEXT-REPORT-LINE.
00352   030700        PERFORM 240-PRINT-REPORT-LINE.
00353   030800        MOVE 1 TO SPACE-CONTROL.
00354   030900*
00355   031000 230-READ-SALESMAN-RECORD.
00356   031100*
00357   031200        READ SALESMN
00358   031300            INVALID KEY
00359   031400                MOVE 'N' TO RECORD-FOUND-SW.
00360   031500*
00361   031600 240-PRINT-REPORT-LINE.
00362   031700*
00363   031800        IF LINE-COUNT GREATER LINES-ON-PAGE
00364   031900            PERFORM 250-PRINT-HEADING-LINES.
00365   032000        MOVE NEXT-REPORT-LINE TO PRINT-AREA.
00366   032100        PERFORM 270-WRITE-REPORT-LINE.
00367   032200*
00368   032300 250-PRINT-HEADING-LINES.
00369   032400*
00370   032500        ADD 1               TO PAGE-COUNT.
00371   032600        MOVE PAGE-COUNT     TO HDG1-PAGE-NUMBER.
00372   032700        MOVE HEADING-LINE-1 TO PRINT-AREA.
00373   032800        PERFORM 260-WRITE-PAGE-TOP-LINE.
00374   032900        MOVE HEADING-LINE-2 TO PRINT-AREA.
00375   033000        MOVE 1              TO SPACE-CONTROL.
00376   033100        PERFORM 270-WRITE-REPORT-LINE.
00377   033200        MOVE HEADING-LINE-3 TO PRINT-AREA.
00378   033300        PERFORM 270-WRITE-REPORT-LINE.
00379   033400        MOVE HEADING-LINE-4 TO PRINT-AREA.
00380   033500        MOVE 2              TO SPACE-CONTROL.
00381   033600        PERFORM 270-WRITE-REPORT-LINE.
00382   033700        MOVE HEADING-LINE-5 TO PRINT-AREA.
00383   033800        MOVE 1              TO SPACE-CONTROL.
00384   033900        PERFORM 270-WRITE-REPORT-LINE.
00385   034000        MOVE 2              TO SPACE-CONTROL.
00386   034100*
00387   034200 260-WRITE-PAGE-TOP-LINE.
00388   034300*
00389   034400        WRITE PRINT-AREA
00390   034500            AFTER ADVANCING PAGE.
00391   034600        MOVE 1 TO LINE-COUNT.
00392   034700*
00393   034800 270-WRITE-REPORT-LINE.
00394   034900*
00395   035000        WRITE PRINT-AREA
00396   035100            AFTER ADVANCING SPACE-CONTROL LINES.
00397   035200        ADD SPACE-CONTROL TO LINE-COUNT.
00398   035300*
00399   035400 280-ACCUMULATE-SALES-TOTALS.
00400   035500*
00401   035600        ADD CM-SALES-THIS-YTD TO SALESMAN-TOTAL-THIS-YTD.
```

```
00402   035700       ADD CM-SALES-LAST-YTD TO SALESMAN-TOTAL-LAST-YTD.
00403   035800       ADD CM-SALES-THIS-YTD TO BRANCH-TOTAL-THIS-YTD.
00404   035900       ADD CM-SALES-LAST-YTD TO BRANCH-TOTAL-LAST-YTD.
00405   036000       ADD CM-SALES-THIS-YTD TO TOTAL-SALES-THIS-YTD.
00406   036100       ADD CM-SALES-LAST-YTD TO TOTAL-SALES-LAST-YTD.
00407   036200*
00408   036300 290-PRINT-SALESMAN-TOTAL-LINE.
00409   036400*
00410   036500       MOVE SALESMAN-TOTAL-THIS-YTD TO SL-SALES-THIS-YTD.
00411   036600       MOVE SALESMAN-TOTAL-LAST-YTD TO SL-SALES-LAST-YTD.
00412   036700       COMPUTE CHANGE-AMOUNT = SALESMAN-TOTAL-THIS-YTD
00413   036800                             - SALESMAN-TOTAL-LAST-YTD.
00414   036900       MOVE CHANGE-AMOUNT TO SL-CHANGE-AMOUNT.
00415   037000       IF SALESMAN-TOTAL-LAST-YTD NOT EQUAL ZERO
00416   037100           COMPUTE CHANGE-PERCENT ROUNDED = CHANGE-AMOUNT
00417   037200                                 / SALESMAN-TOTAL-LAST-YTD
00418   037300                                 * 100
00419   037400           MOVE CHANGE-PERCENT TO SL-CHANGE-PERCENT
00420   037500       ELSE
00421   037600           MOVE 'N/A' TO SL-CHANGE-PERCENT-R.
00422   037700       MOVE SALESMAN-TOTAL-LINE TO NEXT-REPORT-LINE.
00423   037800       MOVE 2                   TO SPACE-CONTROL.
00424   037900       PERFORM 240-PRINT-REPORT-LINE.
00425   038000       MOVE ZERO TO SALESMAN-TOTAL-THIS-YTD
00426   038100                    SALESMAN-TOTAL-LAST-YTD.
00427   038200*
00428   038300 300-PRINT-BRANCH-TOTAL-LINE.
00429   038400*
00430   038500       MOVE BRANCH-TOTAL-THIS-YTD TO BL-SALES-THIS-YTD.
00431   038600       MOVE BRANCH-TOTAL-LAST-YTD TO BL-SALES-LAST-YTD.
00432   038700       COMPUTE CHANGE-AMOUNT = BRANCH-TOTAL-THIS-YTD
00433   038800                             - BRANCH-TOTAL-LAST-YTD.
00434   038900       MOVE CHANGE-AMOUNT TO BL-CHANGE-AMOUNT.
00435   039000       IF BRANCH-TOTAL-LAST-YTD NOT EQUAL ZERO
00436   039100           COMPUTE CHANGE-PERCENT ROUNDED = CHANGE-AMOUNT
00437   039200                                 / BRANCH-TOTAL-LAST-YTD
00438   039300                                 * 100
00439   039400           MOVE CHANGE-PERCENT TO BL-CHANGE-PERCENT
00440   039500       ELSE
00441   039600           MOVE 'N/A' TO BL-CHANGE-PERCENT-R.
00442   039700       MOVE BRANCH-TOTAL-LINE TO NEXT-REPORT-LINE.
00443   039800       MOVE 3                   TO SPACE-CONTROL.
00444   039900       PERFORM 240-PRINT-REPORT-LINE.
00445   040000       MOVE ZERO TO BRANCH-TOTAL-THIS-YTD
00446   040100                    BRANCH-TOTAL-LAST-YTD.
00447   040200*
00448   040300 400-PRINT-GRAND-TOTAL-LINE.
00449   040400*
00450   040500       MOVE TOTAL-SALES-THIS-YTD TO GTL-SALES-THIS-YTD.
00451   040600       MOVE TOTAL-SALES-LAST-YTD TO GTL-SALES-LAST-YTD.
00452   040700       COMPUTE CHANGE-AMOUNT = TOTAL-SALES-THIS-YTD
00453   040800                             - TOTAL-SALES-LAST-YTD.
00454   040900       MOVE CHANGE-AMOUNT TO GTL-CHANGE-AMOUNT.
00455   041000       IF TOTAL-SALES-LAST-YTD NOT EQUAL ZERO
00456   041100           COMPUTE CHANGE-PERCENT ROUNDED = CHANGE-AMOUNT
00457   041200                                 / TOTAL-SALES-LAST-YTD
00458   041300                                 * 100
00459   041400           MOVE CHANGE-PERCENT TO GTL-CHANGE-PERCENT
00460   041500       ELSE
00461   041600           MOVE 'N/A' TO GTL-CHANGE-PERCENT-R.
00462   041700       MOVE GRAND-TOTAL-LINE TO NEXT-REPORT-LINE.
00463   041800       PERFORM 240-PRINT-REPORT-LINE.
```

MIKE MURACH & ASSOCIATES, INC.

YEAR-TO-DATE SALES REPORT

BRANCH NO	SALESMAN NO	SALESMAN NAME	CUSTOMER NO	CUSTOMER NAME	SALES THIS YTD	SALES LAST YTD	CHANGE AMOUNT	CHANGE %
01	01	LINDA HUGHES	1	GEORGE DONALDSON	456.38	235.49	220.89	93
			2	BONNIE BRENDT	52.39	425.39	373.00-	87-
			5	YOLANDA PEREZ	129.38	0.00	129.38	N/A
			7	CELIA PRICE	0.00	253.49	253.49-	100-
			12	GEORGE THOMAS	1,253.39	538.49	714.90	132
				SALESMAN TOTALS:	1,891.54	1,452.86	438.68	30
	02	WILLIAM YOUNG	3	KENNY WRIGHT	389.38	629.39	240.01-	38-
			8	ALEX JONAS	0.00	0.00	0.00	N/A
			13	JOHN JOHNSON	35.38	74.39	39.01-	52-
				SALESMAN TOTALS:	424.76	703.78	279.02-	39-
	03	ANTHONY LUND	1	PATTI LANGE	545.39	235.49	309.90	131
			4	INEZ WHITE	45.29	125.39	80.10-	63-
			9	FARRIN LONG	0.00	35.28	35.28-	100-
			17	TINA RANDALL	37.49	58.54	21.05-	35-
			19	THOMAS RICE	254.39	386.39	132.00-	34-
				SALESMAN TOTALS:	882.56	841.09	41.47	4
	04	PETER PIPPIN	4	LARRY UPTON	59.38	0.00	59.38	N/A
				SALESMAN TOTALS:	59.38	0.00	59.38	N/A
	05	TRICIA REED	7	LINDA WENDT	39.49	564.39	524.90-	93-
			9	JOHN KELLY	465.39	253.39	212.00	83
			21	PATRICIA HARRISON	49.30	69.38	20.08-	28-
				SALESMAN TOTALS:	554.18	887.16	332.98-	37-
				BRANCH TOTALS:	3,812.42	3,884.89	72.47-	1-
02	01	PAUL JOHNSON	11	KELLY FLOYD	90.39	154.29	63.90-	41-
			13	SONYA SIMPSON	75.39	153.29	77.90-	50-
			17	HENRY HART	89.30	523.39	434.09-	82-
				SALESMAN TOTALS:	255.08	830.97	575.89-	69-
	02	GEORGE HARVEY	2	FRED RICE	253.39	453.39	200.00-	44-
			6	TOMMY HYDE	85.39	25.39	60.00	236
			7	RALPH HARPER	93.48	142.39	48.91-	34-
				SALESMAN TOTALS:	432.26	621.17	188.91-	30-

The report-
preparation program

DATE: 10/25/84
TIME: 3:45 PM

MIKE MURACH & ASSOCIATES, INC.

YEAR-TO-DATE SALES REPORT

BRANCH NO	SALESMAN NO	SALESMAN NAME	CUSTOMER NO	CUSTOMER NAME	SALES THIS YTD	SALES LAST YTD	CHANGE AMOUNT	CHANGE %
03	03	DONNA TRENT	12	SHEILA BARBER	79.39	0.00	79.39	N/A
			24	HARVEY HILL	0.00	79.49	79.49-	100-
			22	JOHN FRENCH	94.38	143.29	48.91-	34-
			23	SIDNEY TINSLEY	834.48	453.49	380.99	84
			25	PATRICK LANGE	732.38	938.29	205.91-	21-
				SALESMAN TOTALS:	1,740.63	1,614.56	126.07	7
	04	BETTY KENT	1	DOUG ALLEN	593.49	432.53	160.96	37
			2	STEVE QUEEN	634.39	243.49	390.90	160
			5	PENNY UPTON	48.39	153.29	104.90-	68-
			9	LAURA HARVEY	49.39	253.49	204.10-	80-
				SALESMAN TOTALS:	1,325.66	1,082.80	242.86	22
				BRANCH TOTALS:	3,753.63	4,149.50	395.87-	9-
03	01	CLARK PARKER	4	SANDY LOWE	93.28	24.39	68.89	282
			6	PAT KEMMER	78.39	293.48	215.09-	73-
			9	CORY WISE	0.00	0.00	0.00	N/A
			11	RONALD FAYE	48.39	24.39	24.00	98
			15	CINDY VANCE	143.29	13.29	130.00	978
				SALESMAN TOTALS:	363.35	355.55	7.80	2
	03	EDWARD RAND	7	RANDALL TREET	58.39	53.39	5.00	9
			9	JUDY TRUDEAU	94.39	423.49	329.10-	77-
			10	BARBARA BRICE	94.38	35.49	58.89	165
			14	PETER NASH	745.29	253.49	491.80	194
			17	ALAN WHITE	953.39	534.39	419.00	78
			25	SIDNEY POTTER	84.39	35.49	48.90	137
				SALESMAN TOTALS:	2,030.23	1,335.74	694.49	51
	04	THOMAS TINKER	11	HAROLD SMITH	49.39	243.49	194.10-	79-
			15	CAROL BAKER	475.39	243.49	231.90	95
			21	LINDSEY GREEN	74.39	243.54	169.15-	69-
				SALESMAN TOTALS:	599.17	730.52	131.35-	17-
	05	LARRY DARREN	3	DONALD NANCE	0.00	253.49	253.49-	100-
			8	PAULA JOHNSON	74.39	253.48	179.09-	70-
			9	TIMOTHY SMITH	245.39	0.00	245.39	N/A
			12	STEVE SANDERS	83.29	43.29	40.00	92
			17	SALLY FRY	89.39	35.49	53.90	151

MIKE MURACH & ASSOCIATES, INC.

YEAR-TO-DATE SALES REPORT

BRANCH NO	SALESMAN NO	SALESMAN NAME	CUSTOMER NO	CUSTOMER NAME	SALES THIS YTD	SALES LAST YTD	CHANGE AMOUNT	CHANGE %
			19	MANNY MANFRED	384.39	243.49	140.90	57
					876.85	829.24	47.61	5
				SALESMAN TOTALS:				
				BRANCH TOTALS:	3,869.60	3,251.05	618.55	19
04	05	SALESMAN RECORD NOT FOUND	12	TYRONE WHITE	253.39	429.38	175.99-	40-
				SALESMAN TOTALS:	253.39	429.38	175.99-	40-
				BRANCH TOTALS:	253.39	429.38	175.99-	40-
				GRAND TOTALS:	11,689.04	11,714.82	25.78-	0

The report-
preparation program

Batch model programs   211

Model program 3

The sequential file-maintenance program

Input/output specifications

File	Description	Use
OLDMAST	Old inventory master file	Input
MNTTRAN	Maintenance transaction file	Input
NEWMAST	New inventory master file	Output
ERRTRAN	Maintenance transaction error file	Output
MNTLIST	Print file: Inventory maintenance listing	Output

Process specifications

Use the transaction records to maintain the master records. A transaction record may change, add, or delete a master file record. There may be none, one, or several transactions for each master. Since the fields in the transaction record have already been edited, this program does not have to do any field editing.

The master file is in sequence by item number. The transaction file is in sequence by action code within item number. That means that for any one item number, the types of transactions are in this sequence: delete, add, changes. So it is possible to delete an item number, add a new record with the same item number to the file, and then update the new record.

The maintenance listing is to be printed with one line for each valid transaction record as shown on the print chart. The totals for the program are to be printed on a separate output page.

If an unmatched deletion or change transaction, or a matched addition transaction is detected, write a record in the error file. The error record should have the same format as the transaction record.

Process specifications

The basic processing requirements follow:

Do until all records have been processed:

1. Read an inventory transaction record.

2. Get inventory master records until a record with a matching or greater item number is found. This includes writing the previous master record to the new master file if there aren't any more transactions for the record and the record wasn't deleted.

3. Determine the processing to be performed--deletion, addition, change, or error.

4. For a delete transaction, mark the record as deleted and print a line on the maintenance listing.

5. For an add transaction, format the addition record and print a line on the maintenance listing.

6. For a change transaction, make the indicated changes and print a line on the maintenance listing.

7. For an error transaction, write a record to the error transaction file.

After all records have been processed, print the transaction totals on the last page of the maintenance listing.

```
BKEND    C.INVMAST

*
01   INVENTORY-MASTER-RECORD.
*
     05   IM-ITEM-NUMBER           PIC X(5).
     05   IM-ITEM-DESCRIPTION      PIC X(20).
     05   IM-UNIT-COST             PIC S9(3)V99    COMP-3.
     05   IM-UNIT-PRICE            PIC S9(3)V99    COMP-3.
     05   IM-ON-HAND-BALANCE       PIC S9(3)       COMP-3.
     05   IM-SALES-THIS-MONTH      PIC S9(5)V99    COMP-3.
     05   IM-RECEIPTS-THIS-MONTH   PIC S9(5)V99    COMP-3.
     05   IM-SALES-THIS-YEAR       PIC S9(7)V99    COMP-3.
     05   IM-RECEIPTS-THIS-YEAR    PIC S9(7)V99    COMP-3.

BKEND
```

```
BKEND    C.MNTTRAN

*
01   MAINTENANCE-TRANSACTION.
*
     05   MT-ACTION-CODE              PIC X.
          88   MT-DELETION            VALUE '1'.
          88   MT-ADDITION            VALUE '2'.
          88   MT-CHANGE              VALUE '3'.
     05   MT-INVENTORY-DATA.
          10   MT-ITEM-NUMBER         PIC X(5).
          10   MT-ITEM-DESCRIPTION    PIC X(20).
          10   MT-UNIT-COST           PIC S9(3)V99   COMP-3.
          10   MT-UNIT-PRICE          PIC S9(3)V99   COMP-3.
          10   MT-ON-HAND-BALANCE     PIC S9(3)      COMP-3.

BKEND
```

Document name Inventory Maintenance Listing   **Date** 8-30-84

Program name MNT1500   **Designer** Anne Prince

Record Name	Print layout
Heading-Line-1	1 DATE: 99/99/99 MIKE MURACH & ASSOCIATES, INC. PAGE: ZZ9
Heading-Line-2	2 TIME: 99:99 XX INVENTORY MAINTENANCE LISTING MNT1500
Heading-Line-3	3
	4
Heading-Line-4	5 ITEM NO. ITEM DESCRIPTION UNIT COST UNIT PRICE ON HAND ACTION
	6
Maintenance-Line	7 XXXXXXXXXXXXX ZZ9.99 ZZ9.99 ZZ9 CHANGED
	8 XXXXXXXXXXXXX ZZ9.99 ZZ9.99 ZZ9 ADDED
	9 ZZ9.99 ZZ9.99 ZZ9 DELETED
	10
	11
	12
	13
Total page data to be printed after the first two lines of the standard heading:	14 / 15 / 16 / 17 / 18
Total-Line-1	19 SUMMARY FOR INVENTORY MAINTENANCE RUN
	20
Total-Line-2	21 DELETIONS ZZ,ZZ9
Total-Line-3	22 ADDITIONS ZZ,ZZ9
Total-Line-4	23 CHANGES ZZ,ZZ9
Total-Line-5	24 TOTAL ZZ,ZZ9 *
	25
Total-Line-6	26 ERRORS ZZ,ZZ9
	27
Total-Line-7	28 TRANSACTIONS PROCESSED ZZZ,ZZ9 **

The sequential file-maintenance program

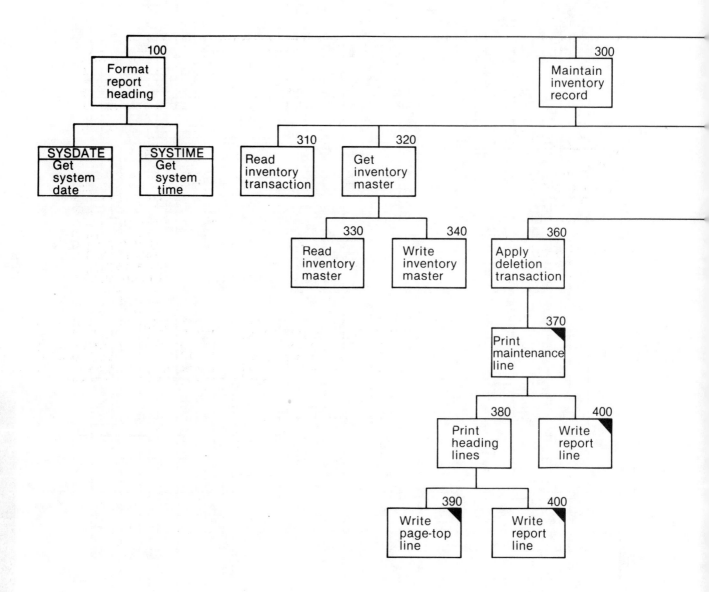

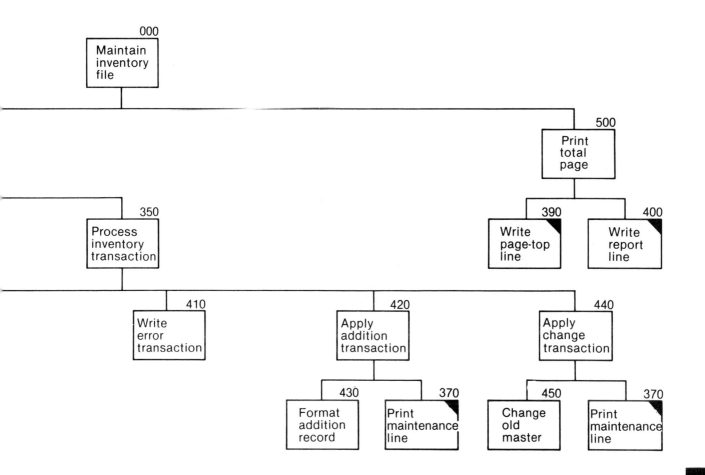

The sequential file-maintenance program

```
    CBL APOST,LANGLVL(1),LIB
00001    000100 IDENTIFICATION DIVISION.
00002    000200✻
00003    000300 PROGRAM-ID.       MNT1500.
00004    000400✻AUTHOR.           ANNE PRINCE.
00005    000500✻INSTALLATION.     MMA.
00006    000600✻DATE.             SEPTEMBER 10, 1984.
00007    000700✻
00008    000800 ENVIRONMENT DIVISION.
00009    000900✻
00010    001000 CONFIGURATION SECTION.
00011    001100✻
00012    001200 SOURCE-COMPUTER.      IBM-370.
00013    001300 OBJECT-COMPUTER.      IBM-370.
00014    001400✻
00015    001500 INPUT-OUTPUT SECTION.
00016    001600✻
00017    001700 FILE-CONTROL.
00018    001800✻
00019    001900     SELECT OLDMAST   ASSIGN TO SYS005-AS-OLDMAST.
00020    002000     SELECT MNTTRAN   ASSIGN TO SYS009-AS-MNTTRAN.
00021    002100     SELECT NEWMAST   ASSIGN TO SYS008-AS-NEWMAST.
00022    002200     SELECT ERRTRAN   ASSIGN TO SYS007-AS-ERRTRAN.
00023    002300     SELECT MNTLIST   ASSIGN TO SYS006-UR-1403-S.
00024    002400✻
00025    002500 DATA DIVISION.
00026    002600✻
00027    002700 FILE SECTION.
00028    002800✻
00029    002900 FD  OLDMAST
00030    003000     LABEL RECORDS ARE STANDARD
00031    003100     RECORD CONTAINS 51 CHARACTERS.
00032    003200✻
00033    003300 01  OLD-MASTER-RECORD   PIC X(51).
00034    003400✻
00035    003500 FD  MNTTRAN
00036    003600     LABEL RECORDS ARE STANDARD
00037    003700     RECORD CONTAINS 34 CHARACTERS.
00038    003800✻
00039    003900 01  TRANSACTION-RECORD  PIC X(34).
00040    004000✻
00041    004100 FD  NEWMAST
00042    004200     LABEL RECORDS ARE STANDARD
00043    004300     RECORD CONTAINS 51 CHARACTERS.
00044    004400✻
00045    004500 01  NEW-MASTER-RECORD   PIC X(51).
00046    004600✻
00047    004700 FD  ERRTRAN
00048    004800     LABEL RECORDS ARE STANDARD
00049    004900     RECORD CONTAINS 34 CHARACTERS.
00050    005000✻
00051    005100 01  ERROR-TRANSACTION        PIC X(34).
00052    005200✻
00053    005300 FD  MNTLIST
00054    005400     LABEL RECORDS ARE OMITTED
00055    005500     RECORD CONTAINS 132 CHARACTERS.
00056    005600✻
00057    005700 01  PRINT-AREA          PIC X(132).
00058    005800✻
00059    005900 WORKING-STORAGE SECTION.
00060    006000✻
00061    006100 01  SWITCHES.
00062    006200✻
00063    006300     05  FIRST-EXECUTION-SW             PIC X    VALUE 'Y'.
00064    006400         88  FIRST-EXECUTION                     VALUE 'Y'.
00065    006500     05  MASTER-HELD-FOR-ADDITION-SW    PIC X    VALUE 'N'.
00066    006600         88  MASTER-HELD-FOR-ADDITION            VALUE 'Y'.
```

```
00067   006700       05    MASTER-DELETED-SW                      PIC X      VALUE 'N'.
00068   006800           88   MASTER-DELETED                                 VALUE 'Y'.
00069   006900       05    ALL-RECORDS-PROCESSED-SW               PIC X      VALUE 'N'.
00070   007000           88   ALL-RECORDS-PROCESSED                          VALUE 'Y'.
00071   007100*
00072   007200 01    COUNT-FIELDS              COMP-3.
00073   007300*
00074   007400       05    CHANGE-COUNT         PIC S9(5)     VALUE ZERO.
00075   007500       05    ADDITION-COUNT       PIC S9(5)     VALUE ZERO.
00076   007600       05    DELETION-COUNT       PIC S9(5)     VALUE ZERO.
00077   007700       05    VALID-COUNT          PIC S9(5)     VALUE ZERO.
00078   007800       05    ERROR-COUNT          PIC S9(5)     VALUE ZERO.
00079   007900       05    TOTAL-COUNT          PIC S9(7)     VALUE ZERO.
00080   008000*
00081   008100 01    PRINT-FIELDS.
00082   008200*
00083   008300       05    SPACE-CONTROL        PIC S9                    COMP  SYNC.
00084   008400       05    LINE-COUNT           PIC S999      VALUE +999  COMP  SYNC.
00085   008500       05    LINES-ON-PAGE        PIC S999      VALUE +57   COMP  SYNC.
00086   008600       05    PAGE-COUNT           PIC S999      VALUE ZERO  COMP-3.
00087   008700*
00088   008800 01    DATE-FIELDS.
00089   008900*
00090   009000       05    TODAYS-DATE          PIC 9(6).
00091   009100*
00092   009200 01    ACTION-MESSAGES.
00093   009300*
00094   009400       05    CHANGE-MESSAGE       PIC X(10)     VALUE 'CHANGED    '.
00095   009500       05    ADD-MESSAGE          PIC X(10)     VALUE 'ADDED      '.
00096   009600       05    DELETE-MESSAGE       PIC X(10)     VALUE 'DELETED    '.
00097   009700*
00098   009800 01    HELD-MASTER-RECORD        PIC X(51).
00099   009900*
00100   010000 COPY INVMAST.
00101 C      *
00102 C         01    INVENTORY-MASTER-RECORD.
00103 C      *
00104 C          05    IM-ITEM-NUMBER           PIC X(5).
00105 C          05    IM-ITEM-DESCRIPTION      PIC X(20).
00106 C          05    IM-UNIT-COST             PIC S9(3)V99   COMP-3.
00107 C          05    IM-UNIT-PRICE            PIC S9(3)V99   COMP-3.
00108 C          05    IM-ON-HAND-BALANCE       PIC S9(3)      COMP-3.
00109 C          05    IM-SALES-THIS-MONTH      PIC S9(5)V99   COMP-3.
00110 C          05    IM-RECEIPTS-THIS-MONTH   PIC S9(5)V99   COMP-3.
00111 C          05    IM-SALES-THIS-YEAR       PIC S9(7)V99   COMP-3.
00112 C          05    IM-RECEIPTS-THIS-YEAR    PIC S9(7)V99   COMP-3.
00113   010100*
00114   010200 COPY MNTTRAN.
00115 C      *
00116 C         01    MAINTENANCE-TRANSACTION.
00117 C      *
00118 C          05    MT-ACTION-CODE           PIC X.
00119 C             88   MT-DELETION            VALUE '1'.
00120 C             88   MT-ADDITION            VALUE '2'.
00121 C             88   MT-CHANGE              VALUE '3'.
00122 C          05    MT-INVENTORY-DATA.
00123 C             10   MT-ITEM-NUMBER         PIC X(5).
00124 C             10   MT-ITEM-DESCRIPTION    PIC X(20).
00125 C             10   MT-UNIT-COST           PIC S9(3)V99   COMP-3.
00126 C             10   MT-UNIT-PRICE          PIC S9(3)V99   COMP-3.
00127 C             10   MT-ON-HAND-BALANCE     PIC S9(3)      COMP-3.
00128   010300*
00129   010400 01    COMPANY-NAME.
00130   010500*
00131   010600       05    FILLER               PIC X(10)     VALUE SPACE.
00132   010700       05    FILLER               PIC X(20)     VALUE 'MIKE MURACH & ASSOCI'.
00133   010800       05    FILLER               PIC X(20)     VALUE 'ATES, INC.'.
```

The sequential file-maintenance program

```
00134     010900�※
00135     011000 01    REPORT-TITLE.
00136     011100☺
00137     011200       05   FILLER            PIC X(15)      VALUE SPACE.
00138     011300       05   FILLER            PIC X(20)      VALUE 'INVENTORY MAINTENANC'.
00139     011400       05   FILLER            PIC X(20)      VALUE 'E LISTING'.
00140     011500       05   FILLER            PIC X(5)       VALUE SPACE.
00141     011600☺
00142     011700 COPY RPTHDG14.
00143 C        ☺
00144 C          01    HEADING-LINE-1.
00145 C        ☺
00146 C             05   FILLER                   PIC X(7)     VALUE 'DATE:'.
00147 C             05   HDG1-DATE                PIC 99/99/99.
00148 C             05   FILLER                   PIC X(26)    VALUE SPACE.
00149 C             05   HDG1-COMPANY-NAME        PIC X(50).
00150 C             05   FILLER                   PIC X(31)    VALUE SPACE.
00151 C             05   FILLER                   PIC X(6)     VALUE 'PAGE:'.
00152 C             05   HDG1-PAGE-NUMBER         PIC ZZ9.
00153 C        ☺
00154 C          01    HEADING-LINE-2.
00155 C        ☺
00156 C             05   HDG2-TIME-DATA.
00157 C                  10   FILLER              PIC X(7)     VALUE 'TIME:'.
00158 C                  10   HDG2-HOURS          PIC XX.
00159 C                  10   FILLER              PIC X        VALUE ':'.
00160 C                  10   HDG2-MINUTES        PIC XX.
00161 C                  10   FILLER              PIC X        VALUE SPACE.
00162 C                  10   HDG2-TIME-SUFFIX    PIC X(8).
00163 C             05   FILLER                   PIC X(101)   VALUE SPACE.
00164 C             05   HDG2-REPORT-NUMBER       PIC X(10).
00165 C        ☺
00166 C          01    HEADING-LINE-3.
00167 C        ☺
00168 C             05   FILLER                   PIC X(36)    VALUE SPACE.
00169 C             05   HDG3-REPORT-TITLE        PIC X(60).
00170     011800☺
00171     011900 01    HEADING-LINE-4.
00172     012000☺
00173     012100       05   FILLER            PIC X(20)    VALUE 'ITEM NO    ITEM DESC'.
00174     012200       05   FILLER            PIC X(20)    VALUE 'RIPTION        UNIT C'.
00175     012300       05   FILLER            PIC X(20)    VALUE 'OST    UNIT PRICE   O'.
00176     012400       05   FILLER            PIC X(20)    VALUE 'N HAND     ACTION    '.
00177     012500       05   FILLER            PIC X(52)    VALUE SPACE.
00178     012600☺
00179     012700 01    MAINTENANCE-LINE.
00180     012800☺
00181     012900       05   FILLER            PIC X          VALUE SPACE.
00182     013000       05   ML-ITEM-NUMBER    PIC X(5).
00183     013100       05   FILLER            PIC X(5)       VALUE SPACE.
00184     013200       05   ML-ITEM-DESCR     PIC X(20).
00185     013300       05   FILLER            PIC X(4)       VALUE SPACE.
00186     013400       05   ML-UNIT-COST      PIC ZZ9.99.
00187     013500       05   FILLER            PIC X(7)       VALUE SPACE.
00188     013600       05   ML-UNIT-PRICE     PIC ZZ9.99.
00189     013700       05   FILLER            PIC X(7)       VALUE SPACE.
00190     013800       05   ML-ON-HAND        PIC ZZ9.
00191     013900       05   FILLER            PIC X(5)       VALUE SPACE.
00192     014000       05   ML-ACTION         PIC X(10).
00193     014100       05   FILLER            PIC X(53)      VALUE SPACE.
00194     014200☺
00195     014300 01    TOTAL-LINE-1.
00196     014400☺
00197     014500       05   FILLER            PIC X(20)    VALUE 'SUMMARY FOR INVENTOR'.
00198     014600       05   FILLER            PIC X(20)    VALUE 'Y MAINTENANCE RUN   '.
00199     014700       05   FILLER            PIC X(92)    VALUE SPACE.
00200     014800☺
```

```
00201   014900 01  TOTAL-LINE-2.
00202   015000✣
00203   015100     05  FILLER          PIC X(20)    VALUE 'DELETIONS'.
00204   015200     05  FILLER          PIC X(5)     VALUE SPACE.
00205   015300     05  TOT2-DELETIONS  PIC ZZ,ZZ9.
00206   015400     05  FILLER          PIC X(101)   VALUE SPACE.
00207   015500✣
00208   015600 01  TOTAL-LINE-3.
00209   015700✣
00210   015800     05  FILLER          PIC X(20)    VALUE 'ADDITIONS'.
00211   015900     05  FILLER          PIC X(5)     VALUE SPACE.
00212   016000     05  TOT3-ADDITIONS  PIC ZZ,ZZ9.
00213   016100     05  FILLER          PIC X(101)   VALUE SPACE.
00214   016200✣
00215   016300 01  TOTAL-LINE-4.
00216   016400✣
00217   016500     05  FILLER          PIC X(20)    VALUE 'CHANGES'.
00218   016600     05  FILLER          PIC X(5)     VALUE SPACE.
00219   016700     05  TOT4-CHANGES    PIC ZZ,ZZ9.
00220   016800     05  FILLER          PIC X(101)   VALUE SPACE.
00221   016900✣
00222   017000 01  TOTAL-LINE-5.
00223   017100✣
00224   017200     05  FILLER          PIC X(20)    VALUE 'TOTAL UPDATES'.
00225   017300     05  FILLER          PIC X(5)     VALUE SPACE.
00226   017400     05  TOT5-UPDATES    PIC ZZ,ZZ9.
00227   017500     05  FILLER          PIC XX       VALUE ' ✳'.
00228   017600     05  FILLER          PIC X(99)    VALUE SPACE.
00229   017700✣
00230   017800 01  TOTAL-LINE-6.
00231   017900✣
00232   018000     05  FILLER          PIC X(20)    VALUE 'ERRORS'.
00233   018100     05  FILLER          PIC X(5)     VALUE SPACE.
00234   018200     05  TOT6-ERRORS     PIC ZZ,ZZ9.
00235   018300     05  FILLER          PIC X(101)   VALUE SPACE.
00236   018400✣
00237   018500 01  TOTAL-LINE-7.
00238   018600✣
00239   018700     05  FILLER          PIC X(20)    VALUE 'TRANSACTIONS PROCESS'.
00240   018800     05  FILLER          PIC XX       VALUE 'ED'.
00241   018900     05  TOT7-TOTAL      PIC Z,ZZZ,ZZ9.
00242   019000     05  FILLER          PIC X(4)     VALUE ' ✳ ✳'.
00243   019100     05  FILLER          PIC X(97)    VALUE SPACE.
00244   019200✣
00245   019300 PROCEDURE DIVISION.
00246   019400✣
00247   019500 000-MAINTAIN-INVENTORY-FILE.
00248   019600✣
00249   019700     OPEN INPUT   OLDMAST
00250   019800                  MNTTRAN
00251   019900          OUTPUT  NEWMAST
00252   020000                  ERRTRAN
00253   020100                  MNTLIST.
00254   020200     PERFORM 100-FORMAT-REPORT-HEADING.
00255   020300     MOVE LOW-VALUE TO IM-ITEM-NUMBER.
00256   020400     PERFORM 300-MAINTAIN-INVENTORY-RECORD
00257   020500         UNTIL ALL-RECORDS-PROCESSED.
00258   020600     PERFORM 500-PRINT-TOTAL-PAGE.
00259   020700     CLOSE OLDMAST
00260   020800           MNTTRAN
00261   020900           NEWMAST
00262   021000           ERRTRAN
00263   021100           MNTLIST.
00264   021200     STOP RUN.
00265   021300✣
00266   021400 100-FORMAT-REPORT-HEADING.
00267   021500✣
```

The sequential file-
maintenance program

```
00268    021600        CALL 'SYSDATE' USING TODAYS-DATE.
00269    021700        MOVE TODAYS-DATE   TO HDG1-DATE.
00270    021800        MOVE COMPANY-NAME TO HDG1-COMPANY-NAME.
00271    021900        CALL 'SYSTIME' USING HDG2-TIME-DATA.
00272    022000        MOVE 'MNT1500'      TO HDG2-REPORT-NUMBER.
00273    022100        MOVE REPORT-TITLE TO HDG3-REPORT-TITLE.
00274    022200*
00275    022300 300-MAINTAIN-INVENTORY-RECORD.
00276    022400*
00277    022500        PERFORM 310-READ-INVENTORY-TRANSACTION.
00278    022600        PERFORM 320-GET-INVENTORY-MASTER
00279    022700            UNTIL IM-ITEM-NUMBER NOT LESS MT-ITEM-NUMBER.
00280    022800        IF        MT-ITEM-NUMBER = HIGH-VALUE
00281    022900               AND IM-ITEM-NUMBER = HIGH-VALUE
00282    023000            MOVE 'Y' TO ALL-RECORDS-PROCESSED-SW
00283    023100        ELSE
00284    023200            PERFORM 350-PROCESS-INVENTORY-TRAN.
00285    023300*
00286    023400 310-READ-INVENTORY-TRANSACTION.
00287    023500*
00288    023600        READ MNTTRAN INTO MAINTENANCE-TRANSACTION
00289    023700            AT END
00290    023800                MOVE HIGH-VALUES TO MT-ITEM-NUMBER.
00291    023900        IF MT-ITEM-NUMBER NOT = HIGH-VALUES
00292    024000            ADD 1 TO TOTAL-COUNT.
00293    024100*
00294    024200 320-GET-INVENTORY-MASTER.
00295    024300*
00296    024400        IF FIRST-EXECUTION
00297    024500            PERFORM 330-READ-INVENTORY-MASTER
00298    024600            MOVE 'N' TO FIRST-EXECUTION-SW
00299    024700        ELSE
00300    024800            IF NOT MASTER-DELETED
00301    024900                PERFORM 340-WRITE-INVENTORY-MASTER
00302    025000                IF MASTER-HELD-FOR-ADDITION
00303    025100                    MOVE HELD-MASTER-RECORD
00304    025200                        TO INVENTORY-MASTER-RECORD
00305    025300                    MOVE 'N' TO MASTER-HELD-FOR-ADDITION-SW
00306    025400                ELSE
00307    025500                    PERFORM 330-READ-INVENTORY-MASTER
00308    025600            ELSE
00309    025700                MOVE 'N' TO MASTER-DELETED-SW
00310    025800                IF MASTER-HELD-FOR-ADDITION
00311    025900                    MOVE HELD-MASTER-RECORD
00312    026000                        TO INVENTORY-MASTER-RECORD
00313    026100                    MOVE 'N' TO MASTER-HELD-FOR-ADDITION-SW
00314    026200                ELSE
00315    026300                    PERFORM 330-READ-INVENTORY-MASTER.
00316    026400*
00317    026500 330-READ-INVENTORY-MASTER.
00318    026600*
00319    026700        READ OLDMAST INTO INVENTORY-MASTER-RECORD
00320    026800            AT END
00321    026900                MOVE HIGH-VALUES TO IM-ITEM-NUMBER.
00322    027000*
00323    027100 340-WRITE-INVENTORY-MASTER.
00324    027200*
00325    027300        WRITE NEW-MASTER-RECORD FROM INVENTORY-MASTER-RECORD.
00326    027400*
00327    027500 350-PROCESS-INVENTORY-TRAN.
00328    027600*
00329    027700        IF MT-DELETION
00330    027800            IF IM-ITEM-NUMBER = MT-ITEM-NUMBER
00331    027900                IF NOT MASTER-DELETED
00332    028000                    PERFORM 360-APPLY-DELETION-TRANSACTION
00333    028100                ELSE
00334    028200                    PERFORM 410-WRITE-ERROR-TRANSACTION
```

```
00335   028300              ELSE
00336   028400                  PERFORM 410-WRITE-ERROR-TRANSACTION
00337   028500          ELSE
00338   028600              IF MT-ADDITION
00339   028700                  IF IM-ITEM-NUMBER = MT-ITEM-NUMBER
00340   028800                      IF MASTER-DELETED
00341   028900                          PERFORM 420-APPLY-ADDITION-TRANSACTION
00342   029000                      ELSE
00343   029100                          PERFORM 410-WRITE-ERROR-TRANSACTION
00344   029200                  ELSE
00345   029300                      PERFORM 420-APPLY-ADDITION-TRANSACTION
00346   029400              ELSE
00347   029500                  IF MT-CHANGE
00348   029600                      IF IM-ITEM-NUMBER = MT-ITEM-NUMBER
00349   029700                          IF NOT MASTER-DELETED
00350   029800                              PERFORM 440-APPLY-CHANGE-TRANSACTION
00351   029900                          ELSE
00352   030000                              PERFORM 410-WRITE-ERROR-TRANSACTION
00353   030100                      ELSE
00354   030200                          PERFORM 410-WRITE-ERROR-TRANSACTION.
00355   030300*
00356   030400 360-APPLY-DELETION-TRANSACTION.
00357   030500*
00358   030600          MOVE 'Y'                TO MASTER-DELETED-SW.
00359   030700          MOVE DELETE-MESSAGE TO ML-ACTION.
00360   030800          ADD 1                   TO DELETION-COUNT.
00361   030900          PERFORM 370-PRINT-MAINTENANCE-LINE.
00362   031000*
00363   031100 370-PRINT-MAINTENANCE-LINE.
00364   031200*
00365   031300          IF LINE-COUNT GREATER THAN LINES-ON-PAGE
00366   031400              PERFORM 380-PRINT-HEADING-LINES.
00367   031500          MOVE IM-ITEM-NUMBER        TO ML-ITEM-NUMBER.
00368   031600          MOVE IM-ITEM-DESCRIPTION TO ML-ITEM-DESCR.
00369   031700          MOVE IM-UNIT-COST          TO ML-UNIT-COST.
00370   031800          MOVE IM-UNIT-PRICE         TO ML-UNIT-PRICE.
00371   031900          MOVE IM-ON-HAND-BALANCE  TO ML-ON-HAND.
00372   032000          MOVE MAINTENANCE-LINE      TO PRINT-AREA.
00373   032100          PERFORM 400-WRITE-REPORT-LINE.
00374   032200          MOVE 1 TO SPACE-CONTROL.
00375   032300*
00376   032400 380-PRINT-HEADING-LINES.
00377   032500*
00378   032600          ADD 1                   TO PAGE-COUNT.
00379   032700          MOVE PAGE-COUNT          TO HDG1-PAGE-NUMBER.
00380   032800          MOVE HEADING-LINE-1 TO PRINT-AREA.
00381   032900          PERFORM 390-WRITE-PAGE-TOP-LINE.
00382   033000          MOVE HEADING-LINE-2 TO PRINT-AREA.
00383   033100          MOVE 1                   TO SPACE-CONTROL.
00384   033200          PERFORM 400-WRITE-REPORT-LINE.
00385   033300          MOVE HEADING-LINE-3 TO PRINT-AREA.
00386   033400          PERFORM 400-WRITE-REPORT-LINE.
00387   033500          MOVE HEADING-LINE-4 TO PRINT-AREA.
00388   033600          MOVE 2                   TO SPACE-CONTROL.
00389   033700          PERFORM 400-WRITE-REPORT-LINE.
00390   033800*
00391   033900 390-WRITE-PAGE-TOP-LINE.
00392   034000*
00393   034100          WRITE PRINT-AREA
00394   034200              AFTER ADVANCING PAGE.
00395   034300          MOVE 1 TO LINE-COUNT.
00396   034400*
00397   034500 400-WRITE-REPORT-LINE.
00398   034600*
00399   034700          WRITE PRINT-AREA
00400   034800              AFTER ADVANCING SPACE-CONTROL LINES.
00401   034900          ADD SPACE-CONTROL TO LINE-COUNT.
```

The sequential file-maintenance program

```
00402    035000✣
00403    035100 410-WRITE-ERROR-TRANSACTION.
00404    035200✣
00405    035300        WRITE ERROR-TRANSACTION FROM MAINTENANCE-TRANSACTION.
00406    035400        ADD 1 TO ERROR-COUNT.
00407    035500✣
00408    035600 420-APPLY-ADDITION-TRANSACTION.
00409    035700✣
00410    035800        IF NOT MASTER-DELETED
00411    035900            MOVE INVENTORY-MASTER-RECORD TO HELD-MASTER-RECORD
00412    036000            MOVE 'Y' TO MASTER-HELD-FOR-ADDITION-SW
00413    036100        ELSE
00414    036200            MOVE 'N' TO MASTER-DELETED-SW.
00415    036300        PERFORM 430-FORMAT-ADDITION-RECORD.
00416    036400        MOVE ADD-MESSAGE      TO ML-ACTION.
00417    036500        ADD 1                 TO ADDITION-COUNT.
00418    036600        PERFORM 370-PRINT-MAINTENANCE-LINE.
00419    036700✣
00420    036800 430-FORMAT-ADDITION-RECORD.
00421    036900✣
00422    037000        MOVE MT-ITEM-NUMBER        TO IM-ITEM-NUMBER.
00423    037100        MOVE MT-ITEM-DESCRIPTION   TO IM-ITEM-DESCRIPTION.
00424    037200        MOVE MT-UNIT-COST          TO IM-UNIT-COST.
00425    037300        MOVE MT-UNIT-PRICE         TO IM-UNIT-PRICE.
00426    037400        MOVE MT-ON-HAND-BALANCE    TO IM-ON-HAND-BALANCE.
00427    037500        MOVE ZERO                  TO IM-SALES-THIS-MONTH
00428    037600                                      IM-RECEIPTS-THIS-MONTH
00429    037700                                      IM-SALES-THIS-YEAR
00430    037800                                      IM-RECEIPTS-THIS-YEAR.
00431    037900✣
00432    038000 440-APPLY-CHANGE-TRANSACTION.
00433    038100✣
00434    038200        PERFORM 450-CHANGE-OLD-MASTER-RECORD.
00435    038300        MOVE CHANGE-MESSAGE TO ML-ACTION.
00436    038400        ADD 1                 TO CHANGE-COUNT.
00437    038500        PERFORM 370-PRINT-MAINTENANCE-LINE.
00438    038600✣
00439    038700 450-CHANGE-OLD-MASTER-RECORD.
00440    038800✣
00441    038900        IF MT-ITEM-DESCRIPTION NOT = SPACE
00442    039000            MOVE MT-ITEM-DESCRIPTION TO IM-ITEM-DESCRIPTION.
00443    039100        IF MT-UNIT-COST NOT = ZERO
00444    039200            MOVE MT-UNIT-COST         TO IM-UNIT-COST.
00445    039300        IF MT-UNIT-PRICE NOT = ZERO
00446    039400            MOVE MT-UNIT-PRICE        TO IM-UNIT-PRICE.
00447    039500        IF MT-ON-HAND-BALANCE NOT = ZERO
00448    039600            MOVE MT-ON-HAND-BALANCE   TO IM-ON-HAND-BALANCE.
00449    039700✣
00450    039800 500-PRINT-TOTAL-PAGE.
00451    039900✣
00452    040000        ADD 1                 TO PAGE-COUNT.
00453    040100        MOVE PAGE-COUNT       TO HDG1-PAGE-NUMBER.
00454    040200        MOVE HEADING-LINE-1 TO PRINT-AREA.
00455    040300        PERFORM 390-WRITE-PAGE-TOP-LINE.
00456    040400        MOVE HEADING-LINE-2 TO PRINT-AREA.
00457    040500        MOVE 1                TO SPACE-CONTROL.
00458    040600        PERFORM 400-WRITE-REPORT-LINE.
00459    040700        ADD DELETION-COUNT
00460    040800            ADDITION-COUNT
00461    040900            CHANGE-COUNT GIVING VALID-COUNT.
00462    041000        MOVE TOTAL-LINE-1          TO PRINT-AREA.
00463    041100        MOVE 3                     TO SPACE-CONTROL.
00464    041200        PERFORM 400-WRITE-REPORT-LINE.
00465    041300        MOVE DELETION-COUNT       TO TOT2-DELETIONS.
00466    041400        MOVE TOTAL-LINE-2         TO PRINT-AREA.
00467    041500        MOVE 2                     TO SPACE-CONTROL.
00468    041600        PERFORM 400-WRITE-REPORT-LINE.
```

```
00469    041700    MOVE  ADDITION-COUNT          TO TOT3-ADDITIONS.
00470    041800    MOVE  TOTAL-LINE-3            TO PRINT-AREA.
00471    041900    MOVE  1                       TO SPACE-CONTROL.
00472    042000    PERFORM 400-WRITE-REPORT-LINE.
00473    042100    MOVE  CHANGE-COUNT            TO TOT4-CHANGES.
00474    042200    MOVE  TOTAL-LINE-4            TO PRINT-AREA.
00475    042300    PERFORM 400-WRITE-REPORT-LINE.
00476    042400    MOVE  VALID-COUNT             TO TOT5-UPDATES.
00477    042500    MOVE  TOTAL-LINE-5            TO PRINT-AREA.
00478    042600    PERFORM 400-WRITE-REPORT-LINE.
00479    042700    MOVE  ERROR-COUNT             TO TOT6-ERRORS.
00480    042800    MOVE  TOTAL-LINE-6            TO PRINT-AREA.
00481    042900    MOVE  2                       TO SPACE-CONTROL.
00482    043000    PERFORM 400-WRITE-REPORT-LINE.
00483    043100    MOVE  TOTAL-COUNT             TO TOT7-TOTAL.
00484    043200    MOVE  TOTAL-LINE-7            TO PRINT-AREA.
00485    043300    MOVE  2                       TO SPACE-CONTROL.
00486    043400    PERFORM 400-WRITE-REPORT-LINE.
```

The sequential file-
maintenance program

DATE: 10/25/84
TIME: 3:48 PM

MIKE MURACH & ASSOCIATES, INC.

INVENTORY MAINTENANCE LISTING

ITEM NO	ITEM DESCRIPTION	UNIT COST	UNIT PRICE	ON HAND	ACTION
00003	JOGGING SHORTS	3.47	7.29	50	ADDED
00005	BATTING GLOVE	4.29	7.19	65	DELETED
00006	SOFTBALL GLOVE	22.49	35.29	34	CHANGED
00008	BASEBALL GLOVE	23.19	35.69	61	DELETED
00012	BASKETBALL	7.21	12.38	100	CHANGED
00012	BASKETBALL	7.21	8.79	100	CHANGED
00014	T-SHIRTS	9.28	15.29	18	DELETED
00014	TENNIS SHORTS	9.28	15.29	20	ADDED
00014	TENNIS SHORTS	10.38	15.29	20	CHANGED
00019	WARM-UP SUIT	25.23	42.19	4	DELETED
00021	SOCCER BALL	5.35	8.79	75	ADDED

DATE: 10/25/84
TIME: 3:48 PM

MIKE MURACH & ASSOCIATES, INC.

SUMMARY FOR INVENTORY MAINTENANCE RUN

DELETIONS   4
ADDITIONS   3
CHANGES   4
TOTAL UPDATES   11 *

ERRORS   6

TRANSACTIONS PROCESSED   17 * *

The sequential file-
maintenance program

Model program 4

The random update program with an internal sort

Program:	INV2300 UPDATE INVENTORY FILE	Page:	1
Designer:	Anne Prince	Date:	08-23-84

Input/output specifications

File	Description	Use
RCPTTRAN	Receipt transaction file	Input
INVMAST	Inventory master file	Update
VRCPTRN	Valid receipt transaction file	Output
IRCPTLST	Print file: Invalid inventory receipt listing	Output
SORTFILE	Sorted inventory receipt transaction file	Output

Process specifications

The inventory master file has indexed file organization. It is a large file with low receipt activity.

The input file of receipt transactions is in a random order. Before the transactions are processed, they should be sorted into item-number sequence.

For object-program efficiency, the program should only read and write a master record once for each group of transactions that affect the master record.

The receipts must be edited and only valid receipts should be used to update the master records. The error code on the invalid listing will indicate only the first field that is invalid in each invalid record.

The totals for the update run should be printed on a separate page of printer output.

The random
update program

Process specifications

The basic processing requirements follow:

Sort the inventory transaction file in ascending item number order.

Do until the end of the sorted transaction file:

1. Get the next transaction.

2. Edit the transaction fields.

3. If the transaction is not valid, print a line on the invalid inventory receipts listing.

4. If the transaction is valid and has the same item number as the previous transaction, add the receipt quantity in the transaction record to the on hand balance in the master record, and write a valid transaction record.

5. If the transaction is valid and has a different item number than the previous transaction, rewrite the current master record on the master file and then process the new transaction.

Print the transaction totals on a separate page.

Process specifications

Editing rules for inventory transactions:

RT-ITEM-NUMBER   Must be a valid number in the inventory master file.

RT-VENDOR-NUMBER   Must be numeric and greater than zero.

RT-RECEIPT-DATE   Must be a valid date in the form MMDDYY and the year must be equal to the current year.

RT-RECEIPT-QUANTITY   Must be numeric and greater than zero.

```
        BKEND    C.INVMAST

      ✿
      01    INVENTORY-MASTER-RECORD.
      ✿
            05   IM-ITEM-NUMBER            PIC X(5).
            05   IM-ITEM-DESCRIPTION       PIC X(20).
            05   IM-UNIT-COST              PIC S9(3)V99   COMP-3.
            05   IM-UNIT-PRICE             PIC S9(3)V99   COMP-3.
            05   IM-ON-HAND-BALANCE        PIC S9(3)      COMP-3.
            05   IM-SALES-THIS-MONTH       PIC S9(5)V99   COMP-3.
            05   IM-RECEIPTS-THIS-MONTH    PIC S9(5)V99   COMP-3.
            05   IM-SALES-THIS-YEAR        PIC S9(7)V99   COMP-3.
            05   IM-RECEIPTS-THIS-YEAR     PIC S9(7)V99   COMP-3.

        BKEND
```

```
        BKEND    C.RCPTTRAN

      ✿
      01    RECEIPT-TRANSACTION.
      ✿
            05   RT-ITEM-NUMBER            PIC X(5).
            05   RT-VENDOR-NUMBER          PIC X(3).
            05   RT-RECEIPT-DATE           PIC X(6).
            05   RT-RECEIPT-DATE-R         REDEFINES RT-RECEIPT-DATE.
                 10   RT-RECEIPT-MONTH     PIC 99.
                 10   RT-RECEIPT-DAY       PIC 99.
                 10   RT-RECEIPT-YEAR      PIC 99.
            05   RT-RECEIPT-QUANTITY       PIC S9(3)   COMP-3.

        BKEND
```

The random update program

Document name Invalid Inventory Receipts Listing **Date** 8-23-84

Program name INV2300 **Designer** Anne Prince

Record Name		
Heading-Line-1	1 DATE: 99/99/99	PAGE: ZZ9
Heading-Line-2	2 TIME: 99:99 XX	INV2500
Heading-Line-3	3	MIKE MURACH & ASSOCIATES, INC.
	4	INVALID INVENTORY RECEIPTS LISTING
Heading-Line-4	5 ITEM	ERROR
Heading-Line-5	6 NUMBER VENDOR DATE QUANTITY CODE	
	7 NUMBER RECEIVED	
Invalid-Transaction-Line	8 XXXXX	
	9 XXX XX/XX/XX ZZ9 FIELD 1	
	10 XXXXX	
	11 XXX XX/XX/XX ZZ9 FIELD 2	
	12 XXXXX	
	13 XXX XX/XX/XX ZZ9 FIELD 3	
	14 XXXXX XXX XX/XX/XX ZZ9 FIELD 4	
	15	
	16	
	17	
	18	
Total page data to be printed after the first two lines of the standard heading:	19	
	20	
	21	
	22	
	23	
	24	
Total-Line-1	25 SUMMARY FOR INVENTORY RECEIPTS RUN	
	26	
Total-Line-2	27 ZZ,ZZ9 TRANSACTIONS READ	
Total-Line-3	28 ZZ,ZZ9 VALID TRANSACTIONS	
Total-Line-4	29 ZZ,ZZ9 INVALID TRANSACTIONS	
	30	

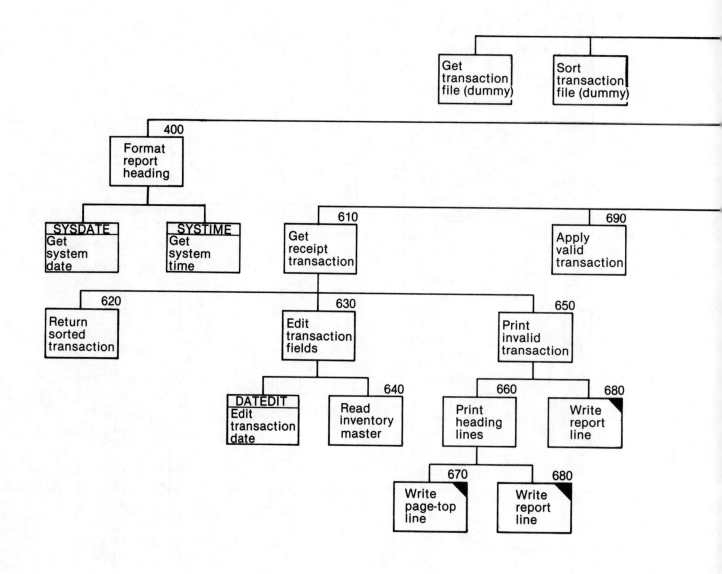

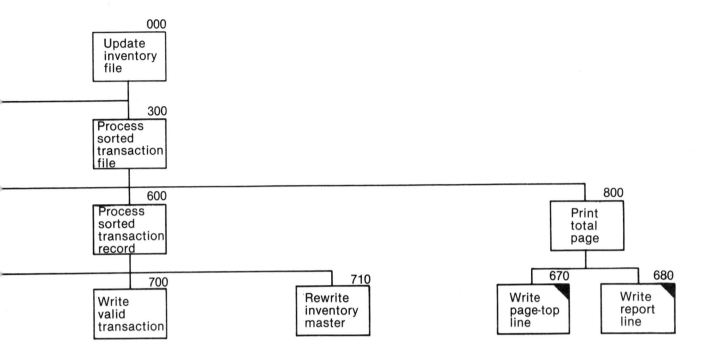

```
       CBL APOST,LANGLVL(1),LIB
00001     000100 IDENTIFICATION DIVISION.
00002     000200✸
00003     000300 PROGRAM-ID.        INV2300.
00004     000400✸AUTHOR.            ANNE PRINCE.
00005     000500✸INSTALLATION.      MMA.
00006     000600✸DATE.              SEPTEMBER 10, 1984.
00007     000700✸
00008     000800 ENVIRONMENT DIVISION.
00009     000900✸
00010     001000 CONFIGURATION SECTION.
00011     001100✸
00012     001200 SOURCE-COMPUTER.   IBM-370.
00013     001300 OBJECT-COMPUTER.   IBM-370.
00014     001400✸
00015     001500 INPUT-OUTPUT SECTION.
00016     001600✸
00017     001700 FILE-CONTROL.
00018     001800     SELECT RCPTTRAN ASSIGN TO SYS008-AS-SORTIN.
00019     001900     SELECT INVMAST  ASSIGN TO SYS005-INVMAST
00020     002000                     ORGANIZATION IS INDEXED
00021     002100                     ACCESS IS RANDOM
00022     002200                     RECORD KEY IS IR-ITEM-NUMBER.
00023     002300     SELECT VRCPTRN  ASSIGN TO SYS007-AS-VRCPTRN.
00024     002400     SELECT IRCPTLST ASSIGN TO SYS006-UR-1403-S.
00025     002500     SELECT SORTFILE ASSIGN TO SYS001-UT-F8A1-S-SORTWK1.
00026     002600✸
00027     002700 DATA DIVISION.
00028     002800✸
00029     002900 FILE SECTION.
00030     003000✸
00031     003100 FD  RCPTTRAN
00032     003200     LABEL RECORDS ARE STANDARD
00033     003300     RECORD CONTAINS 16 CHARACTERS.
00034     003400✸
00035     003500 01  TRANSACTION-RECORD          PIC X(16).
00036     003600✸
00037     003700 FD  INVMAST
00038     003800     LABEL RECORDS ARE STANDARD
00039     003900     RECORD CONTAINS 51 CHARACTERS.
00040     004000✸
00041     004100 01  INVENTORY-RECORD.
00042     004200✸
00043     004300     05  IR-ITEM-NUMBER  PIC X(5).
00044     004400     05  FILLER          PIC X(46).
00045     004500✸
00046     004600 FD  VRCPTRN
00047     004700     LABEL RECORDS ARE STANDARD
00048     004800     RECORD CONTAINS 16 CHARACTERS.
00049     004900✸
00050     005000 01  VALID-RECEIPT-TRANSACTION   PIC X(16).
00051     005100✸
00052     005200 FD  IRCPTLST
00053     005300     LABEL RECORDS ARE OMITTED
00054     005400     RECORD CONTAINS 132 CHARACTERS.
00055     005500✸
00056     005600 01  PRINT-AREA          PIC X(132).
00057     005700✸
00058     005800 SD  SORTFILE
00059     005900     RECORD CONTAINS 16 CHARACTERS.
00060     006000✸
00061     006100 01  SF-RECORD.
00062     006200✸
00063     006300     05  SF-ITEM-NUMBER  PIC X(5).
00064     006400     05  FILLER          PIC X(11).
00065     006500✸
00066     006600 WORKING-STORAGE SECTION.
```

```
00067    006700✷
00068    006800 01   SWITCHES.
00069    006900✷
00070    007000      05   TRAN-EOF-SW          PIC X          VALUE 'N'.
00071    007100           88   TRAN-EOF                        VALUE 'Y'.
00072    007200      05   FIRST-RECORD-SW      PIC X          VALUE 'Y'.
00073    007300           88   FIRST-RECORD                    VALUE 'Y'.
00074    007400      05   VALID-TRAN-SW        PIC X          VALUE 'N'.
00075    007500           88   VALID-TRAN                      VALUE 'Y'.
00076    007600      05   VALID-DATE-SW        PIC X.
00077    007700           88   VALID-DATE                      VALUE 'Y'.
00078    007800      05   MASTER-FOUND-SW      PIC X          VALUE 'Y'.
00079    007900           88   MASTER-FOUND                    VALUE 'Y'.
00080    008000✷
00081    008100 01   CONTROL-FIELDS.
00082    008200✷
00083    008300      05   OLD-ITEM-NUMBER      PIC X(5)     VALUE LOW-VALUE.
00084    008400✷
00085    008500 01   COUNT-FIELDS              COMP-3.
00086    008600✷
00087    008700      05   TRANSACTION-COUNT    PIC S9(5)    VALUE ZERO.
00088    008800      05   VALID-COUNT          PIC S9(5)    VALUE ZERO.
00089    008900      05   INVALID-COUNT        PIC S9(5)    VALUE ZERO.
00090    009000✷
00091    009100 01   PRINT-FIELDS.
00092    009200✷
00093    009300      05   SPACE-CONTROL    PIC S9                  COMP SYNC.
00094    009400      05   LINE-COUNT       PIC S999    VALUE +999  COMP SYNC.
00095    009500      05   LINES-ON-PAGE    PIC S999    VALUE +57   COMP SYNC.
00096    009600      05   PAGE-COUNT       PIC S999    VALUE ZERO  COMP-3.
00097    009700✷
00098    009800 01   DATE-FIELDS.
00099    009900✷
00100    010000      05   TODAYS-DATE          PIC 9(6).
00101    010100      05   TODAYS-DATE-R        REDEFINES TODAYS-DATE.
00102    010200           10   TODAYS-MONTH    PIC 99.
00103    010300           10   TODAYS-DAY      PIC 99.
00104    010400           10   TODAYS-YEAR     PIC 99.
00105    010500✷
00106    010600 COPY RCPTTRAN.
00107 C       ✷
00108 C         01   RECEIPT-TRANSACTION.
00109 C       ✷
00110 C            05   RT-ITEM-NUMBER              PIC X(5).
00111 C            05   RT-VENDOR-NUMBER            PIC X(3).
00112 C            05   RT-RECEIPT-DATE             PIC X(6).
00113 C            05   RT-RECEIPT-DATE-R           REDEFINES RT-RECEIPT-DATE.
00114 C                 10   RT-RECEIPT-MONTH       PIC 99.
00115 C                 10   RT-RECEIPT-DAY         PIC 99.
00116 C                 10   RT-RECEIPT-YEAR        PIC 99.
00117 C            05   RT-RECEIPT-QUANTITY         PIC S9(3)   COMP-3.
00118    010700✷
00119    010800 01   NEXT-INVENTORY-RECORD    PIC X(51).
00120    010900✷
00121    011000 COPY INVMAST.
00122 C       ✷
00123 C         01   INVENTORY-MASTER-RECORD.
00124 C       ✷
00125 C            05   IM-ITEM-NUMBER         PIC X(5).
00126 C            05   IM-ITEM-DESCRIPTION    PIC X(20).
00127 C            05   IM-UNIT-COST           PIC S9(3)V99   COMP-3.
00128 C            05   IM-UNIT-PRICE          PIC S9(3)V99   COMP-3.
00129 C            05   IM-ON-HAND-BALANCE     PIC S9(3)      COMP-3.
00130 C            05   IM-SALES-THIS-MONTH    PIC S9(5)V99   COMP-3.
00131 C            05   IM-RECEIPTS-THIS-MONTH PIC S9(5)V99   COMP-3.
00132 C            05   IM-SALES-THIS-YEAR     PIC S9(7)V99   COMP-3.
00133 C            05   IM-RECEIPTS-THIS-YEAR  PIC S9(7)V99   COMP-3.
```

```
00134    011100✿
00135    011200 01   ERROR-CODES.
00136    011300✿
00137    011400      05   FIELD-1              PIC X(15)    VALUE 'FIELD-1           '.
00138    011500      05   FIELD-2              PIC X(15)    VALUE 'FIELD-2           '.
00139    011600      05   FIELD-3              PIC X(15)    VALUE 'FIELD-3           '.
00140    011700      05   FIELD-4              PIC X(15)    VALUE 'FIELD-4           '.
00141    011800      05   NOT-FOUND            PIC X(15)    VALUE 'NOT FOUND         '.
00142    011900✿
00143    012000 01   COMPANY-NAME.
00144    012100✿
00145    012200      05   FILLER          PIC X(10)    VALUE SPACE.
00146    012300      05   FILLER          PIC X(20)    VALUE 'MIKE MURACH & ASSOCI'.
00147    012400      05   FILLER          PIC X(20)    VALUE 'ATES, INC.'.
00148    012500✿
00149    012600 01   REPORT-TITLE.
00150    012700✿
00151    012800      05   FILLER          PIC X(13)    VALUE SPACE.
00152    012900      05   FILLER          PIC X(20)    VALUE 'INVALID INVENTORY RE'.
00153    013000      05   FILLER          PIC X(20)    VALUE 'CEIPT LISTING       '.
00154    013100      05   FILLER          PIC X(7)     VALUE SPACE.
00155    013200✿
00156    013300 COPY RPTHDG14.
00157 C       ✿
00158 C          01   HEADING-LINE-1.
00159 C       ✿
00160 C             05   FILLER               PIC X(7)     VALUE 'DATE:'.
00161 C             05   HDG1-DATE            PIC 99/99/99.
00162 C             05   FILLER               PIC X(26)    VALUE SPACE.
00163 C             05   HDG1-COMPANY-NAME    PIC X(50).
00164 C             05   FILLER               PIC X(31)    VALUE SPACE.
00165 C             05   FILLER               PIC X(6)     VALUE 'PAGE:'.
00166 C             05   HDG1-PAGE-NUMBER     PIC ZZ9.
00167 C       ✿
00168 C          01   HEADING-LINE-2.
00169 C       ✿
00170 C             05   HDG2-TIME-DATA.
00171 C                10   FILLER            PIC X(7)     VALUE 'TIME:'.
00172 C                10   HDG2-HOURS        PIC XX.
00173 C                10   FILLER            PIC X        VALUE ':'.
00174 C                10   HDG2-MINUTES      PIC XX.
00175 C                10   FILLER            PIC X        VALUE SPACE.
00176 C                10   HDG2-TIME-SUFFIX  PIC X(8).
00177 C             05   FILLER               PIC X(101)   VALUE SPACE.
00178 C             05   HDG2-REPORT-NUMBER   PIC X(10).
00179 C       ✿
00180 C          01   HEADING-LINE-3.
00181 C       ✿
00182 C             05   FILLER               PIC X(36)    VALUE SPACE.
00183 C             05   HDG3-REPORT-TITLE    PIC X(60).
00184    013400✿
00185    013500 01   HEADING-LINE-4.
00186    013600✿
00187    013700      05   FILLER          PIC X(20)    VALUE ' ITEM       VENDOR  '.
00188    013800      05   FILLER          PIC X(20)    VALUE 'DATE              '.
00189    013900      05   FILLER          PIC X(20)    VALUE 'ERROR             '.
00190    014000✿
00191    014100 01   HEADING-LINE-5.
00192    014200✿
00193    014300      05   FILLER          PIC X(20)    VALUE 'NUMBER      NUMBER  RE'.
00194    014400      05   FILLER          PIC X(20)    VALUE 'CEIVED      QUANTITY '.
00195    014500      05   FILLER          PIC X(20)    VALUE 'CODE              '.
00196    014600✿
00197    014700 01   INVALID-TRANSACTION-LINE.
00198    014800✿
00199    014900      05   ITL-ITEM-NUMBER      PIC X(5).
00200    015000      05   FILLER               PIC X(5)     VALUE SPACE.
```

```
00201  015100      05  ITL-VENDOR-NUMBER    PIC X(3).
00202  015200      05  FILLER               PIC X(5)      VALUE SPACE.
00203  015300      05  ITL-DATE             PIC XX/XX/XX.
00204  015400      05  FILLER               PIC X(5)      VALUE SPACE.
00205  015500      05  ITL-RECEIPT-QTY      PIC ZZ9.
00206  015600      05  FILLER               PIC X(6)      VALUE SPACE.
00207  015700      05  ITL-ERROR-CODE       PIC X(15).
00208  015800      05  FILLER               PIC X(77)     VALUE SPACE.
00209  015900*
00210  016000 01  TOTAL-LINE-1.
00211  016100*
00212  016200      05  FILLER          PIC X(20)    VALUE 'SUMMARY FOR INVENTOR'.
00213  016300      05  FILLER          PIC X(20)    VALUE 'Y RECEIPT RUN        '.
00214  016400      05  FILLER          PIC X(92)    VALUE SPACE.
00215  016500*
00216  016600 01  TOTAL-LINE-2.
00217  016700*
00218  016800      05  TOT2-TRAN-CNT   PIC ZZ,ZZ9.
00219  016900      05  FILLER          PIC X(20)    VALUE ' TRANSACTIONS READ  '.
00220  017000      05  FILLER          PIC X(106)   VALUE SPACE.
00221  017100*
00222  017200 01  TOTAL-LINE-3.
00223  017300*
00224  017400      05  TOT3-VAL-CNT    PIC ZZ,ZZ9.
00225  017500      05  FILLER          PIC X(20)    VALUE ' VALID TRANSACTIONS '.
00226  017600      05  FILLER          PIC X(106)   VALUE SPACE.
00227  017700*
00228  017800 01  TOTAL-LINE-4.
00229  017900*
00230  018000      05  TOT4-INV-CNT    PIC ZZ,ZZ9.
00231  018100      05  FILLER          PIC X(20)    VALUE ' INVALID TRANSACTION'.
00232  018200      05  FILLER          PIC X(20)    VALUE 'S                   '.
00233  018300      05  FILLER          PIC X(86)    VALUE SPACE.
00234  018400*
00235  018500 PROCEDURE DIVISION.
00236  018600*
00237  018700 000-UPDATE-INVENTORY-FILE     SECTION.
00238  018800*
00239  018900      OPEN I-O   INVMAST
00240  019000           OUTPUT VRCPTRN
00241  019100                  IRCPTLST.
00242  019200      SORT SORTFILE
00243  019300          ON ASCENDING KEY SF-ITEM-NUMBER
00244  019400          USING RCPTTRAN
00245  019500          OUTPUT PROCEDURE IS 300-PROCESS-SORTED-TRAN-FILE.
00246  019600      IF SORT-RETURN IS NOT ZERO
00247  019700          DISPLAY 'SORT FAILED'.
00248  019800      CLOSE INVMAST
00249  019900            VRCPTRN
00250  020000            IRCPTLST.
00251  020100      STOP RUN.
00252  020200*
00253  020300 300-PROCESS-SORTED-TRAN-FILE     SECTION.
00254  020400*
00255  020500      PERFORM 400-FORMAT-REPORT-HEADING.
00256  020600      PERFORM 600-PROCESS-SORTED-TRAN-RECORD
00257  020700          UNTIL TRAN-EOF.
00258  020800      PERFORM 800-PRINT-TOTAL-PAGE.
00259  020900      GO TO 300-EXIT.
00260  021000*
00261  021100 400-FORMAT-REPORT-HEADING.
00262  021200*
00263  021300      CALL 'SYSDATE' USING TODAYS-DATE.
00264  021400      MOVE TODAYS-DATE   TO HDG1-DATE.
00265  021500      MOVE COMPANY-NAME TO HDG1-COMPANY-NAME.
00266  021600      CALL 'SYSTIME' USING HDG2-TIME-DATA.
00267  021700      MOVE 'INV2300'    TO HDG2-REPORT-NUMBER.
```

The random
update program

```
00268    021800        MOVE REPORT-TITLE TO HDG3-REPORT-TITLE.
00269    021900✢
00270    022000 600-PROCESS-SORTED-TRAN-RECORD.
00271    022100✢
00272    022200        MOVE 'N' TO VALID-TRAN-SW.
00273    022300        PERFORM 610-GET-RECEIPT-TRANSACTION
00274    022400            UNTIL VALID-TRAN.
00275    022500        IF NOT TRAN-EOF
00276    022600            IF FIRST-RECORD
00277    022700                MOVE RT-ITEM-NUMBER         TO OLD-ITEM-NUMBER
00278    022800                MOVE NEXT-INVENTORY-RECORD TO INVENTORY-MASTER-RECORD
00279    022900                MOVE 'N'                   TO FIRST-RECORD-SW.
00280    023000        IF NOT TRAN-EOF
00281    023100            IF RT-ITEM-NUMBER EQUAL OLD-ITEM-NUMBER
00282    023200                PERFORM 690-APPLY-VALID-TRANSACTION
00283    023300                PERFORM 700-WRITE-VALID-TRANSACTION.
00284    023400        IF RT-ITEM-NUMBER GREATER OLD-ITEM-NUMBER
00285    023500            PERFORM 710-REWRITE-INVENTORY-MASTER
00286    023600            IF NOT TRAN-EOF
00287    023700                MOVE NEXT-INVENTORY-RECORD TO INVENTORY-MASTER-RECORD
00288    023800                MOVE RT-ITEM-NUMBER         TO OLD-ITEM-NUMBER
00289    023900                PERFORM 690-APPLY-VALID-TRANSACTION
00290    024000                PERFORM 700-WRITE-VALID-TRANSACTION.
00291    024100✢
00292    024200 610-GET-RECEIPT-TRANSACTION.
00293    024300✢
00294    024400        MOVE 'Y' TO VALID-TRAN-SW.
00295    024500        PERFORM 620-RETURN-SORTED-TRANSACTION.
00296    024600        IF NOT TRAN-EOF
00297    024700            ADD 1 TO TRANSACTION-COUNT
00298    024800            PERFORM 630-EDIT-TRANSACTION-FIELDS
00299    024900            IF NOT VALID-TRAN
00300    025000                PERFORM 650-PRINT-INVALID-TRANSACTION.
00301    025100✢
00302    025200 620-RETURN-SORTED-TRANSACTION.
00303    025300✢
00304    025400        RETURN SORTFILE INTO RECEIPT-TRANSACTION
00305    025500            AT END
00306    025600                MOVE HIGH-VALUE TO RT-ITEM-NUMBER
00307    025700                MOVE 'Y' TO TRAN-EOF-SW.
00308    025800✢
00309    025900 630-EDIT-TRANSACTION-FIELDS.
00310    026000✢
00311    026100        MOVE 'Y' TO MASTER-FOUND-SW.
00312    026200        IF RT-ITEM-NUMBER GREATER OLD-ITEM-NUMBER
00313    026300            MOVE RT-ITEM-NUMBER TO IR-ITEM-NUMBER
00314    026400            PERFORM 640-READ-INVENTORY-MASTER.
00315    026500        IF NOT MASTER-FOUND
00316    026600            MOVE FIELD-1 TO ITL-ERROR-CODE
00317    026700            MOVE 'N'       TO VALID-TRAN-SW
00318    026800        ELSE
00319    026900            IF       RT-VENDOR-NUMBER NOT NUMERIC
00320    027000                OR RT-VENDOR-NUMBER NOT GREATER THAN ZERO
00321    027100                MOVE FIELD-2 TO ITL-ERROR-CODE
00322    027200                MOVE 'N'       TO VALID-TRAN-SW
00323    027300            ELSE
00324    027400                CALL 'DATEDIT' USING RT-RECEIPT-DATE, VALID-DATE-SW
00325    027500                IF NOT VALID-DATE
00326    027600                    MOVE FIELD-3 TO ITL-ERROR-CODE
00327    027700                    MOVE 'N'       TO VALID-TRAN-SW
00328    027800                ELSE IF RT-RECEIPT-YEAR NOT EQUAL TODAYS-YEAR
00329    027900                    MOVE FIELD-3 TO ITL-ERROR-CODE
00330    028000                    MOVE 'N'       TO VALID-TRAN-SW
00331    028100                ELSE IF RT-RECEIPT-QUANTITY NOT GREATER THAN ZERO
00332    028200                    MOVE FIELD-4 TO ITL-ERROR-CODE
00333    028300                    MOVE 'N'       TO VALID-TRAN-SW.
00334    028400✢
```

```
00335    028500 640-READ-INVENTORY-MASTER.
00336    028600✤
00337    028700        READ INVMAST INTO NEXT-INVENTORY-RECORD
00338    028800            INVALID KEY
00339    028900                MOVE 'N' TO MASTER-FOUND-SW.
00340    029000✤
00341    029100 650-PRINT-INVALID-TRANSACTION.
00342    029200✤
00343    029300        IF LINE-COUNT GREATER THAN LINES-ON-PAGE
00344    029400            PERFORM 660-PRINT-HEADING-LINES.
00345    029500        MOVE RT-ITEM-NUMBER              TO ITL-ITEM-NUMBER.
00346    029600        MOVE RT-VENDOR-NUMBER            TO ITL-VENDOR-NUMBER.
00347    029700        MOVE RT-RECEIPT-DATE             TO ITL-DATE.
00348    029800        MOVE RT-RECEIPT-QUANTITY         TO ITL-RECEIPT-QTY.
00349    029900        MOVE INVALID-TRANSACTION-LINE TO PRINT-AREA.
00350    030000        PERFORM 680-WRITE-REPORT-LINE.
00351    030100        ADD 1 TO INVALID-COUNT.
00352    030200✤
00353    030300 660-PRINT-HEADING-LINES.
00354    030400✤
00355    030500        ADD 1                   TO PAGE-COUNT.
00356    030600        MOVE PAGE-COUNT         TO HDG1-PAGE-NUMBER.
00357    030700        MOVE HEADING-LINE-1 TO PRINT-AREA.
00358    030800        PERFORM 670-WRITE-PAGE-TOP-LINE.
00359    030900        MOVE HEADING-LINE-2 TO PRINT-AREA.
00360    031000        MOVE 1                  TO SPACE-CONTROL.
00361    031100        PERFORM 680-WRITE-REPORT-LINE.
00362    031200        MOVE HEADING-LINE-3 TO PRINT-AREA.
00363    031300        PERFORM 680-WRITE-REPORT-LINE.
00364    031400        MOVE HEADING-LINE-4 TO PRINT-AREA.
00365    031500        MOVE 2                  TO SPACE-CONTROL.
00366    031600        PERFORM 680-WRITE-REPORT-LINE.
00367    031700        MOVE HEADING-LINE-5 TO PRINT-AREA.
00368    031800        MOVE 1                  TO SPACE-CONTROL.
00369    031900        PERFORM 680-WRITE-REPORT-LINE.
00370    032000        MOVE 2                  TO SPACE-CONTROL.
00371    032100✤
00372    032200 670-WRITE-PAGE-TOP-LINE.
00373    032300✤
00374    032400        WRITE PRINT-AREA
00375    032500            AFTER ADVANCING PAGE.
00376    032600        MOVE 1 TO LINE-COUNT.
00377    032700✤
00378    032800 680-WRITE-REPORT-LINE.
00379    032900✤
00380    033000        WRITE PRINT-AREA
00381    033100            AFTER ADVANCING SPACE-CONTROL LINES.
00382    033200        ADD SPACE-CONTROL TO LINE-COUNT.
00383    033300✤
00384    033400 690-APPLY-VALID-TRANSACTION.
00385    033500✤
00386    033600        ADD RT-RECEIPT-QUANTITY TO IM-ON-HAND-BALANCE.
00387    033700✤
00388    033800 700-WRITE-VALID-TRANSACTION.
00389    033900✤
00390    034000        WRITE VALID-RECEIPT-TRANSACTION FROM RECEIPT-TRANSACTION.
00391    034100        ADD 1 TO VALID-COUNT.
00392    034200✤
00393    034300 710-REWRITE-INVENTORY-MASTER.
00394    034400✤
00395    034500        REWRITE INVENTORY-RECORD FROM INVENTORY-MASTER-RECORD.
00396    034600✤
00397    034700 800-PRINT-TOTAL-PAGE.
00398    034800✤
00399    034900        ADD 1                   TO PAGE-COUNT.
00400    035000        MOVE PAGE-COUNT         TO HDG1-PAGE-NUMBER.
00401    035100        MOVE HEADING-LINE-1     TO PRINT-AREA.
```

The random
update program

```
00402    035200        PERFORM 670-WRITE-PAGE-TOP-LINE.
00403    035300        MOVE HEADING-LINE-2       TO PRINT-AREA.
00404    035400        MOVE 1                    TO SPACE-CONTROL.
00405    035500        PERFORM 680-WRITE-REPORT-LINE.
00406    035600        MOVE TOTAL-LINE-1         TO PRINT-AREA.
00407    035700        MOVE 3                    TO SPACE-CONTROL.
00408    035800        PERFORM 680-WRITE-REPORT-LINE.
00409    035900        MOVE TRANSACTION-COUNT TO TOT2-TRAN-CNT.
00410    036000        MOVE TOTAL-LINE-2         TO PRINT-AREA.
00411    036100        MOVE 2                    TO SPACE-CONTROL.
00412    036200        PERFORM 680-WRITE-REPORT-LINE.
00413    036300        MOVE VALID-COUNT          TO TOT3-VAL-CNT.
00414    036400        MOVE TOTAL-LINE-3         TO PRINT-AREA.
00415    036500        MOVE 1                    TO SPACE-CONTROL.
00416    036600        PERFORM 680-WRITE-REPORT-LINE.
00417    036700        MOVE INVALID-COUNT        TO TOT4-INV-CNT.
00418    036800        MOVE TOTAL-LINE-4         TO PRINT-AREA.
00419    036900        PERFORM 680-WRITE-REPORT-LINE.
00420    037000*
00421    037100 300-EXIT.
00422    037200*
00423    037300        EXIT.
```

DATE: 10/25/84
TIME: 3:53 PM

MIKE MURACH & ASSOCIATES, INC.

INVALID INVENTORY RECEIPT LISTING

ITEM NUMBER	VENDOR NUMBER	DATE RECEIVED	QUANTITY	ERROR CODE
00000	053	02/29/84	75	FIELD-1
00002	000	03/12/84	25	FIELD-2
00004	21	03/09/84	100	FIELD-2
00005	074	02/31/84	35	FIELD-3
00006	103	03/03/83	50	FIELD-3
00007	072	02/27/84	0	FIELD-4
00010	085	03/14/84	75	FIELD-1
2	008	03/15/84	50	FIELD-1

The random
update program

DATE: 10/25/84
TIME: 3:53 PM

MIKE MURACH & ASSOCIATES, INC.

SUMMARY FOR INVENTORY RECEIPT RUN

15 TRANSACTIONS READ
 7 VALID TRANSACTIONS
 8 INVALID TRANSACTIONS

Section 6

Interactive model programs

This section presents three interactive programs that are intended to be models for the development of other interactive programs. The model programs represent solutions for the same interactive programming problem, but they show how the solutions are implemented on three different types of computer systems.

The first program shows a solution using Microsoft COBOL on an IBM PC. The second program shows a solution using Wang VS COBOL on a Wang VS system. The third program shows a solution using CICS on an IBM 4300 running under DOS/VSE. We decided to use these systems because they represent the development practices common to the vast majority of modern computer systems. As a result, if you're not using one of these systems, one of them should be enough like your system so its model program will be useful to you.

Model program 5

The interactive file-maintenance program using Microsoft COBOL on an IBM PC

| Program: | MNT2100   Maintain customer file | Page: 1 |
| | Microsoft COBOL on the IBM PC | |

| Designer: Steve Eckols | Date: 08-26-84 |

Input/output specifications

File	Description	Use
CUSTMAST	Customer master file	Update

Process specifications

Until the operator indicates end of program by pressing function key
10 in step 1:

1.   Get a valid combination of action code and customer code from
     the ACTION SCREEN. Use the operator-entered customer code as
     the primary key for a random read on CUSTMAST. If the action is
     addition, there shouldn't be a record for the customer code in
     the customer file; if the action is deletion or change, there
     should be a record for the customer code in the customer file.

2.   For an addition transaction, get the valid customer entries from
     the CUSTOMER ENTRY SCREEN. Then, get a valid verification entry
     from the TRANSACTION VERIFICATION SCREEN. If the transaction is
     accepted, write the new record on the customer file. If the
     transaction is to be modified, repeat this step. If the
     transaction is to be cancelled, cancel this transaction and
     continue with step 1.

3.   For a change transaction, get the valid change entries from the
     CUSTOMER ENTRY SCREEN. Then, get a valid verification entry
     from the TRANSACTION VERIFICATION SCREEN. If the transaction is
     accepted, write the changed record back onto the customer file.
     If the transaction is to be modified, repeat this step. If the
     transaction is to be cancelled, cancel this transaction and
     continue with step 1.

Program: **MNT2100** **Maintain customer file**
Microsoft COBOL on the IBM PC
Page: 2

Designer: **Steve Eckols**
Date: 08-26-84

Process specifications

4. **For a deletion transaction, get a valid verification entry from the TRANSACTION VERIFICATION SCREEN. If the transaction is accepted, delete the record from the customer file. If the transaction is to be cancelled, cancel this transaction and continue with step 1.**

<u>Editing rules</u>

CM-CUSTOMER-CODE	Must be non-blank.
CM-NAME	Must be non-blank.
CM-ADDRESS	Must be non-blank.
CM-CITY	Must be non-blank.
CM-STATE	Must be a valid United States Postal Service state code. Use the installation subprogram STATEDIT to validate the entry.
CM-ZIP-CODE	Must be a valid United States Postal Service zip code valid for CM-STATE. Use the installation subprogram ZIPEDIT to validate the entry.

```
*
 01   CUSTOMER-MASTER-RECORD.
*
      05   CM-CUSTOMER-CODE        PIC X(5).
      05   CM-NAME                 PIC X(30).
      05   CM-ADDRESS              PIC X(30).
      05   CM-CITY                 PIC X(21).
      05   CM-STATE                PIC XX.
      05   CM-ZIP-CODE             PIC X(5).
```

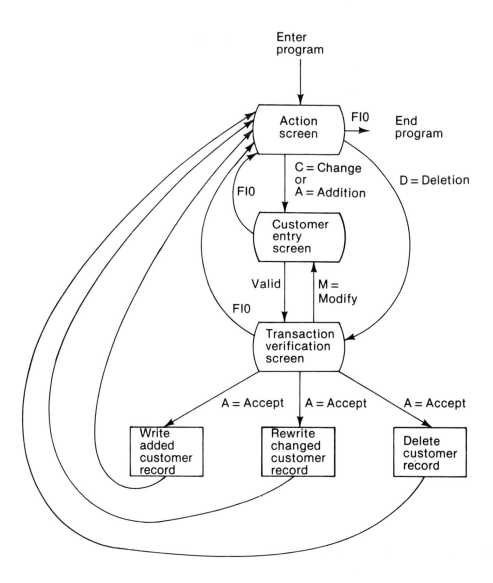

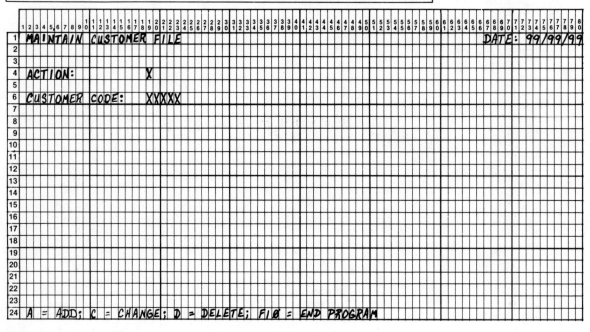

Screen name *Action*   **Date** *8-26-84*

Program name *MNT2100*   **Designer** *SLE*

```
 1 MAINTAIN CUSTOMER FILE                                    DATE: 99/99/99
 2
 3
 4 ACTION:        X
 5
 6 CUSTOMER CODE:  XXXXX
 7
 8
 9
10
11
12
13
14
15
16
17
18
19
20
21
22
23
24 A = ADD; C = CHANGE; D = DELETE; F10 = END PROGRAM
```

Screen name *Customer entry*   **Date** *8-26-84*

Program name *MNT2100*   **Designer** *SLE*

```
 1 MAINTAIN CUSTOMER FILE                                    DATE: 99/99/99
 2
 3
 4
 5
 6 CUSTOMER CODE:   XXXXX
 7
 8 NAME:           X                        X
 9 ADDRESS:        X                        X
10 CITY/STATE/ZIP: X                X XX XXXXX
11
12
13
14
15
16
17
18
19
20
21
22
23
24 F10 = CANCEL ENTRY
```

Screen name _Transaction verification_   Date _8-26-84_

Program name _MNT2100_   Designer _SLE_

```
 1  MAINTAIN CUSTOMER FILE                                              DATE: 99/99/99
 2
 3
 4
 5
 6  CUSTOMER CODE:     XXXXX
 7
 8  NAME:             X                                            X
 9  ADDRESS:          X                                            X
10  CITY/STATE/ZIP:   X                             X XX XXXXX
11
12  VERIFICATION:     X
13
14
15
16
17
18
19
20
21
22
23
*24  A = ACCEPT; M = MODIFY; F10 = CANCEL ENTRY
```

* For a deletion verification the operator message is
   A = DELETE THIS RECORD; F10 = CANCEL ENTRY

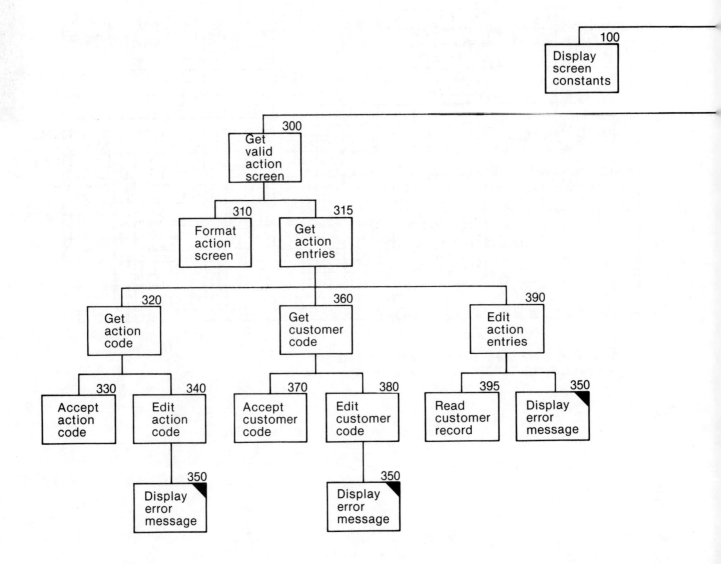

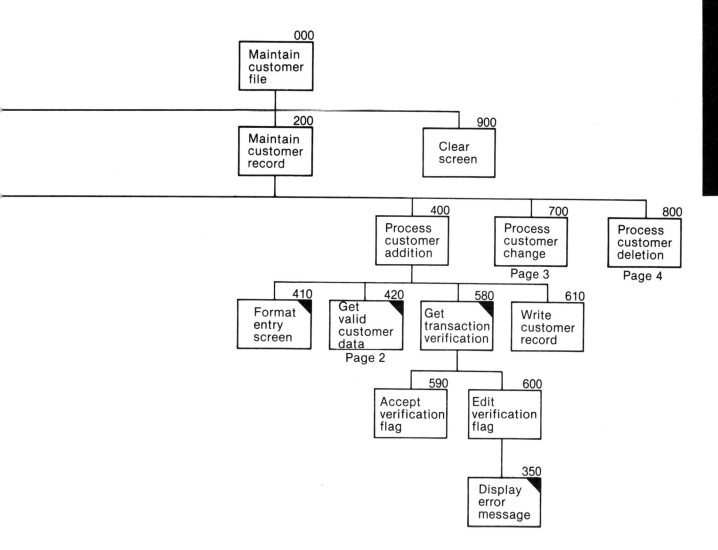

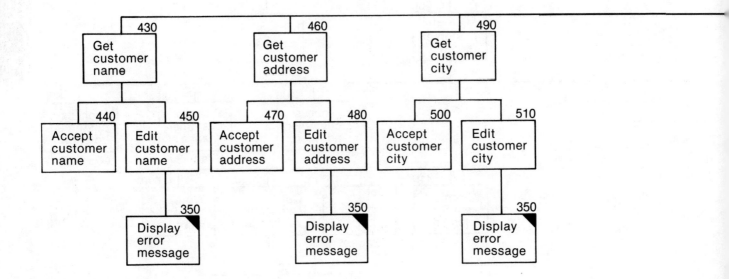

From page 1

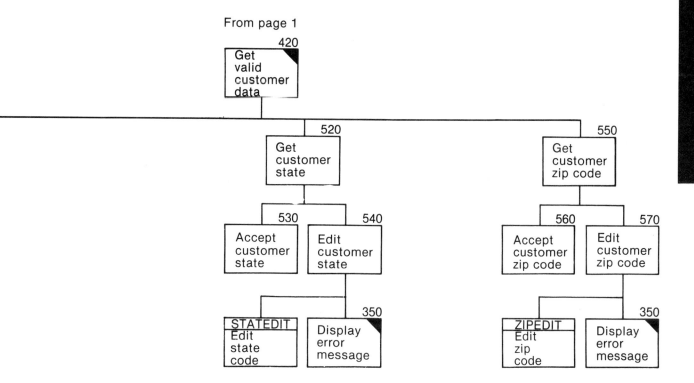

From page 1

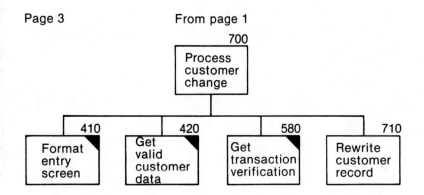

From page 1

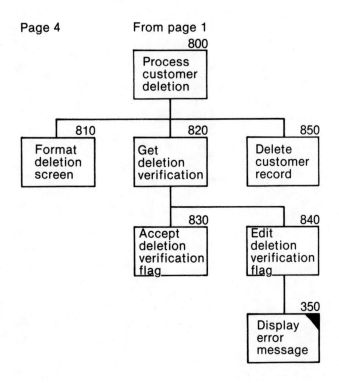

```
     1          IDENTIFICATION DIVISION.
     2          *
     3          PROGRAM-ID.            MNT2100.
     4          *
     5          ENVIRONMENT DIVISION.
     6          *
     7          CONFIGURATION SECTION.
     8          *
     9          INPUT-OUTPUT SECTION.
    10          *
    11          FILE-CONTROL.
    12          *
    13              SELECT CUSTMAST ASSIGN TO DISK
    14                            ORGANIZATION IS INDEXED
    15                            ACCESS IS DYNAMIC
    16                            RECORD KEY IS CM-KEY.
    17          *
    18          DATA DIVISION.
    19          *
    20          FILE SECTION.
    21          *
    22          FD  CUSTMAST
    23              LABEL RECORDS ARE STANDARD
    24              VALUE OF FILE-ID IS "B:CUSTMAST.DAT".
    25          *
    26          01  CM-RECORD.
    27          *
    28              05  CM-KEY                 PIC X(5).
    29              05  FILLER                 PIC X(88).
    30          *
    31          WORKING-STORAGE SECTION.
    32          *
    33          01  SWITCHES.
    34          *
    35              05  END-PROGRAM-SW         PIC X    VALUE "N".
    36                  88  END-PROGRAM                 VALUE "Y".
    37              05  CANCEL-ENTRY-SW        PIC X    VALUE "N".
    38                  88  CANCEL-ENTRY                VALUE "Y".
    39              05  RECORD-FOUND-SW        PIC X    VALUE "Y".
    40                  88  RECORD-FOUND                VALUE "Y".
    41              05  VALID-ACTION-SW        PIC X    VALUE "N".
    42                  88  VALID-ACTION                VALUE "Y".
    43              05  VALID-ENTRY-SW         PIC X    VALUE "N".
    44                  88  VALID-ENTRY                 VALUE "Y".
    45          *
    46          01  FLAGS.
    47          *
    48              05  ACTION-FLAG           PIC X.
    49                  88  ADD-RECORD                  VALUE "A".
    50                  88  CHANGE-RECORD               VALUE "C".
    51                  88  DELETE-RECORD               VALUE "D".
    52              05  VERIFICATION-FLAG     PIC X.
    53                  88  ACCEPT-ENTRY                VALUE "A".
    54                  88  MODIFY-ENTRY                VALUE "M".
    55          *
    56          01  DATE-FIELDS.
    57          *
    58              05  CURRENT-DATE      PIC 9(6).
    59              05  DISPLAY-DATE      PIC 99/99/99.
    60          *
    61          COPY CUSTMAST.CPY.
    62          *
    63          01  CUSTOMER-MASTER-RECORD.
    64          *
    65              05  CM-CUSTOMER-CODE     PIC X(5).
    66              05  CM-NAME              PIC X(30).
```

```
 67                05   CM-ADDRESS                 PIC X(30).
 68                05   CM-CITY                    PIC X(21).
 69                05   CM-STATE                   PIC XX.
 70                05   CM-ZIP-CODE                PIC X(5).
 71          *
 72          01   FUNCTION-KEY                     PIC 99.
 73                88   F10                        VALUE 11.
 74          *
 75          01   OPERATOR-MESSAGES.
 76          *
 77                05   ACTION-OPTIONS-MESSAGE      PIC X(79)
 78                     VALUE "A = ADD; C = CHANGE; D = DELETE; F10 = END PROGRAM
 79          -             " ".
 80                05   CANCEL-ENTRY-MESSAGE        PIC X(79)
 81                     VALUE "F10 = CANCEL ENTRY".
 82                05   ADD-MODIFY-VERIFY-MESSAGE   PIC X(79)
 83                     VALUE "A = ACCEPT; M = MODIFY; F10 = CANCEL ENTRY".
 84                05   DELETE-VERIFY-MESSAGE       PIC X(79)
 85                     VALUE "A = DELETE THIS RECORD; F10 = CANCEL ENTRY".
 86          *
 87          01   DISPLAY-FIELDS.
 88          *
 89                05   BLANK-MESSAGE              PIC X(79)     VALUE SPACE.
 90                05   SCREEN-ERROR-MESSAGE       PIC X(79).
 91          *
 92          PROCEDURE DIVISION.
 93          *
 94          000-MAINTAIN-CUSTOMER-FILE.
 95          *
 96                OPEN I-O CUSTMAST.
 97                PERFORM 100-DISPLAY-SCREEN-CONSTANTS.
 98                PERFORM 200-MAINTAIN-CUSTOMER-RECORD
 99                    UNTIL END-PROGRAM.
100                PERFORM 900-CLEAR-SCREEN.
101                CLOSE CUSTMAST.
102                CHAIN "MNT2000.EXE".
103                STOP RUN.
104          *
105          100-DISPLAY-SCREEN-CONSTANTS.
106          *
107                DISPLAY (1, 1)  ERASE.
108                DISPLAY (1, 2)  "MAINTAIN CUSTOMER FILE".
109                DISPLAY (1, 66) "DATE:".
111                CALL "SYSDATE" USING CURRENT-DATE.
112                MOVE CURRENT-DATE TO DISPLAY-DATE.
113                DISPLAY (1, 72) DISPLAY-DATE.
114          *
115          200-MAINTAIN-CUSTOMER-RECORD.
116          *
117                MOVE SPACE TO CM-KEY
118                             ACTION-FLAG.
119                PERFORM 300-GET-VALID-ACTION-SCREEN.
120                IF NOT END-PROGRAM
121                    MOVE "N"   TO CANCEL-ENTRY-SW
122                    MOVE SPACE TO VERIFICATION-FLAG
123                    IF ADD-RECORD
124                        MOVE SPACE  TO CUSTOMER-MASTER-RECORD
125                        MOVE CM-KEY TO CM-CUSTOMER-CODE
126                        PERFORM 400-PROCESS-CUSTOMER-ADDITION
127                            UNTIL ACCEPT-ENTRY
128                                OR CANCEL-ENTRY
129                    ELSE IF CHANGE-RECORD
130                        PERFORM 700-PROCESS-CUSTOMER-CHANGE
131                            UNTIL ACCEPT-ENTRY
132                                OR CANCEL-ENTRY
```

```
133                         ELSE IF DELETE-RECORD
134                             PERFORM 800-PROCESS-CUSTOMER-DELETION
135                                 UNTIL ACCEPT-ENTRY
136                                     OR CANCEL-ENTRY.
137          *
138            300-GET-VALID-ACTION-SCREEN.
139          *
140                 PERFORM 310-FORMAT-ACTION-SCREEN.
141                 MOVE "N" TO VALID-ACTION-SW.
142                 PERFORM 315-GET-ACTION-ENTRIES
143                     UNTIL VALID-ACTION.
144          *
145            310-FORMAT-ACTION-SCREEN.
146          *
147                 DISPLAY (4, 2)  "ACTION:".
148                 DISPLAY (6, 2)  "CUSTOMER CODE:".
149                 DISPLAY (6, 16) ERASE.
150                 DISPLAY (24, 2) ACTION-OPTIONS-MESSAGE.
151          *
152            315-GET-ACTION-ENTRIES.
153          *
154                 MOVE "Y" TO VALID-ACTION-SW.
155                 MOVE "N" TO VALID-ENTRY-SW.
156                 PERFORM 320-GET-ACTION-CODE
157                     UNTIL VALID-ENTRY.
158                 IF NOT END-PROGRAM
159                     MOVE "N" TO VALID-ENTRY-SW
160                     PERFORM 360-GET-CUSTOMER-CODE
161                         UNTIL VALID-ENTRY.
162                 IF NOT END-PROGRAM
163                     PERFORM 390-EDIT-ACTION-ENTRIES.
164          *
165            320-GET-ACTION-CODE.
166          *
167                 MOVE "Y" TO VALID-ENTRY-SW.
168                 PERFORM 330-ACCEPT-ACTION-CODE.
169                 IF NOT END-PROGRAM
170                     PERFORM 340-EDIT-ACTION-CODE.
171          *
172            330-ACCEPT-ACTION-CODE.
173          *
174                 ACCEPT (4, 19) ACTION-FLAG WITH UPDATE.
175                 ACCEPT FUNCTION-KEY FROM ESCAPE KEY.
176                 IF F10
177                     MOVE "Y" TO END-PROGRAM-SW.
178          *
179            340-EDIT-ACTION-CODE.
180          *
181                 IF          ACTION-FLAG NOT EQUAL "A"
182                     AND ACTION-FLAG NOT EQUAL "C"
183                     AND ACTION-FLAG NOT EQUAL "D"
184                 MOVE "N" TO VALID-ENTRY-SW
185                 MOVE "ACTION:  YOU MUST ENTER A, C, OR D."
186                     TO SCREEN-ERROR-MESSAGE
187                 PERFORM 350-DISPLAY-ERROR-MESSAGE.
188          *
189            350-DISPLAY-ERROR-MESSAGE.
190          *
191                 DISPLAY (23, 2) SCREEN-ERROR-MESSAGE.
192          *
193            360-GET-CUSTOMER-CODE.
194          *
195                 MOVE "Y" TO VALID-ENTRY-SW.
196                 PERFORM 370-ACCEPT-CUSTOMER-CODE.
197                 IF NOT END-PROGRAM
198                     PERFORM 380-EDIT-CUSTOMER-CODE.
```

```
199           *
200              370-ACCEPT-CUSTOMER-CODE.
201           *
202                  ACCEPT (6, 19) CM-KEY WITH UPDATE.
203                  ACCEPT FUNCTION-KEY FROM ESCAPE KEY.
204                  IF F10
205                      MOVE "Y" TO END-PROGRAM-SW.
206           *
207              380-EDIT-CUSTOMER-CODE.
208           *
209                  IF CM-KEY EQUAL SPACE
210                      MOVE "N" TO VALID-ENTRY-SW
211                      MOVE "CODE:   YOU MUST ENTER A CUSTOMER CODE."
212                          TO SCREEN-ERROR-MESSAGE
213                      PERFORM 350-DISPLAY-ERROR-MESSAGE.
214           *
215              390-EDIT-ACTION-ENTRIES.
216           *
217                  MOVE "Y" TO RECORD-FOUND-SW.
218                  PERFORM 395-READ-CUSTOMER-RECORD.
219                  IF NOT RECORD-FOUND
220                      IF       CHANGE-RECORD
221                          OR DELETE-RECORD
222                          MOVE "N" TO VALID-ACTION-SW
223                          MOVE "CODE:   THE CUSTOMER RECORD IS NOT ON FILE.   YOU
224          -               " CANNOT MODIFY OR DELETE IT."
225                              TO SCREEN-ERROR-MESSAGE
226                          PERFORM 350-DISPLAY-ERROR-MESSAGE.
227                  IF RECORD-FOUND
228                      IF ADD-RECORD
229                          MOVE "N" TO VALID-ACTION-SW
230                          MOVE "CODE:   THE CUSTOMER RECORD IS ALREADY ON FILE.
231                              " YOU CANNOT ADD IT."
232                              TO SCREEN-ERROR-MESSAGE
233                          PERFORM 350-DISPLAY-ERROR-MESSAGE.
234           *
235              395-READ-CUSTOMER-RECORD.
236           *
237                  READ CUSTMAST INTO CUSTOMER-MASTER-RECORD
238                      INVALID KEY
239                          MOVE "N" TO RECORD-FOUND-SW.
240           *
241              400-PROCESS-CUSTOMER-ADDITION.
242           *
243                  PERFORM 410-FORMAT-ENTRY-SCREEN.
244                  PERFORM 420-GET-VALID-CUSTOMER-DATA.
245                  IF NOT CANCEL-ENTRY
246                      MOVE SPACE TO VERIFICATION-FLAG
247                      MOVE "N"    TO VALID-ENTRY-SW
248                      PERFORM 580-GET-TRAN-VERIFICATION
249                          UNTIL VALID-ENTRY
250                      IF ACCEPT-ENTRY
251                          PERFORM 610-WRITE-CUSTOMER-RECORD.
252           *
253              410-FORMAT-ENTRY-SCREEN.
254           *
255                  DISPLAY (8, 2)   "NAME:".
256                  DISPLAY (9, 2)   "ADDRESS:".
257                  DISPLAY (10, 2)  "CITY/STATE/ZIP:".
258                  DISPLAY (8, 19)   CM-NAME.
259                  DISPLAY (9, 19)   CM-ADDRESS.
260                  DISPLAY (10, 19)  CM-CITY.
261                  DISPLAY (10, 41)  CM-STATE.
262                  DISPLAY (10, 44)  CM-ZIP-CODE
263                                    ERASE.
264                  DISPLAY (24, 2)   CANCEL-ENTRY-MESSAGE.
```

```
265         *
266           420-GET-VALID-CUSTOMER-DATA.
267         *
268               MOVE "N" TO VALID-ENTRY-SW.
269               PERFORM 430-GET-CUSTOMER-NAME
270                   UNTIL VALID-ENTRY.
271               IF NOT CANCEL-ENTRY
272                   MOVE "N" TO VALID-ENTRY-SW
273                   PERFORM 460-GET-CUSTOMER-ADDRESS
274                       UNTIL VALID-ENTRY.
275               IF NOT CANCEL-ENTRY
276                   MOVE "N" TO VALID-ENTRY-SW
277                   PERFORM 490-GET-CUSTOMER-CITY
278                       UNTIL VALID-ENTRY.
279               IF NOT CANCEL-ENTRY
280                   MOVE "N" TO VALID-ENTRY-SW
281                   PERFORM 520-GET-CUSTOMER-STATE
282                       UNTIL VALID-ENTRY.
283               IF NOT CANCEL-ENTRY
284                   MOVE "N" TO VALID-ENTRY-SW
285                   PERFORM 550-GET-CUSTOMER-ZIP-CODE
286                       UNTIL VALID-ENTRY.
287         *
288           430-GET-CUSTOMER-NAME.
289         *
290               MOVE "Y" TO VALID-ENTRY-SW.
291               PERFORM 440-ACCEPT-CUSTOMER-NAME.
292               IF NOT CANCEL-ENTRY
293                   PERFORM 450-EDIT-CUSTOMER-NAME.
294         *
295           440-ACCEPT-CUSTOMER-NAME.
296         *
297               ACCEPT (8, 19) CM-NAME WITH UPDATE.
298               ACCEPT FUNCTION-KEY FROM ESCAPE KEY.
299               IF F10
300                   MOVE "Y" TO CANCEL-ENTRY-SW.
301               DISPLAY (23, 2) BLANK-MESSAGE.
302         *
303           450-EDIT-CUSTOMER-NAME.
304         *
305               IF CM-NAME = SPACE
306                   MOVE "N" TO VALID-ENTRY-SW
307                   MOVE "NAME:   YOU MUST ENTER A NAME."
308                       TO SCREEN-ERROR-MESSAGE
309                   PERFORM 350-DISPLAY-ERROR-MESSAGE.
310         *
311           460-GET-CUSTOMER-ADDRESS.
312         *
313               MOVE "Y" TO VALID-ENTRY-SW.
314               PERFORM 470-ACCEPT-CUSTOMER-ADDRESS.
315               IF NOT CANCEL-ENTRY
316                   PERFORM 480-EDIT-CUSTOMER-ADDRESS.
317         *
318           470-ACCEPT-CUSTOMER-ADDRESS.
319         *
320               ACCEPT (9, 19) CM-ADDRESS WITH UPDATE.
321               ACCEPT FUNCTION-KEY FROM ESCAPE KEY.
322               IF F10 ,
323                   MOVE "Y" TO CANCEL-ENTRY-SW.
324               DISPLAY (23, 2) BLANK-MESSAGE.
325         *
326           480-EDIT-CUSTOMER-ADDRESS.
327         *
328               IF CM-ADDRESS = SPACE
329                   MOVE "N" TO VALID-ENTRY-SW
330                   MOVE "ADDRESS:  YOU MUST ENTER AN ADDRESS."
```

```
331                         TO SCREEN-ERROR-MESSAGE
332                     PERFORM 350-DISPLAY-ERROR-MESSAGE.
333         *
334       490-GET-CUSTOMER-CITY.
335         *
336             MOVE "Y" TO VALID-ENTRY-SW.
337             PERFORM 500-ACCEPT-CUSTOMER-CITY.
338             IF NOT CANCEL-ENTRY
339                 PERFORM 510-EDIT-CUSTOMER-CITY.
340         *
341       500-ACCEPT-CUSTOMER-CITY.
342         *
343             ACCEPT (10, 19) CM-CITY WITH UPDATE.
344             ACCEPT FUNCTION-KEY FROM ESCAPE KEY.
345             IF F10
346                 MOVE "Y" TO CANCEL-ENTRY-SW.
347             DISPLAY (23, 2) BLANK-MESSAGE.
348         *
349       510-EDIT-CUSTOMER-CITY.
350         *
351             IF CM-CITY = SPACE
352                 MOVE "N" TO VALID-ENTRY-SW
353                 MOVE "CITY:  YOU MUST ENTER A CITY."
354                     TO SCREEN-ERROR-MESSAGE
355                 PERFORM 350-DISPLAY-ERROR-MESSAGE.
356         *
357       520-GET-CUSTOMER-STATE.
358         *
359             MOVE "Y" TO VALID-ENTRY-SW.
360             PERFORM 530-ACCEPT-CUSTOMER-STATE.
361             IF NOT CANCEL-ENTRY
362                 PERFORM 540-EDIT-CUSTOMER-STATE.
363         *
364       530-ACCEPT-CUSTOMER-STATE.
365         *
366             ACCEPT (10, 41) CM-STATE WITH UPDATE.
367             ACCEPT FUNCTION-KEY FROM ESCAPE KEY.
368             IF F10
369                 MOVE "Y" TO CANCEL-ENTRY-SW.
370             DISPLAY (23, 2) BLANK-MESSAGE.
371         *
372       540-EDIT-CUSTOMER-STATE.
373         *
374             IF CM-STATE = SPACE
375                 MOVE "N" TO VALID-ENTRY-SW
376                 MOVE "STATE:  YOU MUST ENTER A STATE."
377                     TO SCREEN-ERROR-MESSAGE
378                 PERFORM 350-DISPLAY-ERROR-MESSAGE
379             ELSE
380                 CALL "STATEDIT" USING CM-STATE
381                                       VALID-ENTRY-SW
382                 IF NOT VALID-ENTRY
383                     MOVE "STATE:  INVALID STATE CODE."
384                         TO SCREEN-ERROR-MESSAGE
385                     PERFORM 350-DISPLAY-ERROR-MESSAGE.
386         *
387       550-GET-CUSTOMER-ZIP-CODE.
388         *
389             MOVE "Y" TO VALID-ENTRY-SW.
390             PERFORM 560-ACCEPT-CUSTOMER-ZIP-CODE
391             IF NOT CANCEL-ENTRY
392                 PERFORM 570-EDIT-CUSTOMER-ZIP-CODE.
393         *
394       560-ACCEPT-CUSTOMER-ZIP-CODE.
395         *
396             ACCEPT (10, 44) CM-ZIP-CODE WITH UPDATE.
```

```
397                     ACCEPT FUNCTION-KEY FROM ESCAPE KEY.
398                     IF F10
399                         MOVE "Y" TO CANCEL-ENTRY-SW.
400                     DISPLAY (23, 2) BLANK-MESSAGE.
401            *
402              570-EDIT-CUSTOMER-ZIP-CODE.
403            *
404                     IF CM-ZIP-CODE = SPACE
405                         MOVE "N" TO VALID-ENTRY-SW
406                         MOVE "ZIP CODE:   YOU MUST ENTER A ZIP CODE."
407                             TO SCREEN-ERROR-MESSAGE
408                         PERFORM 350-DISPLAY-ERROR-MESSAGE
409                     ELSE
410                         CALL "ZIPEDIT" USING CM-STATE
411                                              CM-ZIP-CODE
412                                              VALID-ENTRY-SW
413                         IF NOT VALID-ENTRY
414                             MOVE "ZIP CODE:   ZIP CODE DOESN'T AGREE WITH STATE."
415                                 TO SCREEN-ERROR-MESSAGE
416                             PERFORM 350-DISPLAY-ERROR-MESSAGE.
417            *
418              580-GET-TRAN-VERIFICATION.
419            *
420                     MOVE "Y" TO VALID-ENTRY-SW.
421                     PERFORM 590-ACCEPT-VERIFICATION-FLAG.
422                     IF NOT CANCEL-ENTRY
423                         PERFORM 600-EDIT-VERIFICATION-FLAG.
424            *
425              590-ACCEPT-VERIFICATION-FLAG.
426            *
427                     DISPLAY (12, 2) "VERIFICATION:".
428                     DISPLAY '(24, 2) ADD-MODIFY-VERIFY-MESSAGE.
429                     ACCEPT (12, 19) VERIFICATION-FLAG WITH UPDATE.
430                     ACCEPT FUNCTION-KEY FROM ESCAPE KEY.
431                     IF F10
432                         MOVE "Y" TO CANCEL-ENTRY-SW.
433            *
434              600-EDIT-VERIFICATION-FLAG.
435            *
436                     IF       VERIFICATION-FLAG NOT EQUAL "A"
437                         AND VERIFICATION-FLAG NOT EQUAL "M"
438                         MOVE "N" TO VALID-ENTRY-SW
439                         MOVE "VERIFICATION:   YOU MUST ENTER A OR M."
440                             TO SCREEN-ERROR-MESSAGE
441                         PERFORM 350-DISPLAY-ERROR-MESSAGE.
442            *
443              610-WRITE-CUSTOMER-RECORD.
444            *
445                     WRITE CM-RECORD FROM CUSTOMER-MASTER-RECORD
446                         INVALID KEY
447                             DISPLAY "INVALID WRITE ON CUSTOMER MASTER "
448                                 CM-KEY.
449            *
450              700-PROCESS-CUSTOMER-CHANGE.
451            *
452                     PERFORM 410-FORMAT-ENTRY-SCREEN.
453                     PERFORM 420-GET-VALID-CUSTOMER-DATA.
454                     IF NOT CANCEL-ENTRY
455                         MOVE SPACE TO VERIFICATION-FLAG
456                         MOVE "N"   TO VALID-ENTRY-SW
457                         PERFORM 580-GET-TRAN-VERIFICATION
458                             UNTIL VALID-ENTRY
459                         IF ACCEPT-ENTRY
460                             PERFORM 710-REWRITE-CUSTOMER-RECORD.
461            *
462              710-REWRITE-CUSTOMER-RECORD.
```

```
463          *
464                  REWRITE CM-RECORD FROM CUSTOMER-MASTER-RECORD
465                       INVALID KEY
466                           DISPLAY "INVALID REWRITE ON CUSTOMER FILE "
467                               CM-KEY.
468          *
469          800-PROCESS-CUSTOMER-DELETION.
470          *
471                  PERFORM 810-FORMAT-DELETION-SCREEN.
472                  MOVE SPACE TO VERIFICATION-FLAG.
473                  MOVE "N"   TO VALID-ENTRY-SW.
474                  PERFORM 820-GET-DELETION-VERIFICATION
475                       UNTIL VALID-ENTRY.
476                  IF ACCEPT-ENTRY
477                       PERFORM 850-DELETE-CUSTOMER-RECORD.
478          *
479          810-FORMAT-DELETION-SCREEN.
480          *
481                  DISPLAY (8, 2)    "NAME:".
482                  DISPLAY (9, 2)    "ADDRESS:".
483                  DISPLAY (10, 2)   "CITY/STATE/ZIP:".
484                  DISPLAY (8, 19) CM-NAME.
485                  DISPLAY (9, 19) CM-ADDRESS.
486                  DISPLAY (10, 19) CM-CITY.
487                  DISPLAY (10, 41) CM-STATE.
488                  DISPLAY (10, 44) CM-ZIP-CODE.
489                  DISPLAY (12, 2)   "VERIFICATION:"
490                                    ERASE.
491                  DISPLAY (24, 2)   DELETE-VERIFY-MESSAGE.
492          *
493          820-GET-DELETION-VERIFICATION.
494          *
495                  MOVE "Y" TO VALID-ENTRY-SW.
496                  PERFORM 830-ACCEPT-DELETE-VERIFY-FLAG.
497                  IF NOT CANCEL-ENTRY
498                       PERFORM 840-EDIT-DELETE-VERIFY-FLAG.
499          *
500          830-ACCEPT-DELETE-VERIFY-FLAG.
501          *
502                  ACCEPT (12, 19) VERIFICATION-FLAG WITH UPDATE.
503                  ACCEPT FUNCTION-KEY FROM ESCAPE KEY.
504                  IF F10
505                       MOVE "Y" TO CANCEL-ENTRY-SW.
506          *
507          840-EDIT-DELETE-VERIFY-FLAG.
508          *
509                  IF        VERIFICATION-FLAG NOT EQUAL "A"
510                       MOVE "N" TO VALID-ENTRY-SW
511                       MOVE "VERIFICATION:  YOU MUST ENTER A."
512                            TO SCREEN-ERROR-MESSAGE
513                       PERFORM 350-DISPLAY-ERROR-MESSAGE.
514          *
515          850-DELETE-CUSTOMER-RECORD.
516          *
517                  DELETE CUSTMAST
518                       INVALID KEY
519                           DISPLAY "INVALID DELETE ON CUSTOMER FILE "
520                               CM-KEY.
521          *
522          900-CLEAR-SCREEN.
523          *
524                  DISPLAY (1, 1) ERASE.
```

Model program 6

The interactive file-maintenance program
using VS COBOL on a Wang VS system

Designer: **Steve Eckols**

Date: 09-01-84

Input/output specifications

File	Description	Use
CUSTMAST	Customer master file	Update

Process specifications

Until the operator indicates end of program by using PF16 in step 1:

1.   Get a valid combination of action code and customer code from
      the ACTION SCREEN. Use the operator-entered customer code as
      the primary key for a random read on CUSTMAST. If the action is
      addition, there shouldn't be a record for the customer code in
      the customer file; if the action is deletion or change, there
      should be a record for the customer code in the customer file.

2.   For an addition transaction, get the valid customer entries from
      the CUSTOMER ENTRY SCREEN. Then, get a valid verification entry
      from the TRANSACTION VERIFICATION SCREEN. If the transaction is
      accepted, write the addition record onto the customer file. If
      the transaction is to be modified, repeat this step so the
      operator can modify the entries for the new customer. If the
      transaction is to be cancelled, cancel this transaction and
      continue with step 1.

Process specifications

3. For a change transaction, get the valid change entries from the
    CUSTOMER ENTRY SCREEN. Then, get a valid verification entry
    from the TRANSACTION VERIFICATION SCREEN. If the transaction is
    accepted, write the changed record back onto the customer file.
    If the transaction is to be modified, repeat this step. If the
    transaction is to be cancelled, cancel this transaction and
    continue with step 1.

4. For a deletion transaction, get a valid verification entry from
    the TRANSACTION VERIFICATION SCREEN. If the transaction is
    accepted, delete the record from the customer file. If the
    transaction is to be cancelled, cancel this transaction and
    continue with step 1.

Editing rules

CM-CUSTOMER-CODE	Must be non-blank.
CM-NAME	Must be non-blank.
CM-ADDRESS	Must be non-blank.
CM-CITY	Must be non-blank.
CM-STATE	Must be a valid United States Postal Service state code. Use the installation subprogram **STATEDIT** to validate the entry.
CM-ZIP-CODE	Must be a valid United States Postal Service zip code valid for **CM-STATE**. Use the installation subprogram **ZIPEDIT** to validate the entry.

The interactive file-maintenance program using Wang VS COBOL

```
*
 01   CUSTOMER-MASTER-RECORD.
*
     05   CM-CUSTOMER-CODE          PIC X(5).
     05   CM-NAME                   PIC X(30).
     05   CM-ADDRESS                PIC X(30).
     05   CM-CITY                   PIC X(21).
     05   CM-STATE                  PIC XX.
     05   CM-ZIP-CODE               PIC X(5).
```

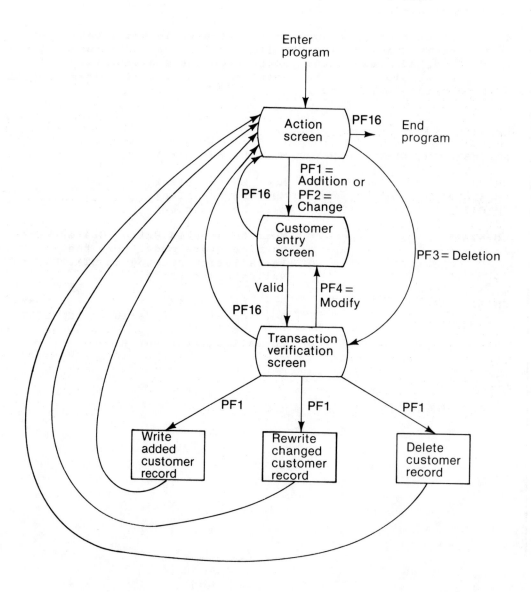

Screen name _Action_   Date _9-1-84_

Program name _MNT2100_   Designer _SLE_

	1 2 3 4 5 6 7 8 9 0	1 1 1 1 1 1 1 1 1 1 2 0 1 2 3 4 5 6 7 8 9 0	2 2 2 2 2 2 2 2 2 3 1 2 3 4 5 6 7 8 9 0	3 3 3 3 3 3 3 3 3 4 1 2 3 4 5 6 7 8 9 0	4 4 4 4 4 4 4 4 4 5 1 2 3 4 5 6 7 8 9 0	5 5 5 5 5 5 5 5 5 6 1 2 3 4 5 6 7 8 9 0	6 6 6 6 6 6 6 6 6 7 1 2 3 4 5 6 7 8 9 0	7 7 7 7 7 7 7 7 7 8 1 2 3 4 5 6 7 8 9 0
1	MAINTAIN CUSTOMER FILE							DATE: 99/99/99
2								
3								
4								
5								
6	CUSTOMER CODE: XXXXX							
7								
8								
9								
10								
11								
12								
13								
14								
15								
16								
17								
18								
19								
20								
21								
22								
23								
24	PF1 = ADD; PF2 = CHANGE; PF3 = DELETE; PF16 = END PROGRAM							

Screen name **Customer entry**   Date **9-1-84**

Program name **MNT2100**   Designer **SLE**

```
     1234567890123456789012345678901234567890123456789012345678901234567890123456789012345
 1  MAINTAIN CUSTOMER FILE                                                      DATE: 99/99/99
 2
 3
 4
 5
 6  CUSTOMER CODE:     XXXXX
 7
 8  NAME:              XXXXXXXXXXXXXXXXXXXXXXXXXXX
 9  ADDRESS:           XXXXXXXXXXXXXXXXXXXXXXXXXXX
10  CITY/STATE/ZIP:    XXXXXXXXXXXXXXXXXXXX XX XXXXX
11
12
13
14
15
16
17
18
19
20
21
22
23
24  PF16 = CANCEL ENTRY
```

Screen name _ *Transaction verification* _ Date 9-1-84

Program name MNT2100 _ Designer SLE

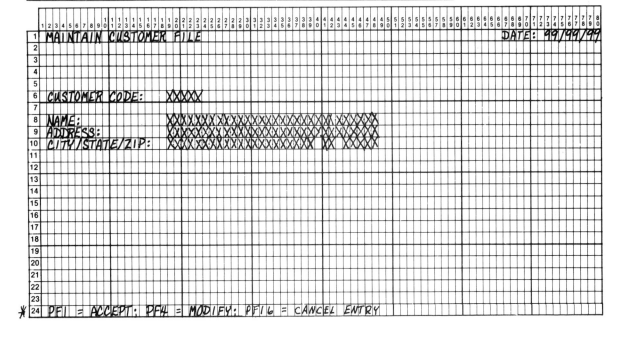

```
    1                1 1 1 1 1 1 1 1 1 1 2 2 2 2 2 2 2 2 2 2 3 3 3 3 3 3 3 3 3 3 4 4 4 4 4 4 4 4 4 4 5 5 5 5 5 5 5 5 5 5 6 6 6 6 6 6 6 6 6 6 7 7 7 7 7 7 7 7 7 7 8
    1 2 3 4 5 6 7 8 9 0 1 2 3 4 5 6 7 8 9 0 1 2 3 4 5 6 7 8 9 0 1 2 3 4 5 6 7 8 9 0 1 2 3 4 5 6 7 8 9 0 1 2 3 4 5 6 7 8 9 0 1 2 3 4 5 6 7 8 9 0 1 2 3 4 5 6 7 8 9 0
 1  MAINTAIN CUSTOMER FILE                                                                                          DATE: 99/99/99
 2
 3
 4
 5
 6  CUSTOMER CODE:      XXXXX
 7
 8  NAME:              XXXXXXX XXXXXXXXXXXXXXXX XXXXXX
 9  ADDRESS:           XXXXXXX XXXXXXXXXXXXXXXXXXXX
10  CITY/STATE/ZIP:    XXXXXXXXXXXXXXXXXXXXX XX XXXXX
11
12
13
14
15
16
17
18
19
20
21
22
23
24  PF1 = ACCEPT; PF4 = MODIFY; PF16 = CANCEL ENTRY
```

*For a deletion verification the operator message is
PF1 = DELETE THIS RECORD; PF16 = CANCEL ENTRY

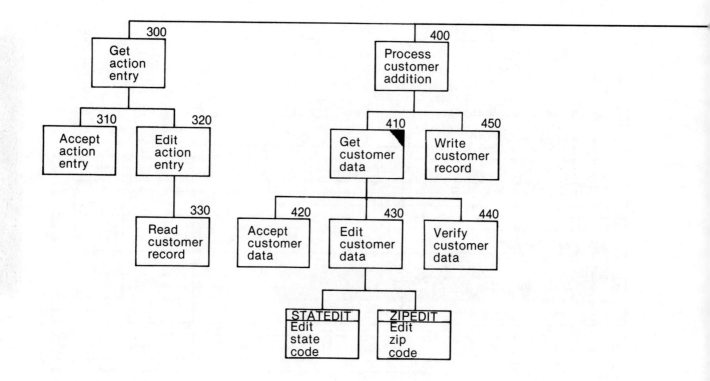

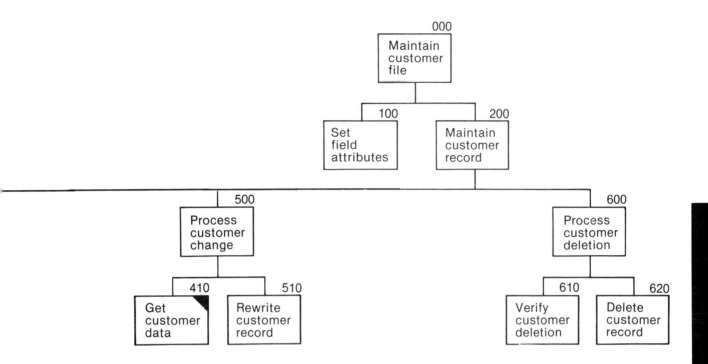

```
     00001     000100 IDENTIFICATION DIVISION.
     00002     000200*
     00003     000300 PROGRAM-ID.          MNT2100.
     00004     000400*
     00005     000500 ENVIRONMENT DIVISION.
     00006     000600*
     00007     000700 CONFIGURATION SECTION.
     00008     000800*
     00009     000900 FIGURATIVE-CONSTANTS.
     00010     001000*
     00011     001100 COPY WCCFIGS.
  +  00012            WCC-UNLOCK IS "A0"
  +  00013            WCC-BEEP   IS "40"
     00014     001200 COPY FIGCONST.
  +  00015            BIT-0              IS "80"
  +  00016            BIT-1              IS "40"
  +  00017            BIT-2              IS "20"
  +  00018            BIT-3              IS "10"
  +  00019            BIT-4              IS "08"
  +  00020            BIT-5              IS "04"
  +  00021            BIT-6              IS "02"
  +  00022            BIT-7              IS "01"
  +  00023            HEX-1              IS "01"
  +  00024            HEX-2              IS "02"
  +  00025            HEX-3              IS "03"
  +  00026            HEX-4              IS "04"
  +  00027            HEX-5              IS "05"
  +  00028            HEX-6              IS "06"
  +  00029            HEX-7              IS "07"
  +  00030            HEX-8              IS "08"
  +  00031            HEX-9              IS "09"
  +  00032            HEX-10             IS "0A"
  +  00033            HEX-11             IS "0B"
  +  00034            HEX-12             IS "0C"
  +  00035            HEX-13             IS "0D"
  +  00036            HEX-14             IS "0E"
  +  00037            HEX-15             IS "0F"
  +  00038            HEX-16             IS "10"
  +  00039            HEX-17             IS "11"
  +  00040            HEX-18             IS "12"
  +  00041            HEX-19             IS "13"
  +  00042            HEX-20             IS "14"
  +  00043            HEX-21             IS "15"
  +  00044            HEX-22             IS "16"
  +  00045            HEX-23             IS "17"
  +  00046            HEX-24             IS "18"
  +  00047            HEX-25             IS "19"
  +  00048            HEX-26             IS "1A"
  +  00049            HEX-27             IS "1B"
  +  00050            HEX-28             IS "1C"
  +  00051            HEX-29             IS "1D"
  +  00052            HEX-30             IS "1E"
  +  00053            HEX-31             IS "1F"
  +  00054            HEX-32             IS "20"
  +  00055            HEX-33             IS "21"
  +  00056            HEX-34             IS "22"
  +  00057            HEX-35             IS "23"
  +  00058            HEX-36             IS "24"
  +  00059            HEX-37             IS "25"
  +  00060            HEX-38             IS "26"
  +  00061            HEX-39             IS "27"
  +  00062            HEX-40             IS "28"
  +  00063            HEX-41             IS "29"
  +  00064            HEX-42             IS "2A"
  +  00065            HEX-43             IS "2B"
  +  00066            HEX-44             IS "2C"
  +  00067            HEX-45             IS "2D"
```

```
+ 00068                HEX-46                IS "2E"
+ 00069                HEX-47                IS "2F"
+ 00070                HEX-48                IS "30"
+ 00071                HEX-49                IS "31"
+ 00072                HEX-50                IS "32"
+ 00073                HEX-51                IS "33"
+ 00074                HEX-52                IS "34"
+ 00075                HEX-53                IS "35"
+ 00076                HEX-54                IS "36"
+ 00077                HEX-55                IS "37"
+ 00078                HEX-56                IS "38"
+ 00079                HEX-57                IS "39"
+ 00080                HEX-58                IS "3A"
+ 00081                HEX-59                IS "3B"
+ 00082                HEX-60                IS "3C"
+ 00083                HEX-61                IS "3D"
+ 00084                HEX-62                IS "3E"
+ 00085                HEX-63                IS "3F"
+ 00086                HEX-64                IS "40"
+ 00087                HEX-65                IS "41"
+ 00088                HEX-66                IS "42"
+ 00089                HEX-67                IS "43"
+ 00090                HEX-68                IS "44"
+ 00091                HEX-69                IS "45"
+ 00092                HEX-70                IS "46"
+ 00093                HEX-71                IS "47"
+ 00094                HEX-72                IS "48"
+ 00095                HEX-73                IS "49"
+ 00096                HEX-74                IS "4A"
+ 00097                HEX-75                IS "4B"
+ 00098                HEX-76                IS "4C"
+ 00099                HEX-77                IS "4D"
+ 00100                HEX-78                IS "4E"
+ 00101                HEX-79                IS "4F"
+ 00102                HEX-80                IS "50"
+ 00103                FAC-BRT-MOD-ALL       IS "80"
+ 00104                FAC-BRT-MOD-ALL-UL    IS "A0"
+ 00105                FAC-BRT-MOD-UC        IS "81"
+ 00106                FAC-BRT-MOD-UC-UL     IS "A1"
+ 00107                FAC-BRT-MOD-NUM       IS "82"
+ 00108                FAC-BRT-MOD-NUM-UL    IS "A2"
+ 00109                FAC-BRT-PRO-ALL       IS "84"
+ 00110                FAC-BRT-PRO-ALL-UL    IS "A4"
+ 00111                FAC-BRT-PRO-UC        IS "85"
+ 00112                FAC-BRT-PRO-UC-UL     IS "A5"
+ 00113                FAC-BRT-PRO-NUM       IS "86"
+ 00114                FAC-BRT-PRO-NUM-UL    IS "A6"
+ 00115                FAC-DIM-MOD-ALL       IS "88"
+ 00116                FAC-DIM-MOD-ALL-UL    IS "A8"
+ 00117                FAC-DIM-MOD-UC        IS "89"
+ 00118                FAC-DIM-MOD-UC-UL     IS "A9"
+ 00119                FAC-DIM-MOD-NUM       IS "8A"
+ 00120                FAC-DIM-MOD-NUM-UL    IS "AA"
+ 00121                FAC-DIM-PRO-ALL       IS "8C"
+ 00122                FAC-DIM-PRO-ALL-UL    IS "AC"
+ 00123                FAC-DIM-PRO-UC        IS "8D"
+ 00124                FAC-DIM-PRO-UC-UL     IS "AD"
+ 00125                FAC-DIM-PRO-NUM       IS "8E"
+ 00126                FAC-DIM-PRO-NUM-UL    IS "AE"
+ 00127                FAC-BLI-MOD-ALL       IS "90"
+ 00128                FAC-BLI-MOD-ALL-UL    IS "B0"
+ 00129                FAC-BLI-MOD-UC        IS "91"
+ 00130                FAC-BLI-MOD-UC-UL     IS "B1"
+ 00131                FAC-BLI-MOD-NUM       IS "92"
+ 00132                FAC-BLI-MOD-NUM-UL    IS "B2"
+ 00133                FAC-BLI-PRO-ALL       IS "94"
+ 00134                FAC-BLI-PRO-ALL-UL    IS "B4"
```

```
+ 00135                    FAC-BLI-PRO-UC          IS "95"
+ 00136                    FAC-BLI-PRO-UC-UL       IS "B5"
+ 00137                    FAC-BLI-PRO-NUM         IS "96"
+ 00138                    FAC-BLI-PRO-NUM-UL      IS "B6"
+ 00139                    FAC-BLA-MOD-ALL         IS "98"
+ 00140                    FAC-BLA-MOD-ALL-UL      IS "B8"
+ 00141                    FAC-BLA-MOD-UC          IS "99"
+ 00142                    FAC-BLA-MOD-UC-UL       IS "B9"
+ 00143                    FAC-BLA-MOD-NUM         IS "9A"
+ 00144                    FAC-BLA-MOD-NUM-UL      IS "BA"
+ 00145                    FAC-BLA-PRO-ALL         IS "9C"
+ 00146                    FAC-BLA-PRO-ALL-UL      IS "BC"
+ 00147                    FAC-BLA-PRO-UC          IS "9D"
+ 00148                    FAC-BLA-PRO-UC-UL       IS "BD"
+ 00149                    FAC-BLA-PRO-NUM         IS "9E"
+ 00150                    FAC-BLA-PRO-NUM-UL      IS "BE"
+ 00151                    FAC-DISPLAY-DIM         IS "8C"
+ 00152                    FAC-DISPLAY-BRIGHT      IS "84"
+ 00153                    FAC-ALPHA-ENTRY         IS "81"
+ 00154                    FAC-NUMERIC-ENTRY       IS "82"
+ 00155                    FAC-BLINK               IS "91"
+ 00156                    FAC-BLANK               IS "9C"
+ 00157                    WCC-POSITION-CURSOR     IS "A0"
+ 00158                    WCC-ALARM               IS "E0"
+ 00159                    WP-RETURN-CHAR          IS "03"
+ 00160                    WP-MERGE-CHAR           IS "0D".
  00161     001300*
  00162     001400 INPUT-OUTPUT SECTION.
  00163     001500*
  00164     001600 FILE-CONTROL.
  00165     001700*
  00166     001800        SELECT CUSTMAST ASSIGN TO "CUSTMAST" "DISK" NODISPLAY
  00167     001900                        ORGANIZATION IS INDEXED
  00168     002000                        ACCESS IS DYNAMIC
  00169     002100                        RECORD KEY IS CM-KEY.
  00170     002200*
  00171     002300        SELECT SCREEN   ASSIGN TO "SCREEN" "DISPLAY"
  00172     002400                        ACCESS MODE IS RANDOM
  00173     002500                        PFKEY IS FUNCTION-KEY.
  00174     002600*
  00175     002700 DATA DIVISION.
  00176     002800*
  00177     002900 FILE SECTION.
  00178     003000*
  00179     003100 FD  CUSTMAST
  00180     003200        LABEL RECORDS ARE STANDARD
  00181     003300        VALUE OF FILENAME IS "CUSTMAST".
  00182     003400*
  00183     003500 01  CM-RECORD.
  00184     003600*
  00185     003700        05  CM-KEY       PIC X(5).
  00186     003800        05  FILLER       PIC X(88).
  00187     003900*
  00188     004000 FD  SCREEN
  00189     004100        LABEL RECORDS ARE OMITTED.
  00190     004200*
  00191     004300 01  SCREEN-AREA     PIC X(1924).
  00192     004400*
  00193     004500 WORKING-STORAGE SECTION.
  00194     004600*
  00195     004700 01  FUNCTION-KEY    PIC 99.
  00196     004800*
  00197     004900 01  SWITCHES.
  00198     005000*
  00199     005100        05  END-PROGRAM-SW          PIC X    VALUE "N".
  00200     005200            88  END-PROGRAM                  VALUE "Y".
  00201     005300        05  CANCEL-ENTRY-SW         PIC X    VALUE "N".
```

```
00202   005400           88  CANCEL-ENTRY                        VALUE "Y".
00203   005500       05  RECORD-FOUND-SW         PIC X     VALUE "Y".
00204   005600           88  RECORD-FOUND                        VALUE "Y".
00205   005700       05  VALID-ACTION-SW         PIC X     VALUE "N".
00206   005800           88  VALID-ACTION                        VALUE "Y".
00207   005900       05  VALID-ENTRY-SW          PIC X     VALUE "N".
00208   006000           88  VALID-ENTRY                         VALUE "Y".
00209   006100       05  VALID-STATE-SW          PIC X     VALUE "N".
00210   006200           88  VALID-STATE                         VALUE "Y".
00211   006300       05  VALID-ZIP-CODE-SW       PIC X     VALUE "N".
00212   006400           88  VALID-ZIP-CODE                      VALUE "Y".
00213   006500*
00214   006600 01  DATE-FIELDS.
00215   006700*
00216   006800       05  CURRENT-DATE    PIC 9(6).
00217   006900*
00218   007000 COPY CUSTMAST.
+ 00219        *
+ 00220          01  CUSTOMER-MASTER-RECORD.
+ 00221        *
+ 00222              05  CM-CUSTOMER-CODE        PIC X(5).
+ 00223              05  CM-NAME                 PIC X(30).
+ 00224              05  CM-ADDRESS              PIC X(30).
+ 00225              05  CM-CITY                 PIC X(21).
+ 00226              05  CM-STATE                PIC XX.
+ 00227              05  CM-ZIP-CODE             PIC X(5).
00228   007100*
00229   007200 COPY ORDRAREA.
+ 00230          01  SCREEN-ORDER-AREA.
+ 00231        *
+ 00232              05  SOA-RECORD-NO       PIC X     VALUE HEX-1.
+ 00233              05  SOA-WCC             PIC X     VALUE LOW-VALUE.
+ 00234              05  SOA-COLUMN-NO       PIC X     VALUE HEX-1.
+ 00235              05  SOA-ROW-NO          PIC X     VALUE HEX-1.
00236   007300*
00237   007400 COPY WSSCREEN.
+ 00238          01  DSP-HEADING-LINE.
+ 00239        *
+ 00240              05  FILLER              PIC X         VALUE FAC-DIM-PRO-UC-UL.
+ 00241              05  DSP-PROGRAM-NAME    PIC X(50).
+ 00242              05  FILLER              PIC X(15)  VALUE SPACE.
+ 00243              05  FILLER              PIC X(6)   VALUE "DATE: ".
+ 00244              05  DSP-SYSTEM-DATE     PIC 99/99/99.
+ 00245        *
+ 00246          01  DSP-LINE-22.
+ 00247        *
+ 00248              05  FILLER              PIC X         VALUE FAC-DIM-PRO-UC-UL.
+ 00249              05  FILLER              PIC X(79)  VALUE SPACE.
+ 00250        *
+ 00251          01  DSP-MESSAGE-LINE.
+ 00252        *
+ 00253              05  DSP-MESSAGE-FAC     PIC X         VALUE FAC-BRT-PRO-ALL.
+ 00254              05  DSP-MESSAGE-AREA    PIC X(79)  VALUE SPACE.
+ 00255        *
+ 00256          01  DSP-ERROR-LINE.
+ 00257        *
+ 00258              05  DSP-ERROR-FAC       PIC X         VALUE FAC-BRT-PRO-ALL.
+ 00259              05  DSP-ERROR-MESSAGE PIC X(79)  VALUE SPACE.
00260   007500*
00261   007600 01  ACTION-SCREEN           DISPLAY-WS.
00262   007700*
00263   007800       05  FILLER            LINE 1
00264   007900                             COLUMN 1
00265   008000                             PIC X(80)
00266   008100                             SOURCE DSP-HEADING-LINE.
00267   008200       05   FILLER           LINE 6
00268   008300                             COLUMN 2
```

The interactive file-maintenance program using Wang VS COBOL

```
00269    008400                              PIC X(14)
00270    008500                              VALUE "CUSTOMER CODE:".
00271    008600        05    AS-CUST-CODE    LINE 6
00272    008700                              COLUMN 19
00273    008800                              PIC X(5)
00274    008900                              SOURCE CM-KEY
00275    009000                              OBJECT CM-KEY.
00276    009100        05    FILLER          LINE 22
00277    009200                              COLUMN 1
00278    009300                              PIC X(80)
00279    009400                              SOURCE DSP-LINE-22.
00280    009500        05    FILLER          LINE 23
00281    009600                              COLUMN 1
00282    009700                              PIC X(80)
00283    009800                              SOURCE DSP-ERROR-LINE.
00284    009900        05    FILLER          LINE 24
00285    010000                              COLUMN 1
00286    010100                              PIC X(80)
00287    010200                              SOURCE DSP-MESSAGE-LINE.
00288    010300*
00289    010400 01    CUSTOMER-ENTRY-SCREEN   DISPLAY-WS.
00290    010500*
00291    010600        05    FILLER          LINE 1
00292    010700                              COLUMN 1
00293    010800                              PIC X(80)
00294    010900                              SOURCE DSP-HEADING-LINE.
00295    011000        05    FILLER          LINE 6
00296    011100                              COLUMN 2
00297    011200                              PIC X(14)
00298    011300                              VALUE "CUSTOMER CODE:".
00299    011400        05    CES-CUST-CODE   LINE 6
00300    011500                              COLUMN 19
00301    011600                              PIC X(5)
00302    011700                              SOURCE CM-CUSTOMER-CODE.
00303    011800        05    FILLER          LINE 8
00304    011900                              COLUMN 2
00305    012000                              PIC X(5)
00306    012100                              VALUE "NAME:".
00307    012200        05    CES-NAME        LINE 8
00308    012300                              COLUMN 19
00309    012400                              PIC X(30)
00310    012500                              SOURCE CM-NAME
00311    012600                              OBJECT CM-NAME.
00312    012700        05    FILLER          LINE 9
00313    012800                              COLUMN 2
00314    012900                              PIC X(8)
00315    013000                              VALUE "ADDRESS:".
00316    013100        05    CES-ADDRESS     LINE 9
00317    013200                              COLUMN 19
00318    013300                              PIC X(30)
00319    013400                              SOURCE CM-ADDRESS
00320    013500                              OBJECT CM-ADDRESS.
00321    013600        05    FILLER          LINE 10
00322    013700                              COLUMN 2
00323    013800                              PIC X(8)
00324    013900                              VALUE "CITY:".
00325    014000        05    CES-CITY        LINE 10
00326    014100                              COLUMN 19
00327    014200                              PIC X(21)
00328    014300                              SOURCE CM-CITY
00329    014400                              OBJECT CM-CITY.
00330    014500        05    CES-STATE       LINE 10
00331    014600                              COLUMN 41
00332    014700                              PIC XX
00333    014800                              SOURCE CM-STATE
00334    014900                              OBJECT CM-STATE.
00335    015000        05    CES-ZIP-CODE    LINE 10
```

```
00336   015100                                   COLUMN 44
00337   015200                                   PIC X(5)
00338   015300                                   SOURCE CM-ZIP-CODE
00339   015400                                   OBJECT CM-ZIP-CODE.
00340   015500        05   FILLER                LINE 22
00341   015600                                   COLUMN 1
00342   015700                                   PIC X(80)
00343   015800                                   SOURCE DSP-LINE-22.
00344   015900        05   FILLER                LINE 23
00345   016000                                   COLUMN 1
00346   016100                                   PIC X(80)
00347   016200                                   SOURCE DSP-ERROR-LINE.
00348   016300        05   FILLER                LINE 24
00349   016400                                   COLUMN 1
00350   016500                                   PIC X(80)
00351   016600                                   SOURCE DSP-MESSAGE-LINE.
00352   016700*
00353   016800 01   TRAN-VERIFICATION-SCREEN          DISPLAY-WS.
00354   016900*
00355   017000        05   FILLER                LINE 1
00356   017100                                   COLUMN 1
00357   017200                                   PIC X(80)
00358   017300                                   SOURCE DSP-HEADING-LINE.
00359   017400        05   FILLER                LINE 6
00360   017500                                   COLUMN 2
00361   017600                                   PIC X(14)
00362   017700                                   VALUE "CUSTOMER CODE:".
00363   017800        05   TVS-CODE              LINE 6
00364   017900                                   COLUMN 19
00365   018000                                   PIC X(5)
00366   018100                                   SOURCE CM-CUSTOMER-CODE.
00367   018200        05   FILLER                LINE 8
00368   018300                                   COLUMN 2
00369   018400                                   PIC X(5)
00370   018500                                   VALUE "NAME:".
00371   018600        05   TVS-NAME              LINE 8
00372   018700                                   COLUMN 19
00373   018800                                   PIC X(30)
00374   018900                                   SOURCE CM-NAME.
00375   019000        05   FILLER                LINE 9
00376   019100                                   COLUMN 2
00377   019200                                   PIC X(8)
00378   019300                                   VALUE "ADDRESS:".
00379   019400        05   TVS-ADDRESS           LINE 9
00380   019500                                   COLUMN 19
00381   019600                                   PIC X(30)
00382   019700                                   SOURCE CM-ADDRESS.
00383   019800        05   FILLER                LINE 10
00384   019900                                   COLUMN 2
00385   020000                                   PIC X(5)
00386   020100                                   VALUE "CITY:".
00387   020200        05   TVS-CITY              LINE 10
00388   020300                                   COLUMN 19
00389   020400                                   PIC X(21)
00390   020500                                   SOURCE CM-CITY.
00391   020600        05   TVS-STATE             LINE 10
00392   020700                                   COLUMN 41
00393   020800                                   PIC XX
00394   020900                                   SOURCE CM-STATE.
00395   021000        05   TVS-ZIP-CODE          LINE 10
00396   021100                                   COLUMN 44
00397   021200                                   PIC X(5)
00398   021300                                   SOURCE CM-ZIP-CODE.
00399   021400        05   FILLER                LINE 22
00400   021500                                   COLUMN 1
00401   021600                                   PIC X(80)
00402   021700                                   SOURCE DSP-LINE-22.
```

The interactive file-maintenance program using Wang VS COBOL

```
00403    021800      05  FILLER          LINE 24
00404    021900                          COLUMN 1
00405    022000                          PIC X(80)
00406    022100                          SOURCE DSP-MESSAGE-LINE.
00407    022200*
00408    022300 PROCEDURE DIVISION.
00409    022400*
00410    022500 000-MAINTAIN-CUSTOMER-FILE.
00411    022600*
00412    022700      CALL "SYSDATE" USING CURRENT-DATE.
00413    022800      MOVE CURRENT-DATE              TO DSP-SYSTEM-DATE.
00414    022900      MOVE "MAINTAIN CUSTOMER FILE" TO DSP-PROGRAM-NAME.
00415    023000      OPEN SHARED CUSTMAST
00416    023100           I-O     SCREEN.
00417    023200      PERFORM 100-SET-FIELD-ATTRIBUTES.
00418    023300      PERFORM 200-MAINTAIN-CUSTOMER-RECORD
00419    023400          UNTIL END-PROGRAM.
00420    023500      CLOSE CUSTMAST
00421    023600            SCREEN.
00422    023700      STOP RUN.
00423    023800*
00424    023900 100-SET-FIELD-ATTRIBUTES.
00425    024000*
00426    024100      MOVE FAC-BRT-PRO-ALL TO FAC OF TVS-CODE
00427    024200                              FAC OF TVS-NAME
00428    024300                              FAC OF TVS-ADDRESS
00429    024400                              FAC OF TVS-CITY
00430    024500                              FAC OF TVS-STATE
00431    024600                              FAC OF TVS-ZIP-CODE.
00432    024700      SET WCC-UNLOCK IN SOA-WCC ON.
00433    024800      SET WCC-BEEP   IN SOA-WCC OFF.
00434    024900*
00435    025000 200-MAINTAIN-CUSTOMER-RECORD.
00436    025100*
00437    025200      MOVE SPACE   TO CM-KEY
00438    025300                      DSP-ERROR-MESSAGE.
00439    025400      MOVE HEX-6  TO SOA-ROW-NO.
00440    025500      MOVE HEX-19 TO SOA-COLUMN-NO.
00441    025600      MOVE "N"    TO VALID-ACTION-SW.
00442    025700      PERFORM 300-GET-ACTION-ENTRY
00443    025800          UNTIL VALID-ACTION.
00444    025900      IF NOT END-PROGRAM
00445    026000          MOVE "N" TO CANCEL-ENTRY-SW
00446    026100          IF FUNCTION-KEY EQUAL 1
00447    026200              PERFORM 400-PROCESS-CUSTOMER-ADDITION
00448    026300          ELSE IF FUNCTION-KEY EQUAL 2
00449    026400              PERFORM 500-PROCESS-CUSTOMER-CHANGE
00450    026500          ELSE IF FUNCTION-KEY EQUAL 3
00451    026600              PERFORM 600-PROCESS-CUSTOMER-DELETION.
00452    026700*
00453    026800 300-GET-ACTION-ENTRY.
00454    026900*
00455    027000      MOVE "Y" TO VALID-ACTION-SW.
00456    027100      PERFORM 310-ACCEPT-ACTION-ENTRY.
00457    027200      IF NOT END-PROGRAM
00458    027300          MOVE SPACE TO DSP-ERROR-MESSAGE
00459    027400          PERFORM 320-EDIT-ACTION-ENTRY.
00460    027500*
00461    027600 310-ACCEPT-ACTION-ENTRY.
00462    027700*
00463    027800      MOVE "PF1 = ADD; PF2 = CHANGE; PF3 = DELETE; PF16 = END PROGR
00464    027900-          "AM" TO DSP-MESSAGE-AREA.
00465    028000      MOVE SCREEN-ORDER-AREA
00466    028100          TO ORDER-AREA OF ACTION-SCREEN.
00467    028200      DISPLAY AND READ ACTION-SCREEN ON SCREEN
00468    028300          ONLY PFKEYS 1, 2, 3, 16.
00469    028400      IF FUNCTION-KEY EQUAL 16
```

```
00470   028500          MOVE "Y" TO END-PROGRAM-SW.
00471   028600          SET WCC-BEEP IN SOA-WCC OFF.
00472   028700*
00473   028800 320-EDIT-ACTION-ENTRY.
00474   028900*
00475   029000          IF CM-KEY EQUAL SPACE
00476   029100              MOVE "N" TO VALID-ACTION-SW
00477   029200              MOVE FAC-BLINK TO FAC OF AS-CUST-CODE
00478   029300              SET WCC-BEEP IN SOA-WCC ON
00479   029400              MOVE "CODE:  YOU MUST ENTER A CUSTOMER CODE."
00480   029500                  TO DSP-ERROR-MESSAGE
00481   029600          ELSE
00482   029700              MOVE "Y" TO RECORD-FOUND-SW.
00483   029800              PERFORM 330-READ-CUSTOMER-RECORD.
00484   029900          IF NOT RECORD-FOUND
00485   030000              IF            FUNCTION-KEY EQUAL 2
00486   030100                         OR FUNCTION-KEY EQUAL 3
00487   030200                  MOVE "N"        TO VALID-ACTION-SW
00488   030300                  MOVE FAC-BLINK TO FAC OF AS-CUST-CODE
00489   030400                  SET WCC-BEEP IN SOA-WCC ON
00490   030500                  MOVE "CODE:  THE CUSTOMER RECORD IS NOT ON FILE.
00491   030600-                      " YOU CANNOT MODIFY OR DELETE IT."
00492   030700                      TO DSP-ERROR-MESSAGE.
00493   030800          IF VALID-ACTION
00494   030900              IF RECORD-FOUND
00495   031000                  IF FUNCTION-KEY EQUAL 1
00496   031100                      MOVE "N"        TO VALID-ACTION-SW
00497   031200                      MOVE FAC-BLINK TO FAC OF AS-CUST-CODE
00498   031300                      SET WCC-BEEP IN SOA-WCC ON
00499   031400                      MOVE "CODE:  THE CUSTOMER RECORD IS ALREADY ON FI
00500   031500-                          "LE.  YOU CANNOT ADD IT."
00501   031600                          TO DSP-ERROR-MESSAGE.
00502   031700*
00503   031800 330-READ-CUSTOMER-RECORD.
00504   031900*
00505   032000          READ CUSTMAST WITH HOLD INTO CUSTOMER-MASTER-RECORD
00506   032100              INVALID KEY
00507   032200                  MOVE "N" TO RECORD-FOUND-SW.
00508   032300*
00509   032400 400-PROCESS-CUSTOMER-ADDITION.
00510   032500*
00511   032600          MOVE SPACE  TO CUSTOMER-MASTER-RECORD.
00512   032700          MOVE CM-KEY TO CM-CUSTOMER-CODE.
00513   032800          MOVE HEX-8  TO SOA-ROW-NO.
00514   032900          MOVE HEX-19 TO SOA-COLUMN-NO.
00515   033000          MOVE "N"    TO VALID-ENTRY-SW.
00516   033100          PERFORM 410-GET-CUSTOMER-DATA
00517   033200              UNTIL VALID-ENTRY.
00518   033300          IF NOT CANCEL-ENTRY
00519   033400              PERFORM 450-WRITE-CUSTOMER-RECORD.
00520   033500*
00521   033600 410-GET-CUSTOMER-DATA.
00522   033700*
00523   033800          MOVE "Y" TO VALID-ENTRY-SW.
00524   033900          PERFORM 420-ACCEPT-CUSTOMER-DATA.
00525   034000          IF NOT CANCEL-ENTRY
00526   034100              MOVE SPACE TO DSP-ERROR-MESSAGE
00527   034200              PERFORM 430-EDIT-CUSTOMER-DATA
00528   034300              IF VALID-ENTRY
00529   034400                  PERFORM 440-VERIFY-CUSTOMER-DATA.
00530   034500*
00531   034600 420-ACCEPT-CUSTOMER-DATA.
00532   034700*
00533   034800          MOVE "PF16 = CANCEL ENTRY" TO DSP-MESSAGE-AREA.
00534   034900          MOVE SCREEN-ORDER-AREA
00535   035000              TO ORDER-AREA OF CUSTOMER-ENTRY-SCREEN.
00536   035100          DISPLAY AND READ CUSTOMER-ENTRY-SCREEN ON SCREEN
```

The interactive file-maintenance program using Wang VS COBOL

```
00537    035200            PFKEY 16
00538    035300            ON PFKEY 16
00539    035400                MOVE "Y" TO CANCEL-ENTRY-SW.
00540    035500        SET WCC-BEEP IN SOA-WCC OFF.
00541    035600*
00542    035700 430-EDIT-CUSTOMER-DATA.
00543    035800*
00544    035900        IF CM-ZIP-CODE = SPACE
00545    036000            MOVE HEX-10    TO SOA-ROW-NO
00546    036100            MOVE HEX-44    TO SOA-COLUMN-NO
00547    036200            MOVE FAC-BLINK TO FAC OF CES-ZIP-CODE
00548    036300            MOVE "ZIP CODE:  YOU MUST ENTER A ZIP CODE."
00549    036400                TO DSP-ERROR-MESSAGE.
00550    036500        IF CM-STATE = SPACE
00551    036600            MOVE HEX-10    TO SOA-ROW-NO
00552    036700            MOVE HEX-41    TO SOA-COLUMN-NO
00553    036800            MOVE FAC-BLINK TO FAC OF CES-STATE
00554    036900            MOVE "STATE:  YOU MUST ENTER A STATE."
00555    037000                TO DSP-ERROR-MESSAGE
00556    037100        ELSE
00557    037200            CALL "STATEDIT" USING CM-STATE
00558    037300                                 VALID-STATE-SW
00559    037400            IF NOT VALID-STATE
00560    037500                MOVE HEX-10    TO SOA-ROW-NO
00561    037600                MOVE HEX-41    TO SOA-COLUMN-NO
00562    037700                MOVE FAC-BLINK TO FAC OF CES-STATE
00563    037800                MOVE "STATE:  INVALID STATE CODE"
00564    037900                    TO DSP-ERROR-MESSAGE.
00565    038000        IF DSP-ERROR-MESSAGE = SPACE
00566    038100            CALL "ZIPEDIT" USING CM-STATE
00567    038200                                 CM-ZIP-CODE
00568    038300                                 VALID-ZIP-CODE-SW
00569    038400            IF NOT VALID-ZIP-CODE
00570    038500                MOVE HEX-10    TO SOA-ROW-NO
00571    038600                MOVE HEX-44    TO SOA-COLUMN-NO
00572    038700                MOVE FAC-BLINK TO FAC OF CES-ZIP-CODE
00573    038800                MOVE "ZIP CODE:  ZIP CODE DOESN'T AGREE WITH STATE CO
00574    038900-                "DE." TO DSP-ERROR-MESSAGE.
00575    039000        IF CM-CITY = SPACE
00576    039100            MOVE HEX-10    TO SOA-ROW-NO
00577    039200            MOVE HEX-19    TO SOA-COLUMN-NO
00578    039300            MOVE FAC-BLINK TO FAC OF CES-CITY
00579    039400            MOVE "CITY:  YOU MUST ENTER A CITY."
00580    039500                TO DSP-ERROR-MESSAGE.
00581    039600        IF CM-ADDRESS = SPACE
00582    039700            MOVE HEX-9     TO SOA-ROW-NO
00583    039800            MOVE HEX-19    TO SOA-COLUMN-NO
00584    039900            MOVE FAC-BLINK TO FAC OF CES-ADDRESS
00585    040000            MOVE "ADDRESS:  YOU MUST ENTER AN ADDRESS."
00586    040100                TO DSP-ERROR-MESSAGE.
00587    040200        IF CM-NAME = SPACE
00588    040300            MOVE HEX-8     TO SOA-ROW-NO
00589    040400            MOVE HEX-19    TO SOA-COLUMN-NO
00590    040500            MOVE FAC-BLINK TO FAC OF CES-NAME
00591    040600            MOVE "NAME:  YOU MUST ENTER A NAME."
00592    040700                TO DSP-ERROR-MESSAGE.
00593    040800        IF DSP-ERROR-MESSAGE NOT = SPACE
00594    040900            MOVE "N" TO VALID-ENTRY-SW
00595    041000            SET WCC-BEEP IN SOA-WCC ON.
00596    041100*
00597    041200 440-VERIFY-CUSTOMER-DATA.
00598    041300*
00599    041400        MOVE HEX-1 TO SOA-ROW-NO.
00600    041500        MOVE HEX-1 TO SOA-COLUMN-NO.
00601    041600        MOVE "PF1 = ACCEPT; PF4 = MODIFY; PF16 = CANCEL ENTRY"
00602    041700            TO DSP-MESSAGE-AREA.
00603    041800        MOVE SCREEN-ORDER-AREA
```

```
00604   041900           TO ORDER-AREA OF TRAN-VERIFICATION-SCREEN.
00605   042000       DISPLAY AND READ TRAN-VERIFICATION-SCREEN ON SCREEN
00606   042100           ONLY PFKEYS 1, 4, 16.
00607   042200       IF FUNCTION-KEY EQUAL 4
00608   042300           MOVE HEX-8  TO SOA-ROW-NO
00609   042400           MOVE HEX-19 TO SOA-COLUMN-NO
00610   042500           MOVE "N"    TO VALID-ENTRY-SW.
00611   042600       IF FUNCTION-KEY EQUAL 16
00612   042700           MOVE "Y" TO CANCEL-ENTRY-SW.
00613   042800*
00614   042900 450-WRITE-CUSTOMER-RECORD.
00615   043000*
00616   043100       WRITE CM-RECORD FROM CUSTOMER-MASTER-RECORD
00617   043200           INVALID KEY
00618   043300               DISPLAY "INVALID WRITE ON CUSTOMER MASTER "
00619   043400                   CM-KEY.
00620   043500*
00621   043600 500-PROCESS-CUSTOMER-CHANGE.
00622   043700*
00623   043800       MOVE HEX-8  TO SOA-ROW-NO.
00624   043900       MOVE HEX-19 TO SOA-COLUMN-NO.
00625   044000       MOVE "N"    TO VALID-ENTRY-SW.
00626   044100       PERFORM 410-GET-CUSTOMER-DATA
00627   044200           UNTIL VALID-ENTRY.
00628   044300       IF NOT CANCEL-ENTRY
00629   044400           PERFORM 510-REWRITE-CUSTOMER-RECORD.
00630   044500*
00631   044600 510-REWRITE-CUSTOMER-RECORD.
00632   044700*
00633   044800       REWRITE CM-RECORD FROM CUSTOMER-MASTER-RECORD
00634   044900           INVALID KEY
00635   045000               DISPLAY "INVALID REWRITE ON CUSTOMER MASTER "
00636   045100                   CM-KEY.
00637   045200*
00638   045300 600-PROCESS-CUSTOMER-DELETION.
00639   045400*
00640   045500       PERFORM 610-VERIFY-CUSTOMER-DELETION.
00641   045600       IF NOT CANCEL-ENTRY
00642   045700           PERFORM 620-DELETE-CUSTOMER-RECORD.
00643   045800*
00644   045900 610-VERIFY-CUSTOMER-DELETION.
00645   046000*
00646   046100       MOVE HEX-1 TO SOA-ROW-NO.
00647   046200       MOVE HEX-1 TO SOA-COLUMN-NO.
00648   046300       MOVE "PF1 = DELETE THIS RECORD; PF16 = CANCEL ENTRY"
00649   046400           TO DSP-MESSAGE-AREA.
00650   046500       MOVE SCREEN-ORDER-AREA
00651   046600           TO ORDER-AREA OF TRAN-VERIFICATION-SCREEN.
00652   046700       DISPLAY AND READ TRAN-VERIFICATION-SCREEN ON SCREEN
00653   046800           ONLY PFKEYS 1, 16.
00654   046900       IF FUNCTION-KEY EQUAL 16
00655   047000           MOVE "Y" TO CANCEL-ENTRY-SW.
00656   047100*
00657   047200 620-DELETE-CUSTOMER-RECORD.
00658   047300*
00659   047400       DELETE CUSTMAST
00660   047500           INVALID KEY
00661   047600               DISPLAY "INVALID REWRITE ON CUSTOMER MASTER "
00662   047700                   CM-KEY.
```

The interactive file-maintenance program using Wang VS COBOL

Model program 7

The interactive file-maintenance program using CICS on an IBM mainframe

| Designer: | **Steve Eckols** | Date: **09-06-84** |

Input/output specifications

File	Description	Use
CUSTMAST	Customer master file	Update

Process specifications

Until the operator indicates end of program by using the CLEAR key in step 1:

1.   Get a valid combination of action code and customer code from the ACTION SCREEN. Use the operator-entered customer code as the primary key for a random read on CUSTMAST. If the action is addition, there shouldn't be a record for the customer code in the customer file; if the action is deletion or change, there should be a record for the customer code in the customer file.

2.   For an addition transaction, get the valid customer entries from the CUSTOMER ENTRY SCREEN. Then, get a valid verification entry from the TRANSACTION VERIFICATION SCREEN. If the transaction is accepted, write the addition record onto the customer file. If the transaction is to be modified, repeat this step so the operator can modify the entries for the new customer. If the transaction is to be cancelled, cancel this transaction and continue with step 1.

Process specifications

3.   For a change transaction, get the valid change entries from the
     CUSTOMER ENTRY SCREEN. Then, get a valid verification entry
     from the TRANSACTION VERIFICATION SCREEN. If the transaction is
     accepted, write the changed record back onto the customer file.
     If the transaction is to be modified, repeat this step. If the
     transaction is to be cancelled, cancel this transaction and
     continue with step 1.

4.   For a deletion transaction, get a valid verification entry from
     the TRANSACTION VERIFICATION SCREEN. If the transaction is
     accepted, delete the record from the customer file. If the
     transaction is to be cancelled, cancel this transaction and
     continue with step 1.

Editing rules

CM-CUSTOMER-CODE	Must be non-blank.
CM-NAME	Must be non-blank.
CM-ADDRESS	Must be non-blank.
CM-CITY	Must be non-blank.
CM-STATE	Must be a valid United States Postal Service state code. Use the installation subprogram STATEDIT to validate the entry.
CM-ZIP-CODE	Must be a valid United States Postal Service zip code valid for CM-STATE. Use the installation subprogram ZIPEDIT to validate the entry.

```
     BKEND    C.CUSTMAST

✿
 01   CUSTOMER-MASTER-RECORD.
✿
      05   CM-CUSTOMER-CODE          PIC X(5).
      05   CM-NAME                   PIC X(30).
      05   CM-ADDRESS                PIC X(30).
      05   CM-CITY                   PIC X(21).
      05   CM-STATE                  PIC XX.
      05   CM-ZIP-CODE               PIC X(5).

      BKEND
```

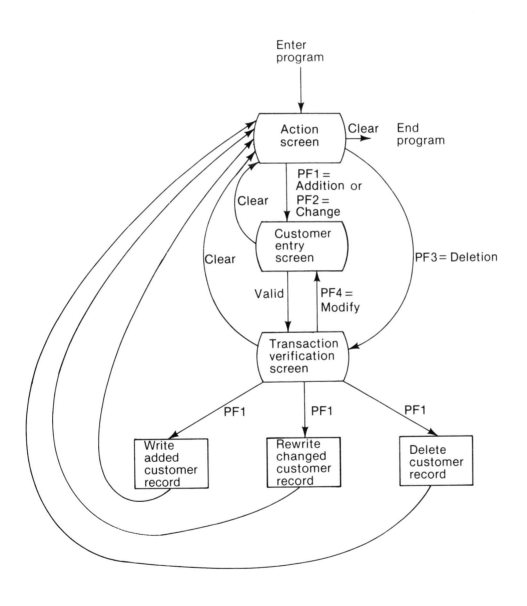

The interactive file-maintenance
program using CICS

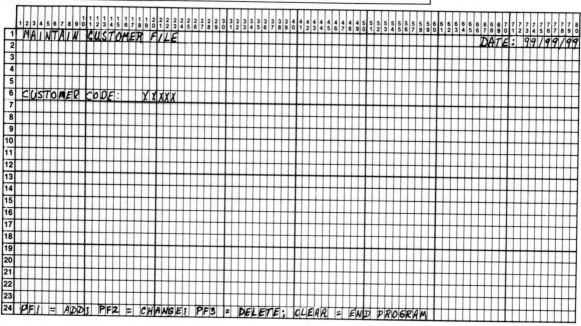

Screen name _Action_ **Date** _9-6-84_

Program name _MNT2100_ **Designer** _SLE_

```
 1 MAINTAIN CUSTOMER FILE                                                    DATE: 99/99/99
 2
 3
 4
 5
 6 CUSTOMER CODE:      XXXXX
 7
 8
 9
10
11
12
13
14
15
16
17
18
19
20
21
22
23
24 PF1 = ADD; PF2 = CHANGE; PF3 = DELETE; CLEAR = END PROGRAM
```

Screen name _Customer entry_ **Date** _9-6-84_

Program name _MNT2100_ **Designer** _SLE_

```
 1 MAINTAIN CUSTOMER FILE                                                    DATE: 99/99/99
 2
 3
 4
 5
 6 CUSTOMER CODE:      XXXXX
 7
 8 NAME:            XXXXXXXXXXXXXXXXXXXXXXXXXXXXXX
 9 ADDRESS:         XXXXXXXXXXXXXXXXXXXXXXXXXXXXXX
10 CITY/STATE/ZIP:  XXXXXXXXXXXXXXXXXXXX XX XXXXX
11
12
13
14
15
16
17
18
19
20
21
22
23
24 CLEAR = CANCEL ENTRY
```

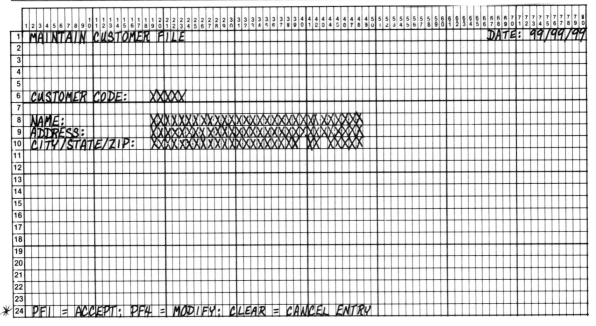

Screen name _Transaction verification_   Date _9-6-84_

Program name _MNT2100_   Designer _SLE_

```
      1234567890123456789012345678901234567890123456789012345678901234567890123456789 0
 1  MAINTAIN CUSTOMER FILE                                                  DATE: 99/99/99
 2
 3
 4
 5
 6  CUSTOMER CODE:      XXXX
 7
 8  NAME:               XXXXXX XXXXXXXXXXXXXXXX XXXXX
 9  ADDRESS:            XXXXXX XXXXXXXXXXXXXXXXXXX XXXX
10  CITY/STATE/ZIP:     XXXXXXXXXXXXXXXXXXXX XX XXXXX
11
12
13
14
15
16
17
18
19
20
21
22
23
24  PFI = ACCEPT; PF4 = MODIFY; CLEAR = CANCEL ENTRY
```

* For a deletion verification the operator message is
  PFI = DELETE THIS RECORD; CLEAR = CANCEL ENTRY

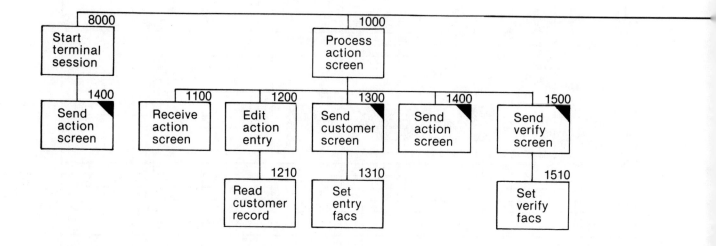

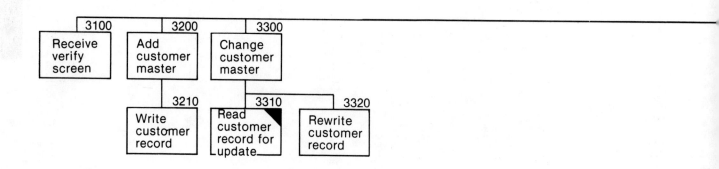

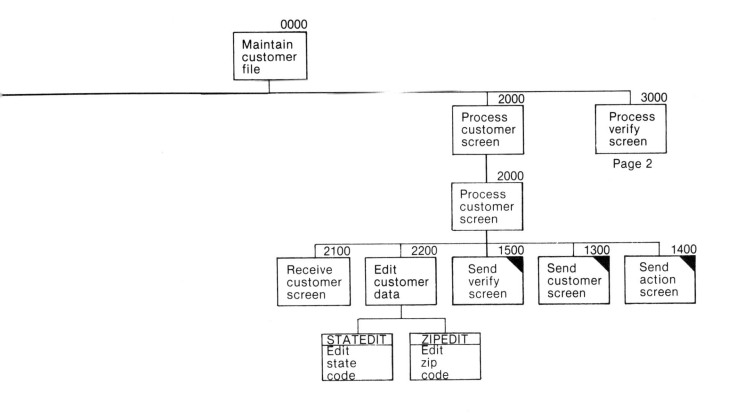

Maintain customer file — 0000

Process customer screen — 2000
Process verify screen — 3000 (Page 2)

Process customer screen — 2000

Receive customer screen — 2100
Edit customer data — 2200
Send verify screen — 1500
Send customer screen — 1300
Send action screen — 1400

STATEDIT — Edit state code
ZIPEDIT — Edit zip code

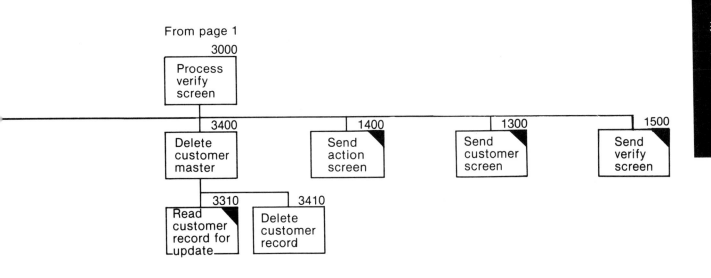

From page 1

Process verify screen — 3000

Delete customer master — 3400
Send action screen — 1400
Send customer screen — 1300
Send verify screen — 1500

Read customer record for update — 3310
Delete customer record — 3410

```
MT21SET    DFHMSD TYPE=&SYSPARM,                                              X
                  LANG=COBOL,                                                 X
                  MODE=INOUT,                                                 X
                  TERM=3270-2,                                                X
                  CTRL=FREEKB,                                                X
                  STORAGE=AUTO,                                               X
                  TIOAPFX=YES
*******************************************************************************
*******************************************************************************
MT21MP1    DFHMDI SIZE=(24,80),                                               X
                  LINE=1,                                                     X
                  COLUMN=1
*******************************************************************************
           DFHMDF POS=(1,1),                                                  X
                  LENGTH=22,                                                  X
                  ATTRB=(BRT,PROT),                                           X
                  INITIAL='MAINTAIN CUSTOMER FILE'
*******************************************************************************
           DFHMDF POS=(1,66),                                                 X
                  LENGTH=5,                                                   X
                  ATTRB=(BRT,PROT),                                           X
                  INITIAL='DATE:'
DATE1      DFHMDF POS=(1,72),                                                 X
                  LENGTH=8,                                                   X
                  ATTRB=(BRT,PROT)
*******************************************************************************
           DFHMDF POS=(6,1),                                                  X
                  LENGTH=14,                                                  X
                  ATTRB=(BRT,PROT),                                           X
                  INITIAL='CUSTOMER CODE:'
CODE1      DFHMDF POS=(6,18),                                                 X
                  LENGTH=5,                                                   X
                  ATTRB=(UNPROT,IC,FSET)
           DFHMDF POS=(6,24),                                                 X
                  LENGTH=1,                                                   X
                  ATTRB=PROT
*******************************************************************************
ERROR1     DFHMDF POS=(23,1),                                                 X
                  LENGTH=79,                                                  X
                  ATTRB=(BRT,PROT)
MESSAG1    DFHMDF POS=(24,1),                                                 X
                  LENGTH=77,                                                  X
                  ATTRB=(BRT,PROT)
DUMMY1     DFHMDF POS=(24,79),                                                X
                  LENGTH=1,                                                   X
                  ATTRB=(DRK,PROT,FSET),                                      X
                  INITIAL=' '
*******************************************************************************
*******************************************************************************
MT21MP2    DFHMDI SIZE=(24,80),                                               X
                  LINE=1,                                                     X
                  COLUMN=1
*******************************************************************************
           DFHMDF POS=(1,1),                                                  X
                  LENGTH=22,                                                  X
                  ATTRB=(BRT,PROT),                                           X
                  INITIAL='MAINTAIN CUSTOMER FILE'
*******************************************************************************
           DFHMDF POS=(1,66),                                                 X
                  LENGTH=5,                                                   X
                  ATTRB=(BRT,PROT),                                           X
                  INITIAL='DATE:'
DATE2      DFHMDF POS=(1,72),                                                 X
                  LENGTH=8,                                                   X
                  ATTRB=(BRT,PROT)
*******************************************************************************
           DFHMDF POS=(6,1),                                                  X
                  LENGTH=14,                                                  X
                  ATTRB=(BRT,PROT),                                           X
                  INITIAL='CUSTOMER CODE:'
```

```
CODE2       DFHMDF POS=(6,18),                                                    X
                   LENGTH=5,                                                      X
                   ATTRB=(PROT,FSET)
            DFHMDF POS=(6,24),                                                    X
                   LENGTH=1,                                                      X
                   ATTRB=PROT
*******************************************************************************
            DFHMDF POS=(8,1),                                                     X
                   LENGTH=14,                                                     X
                   ATTRB=(BRT,PROT),                                              X
                   INITIAL='CUSTOMER NAME:'
NAME        DFHMDF POS=(8,18),                                                    X
                   LENGTH=30,                                                     X
                   ATTRB=(UNPROT,FSET)
            DFHMDF POS=(8,49),                                                    X
                   LENGTH=1,                                                      X
                   ATTRB=ASKIP
*******************************************************************************
            DFHMDF POS=(9,1),                                                     X
                   LENGTH=8,                                                      X
                   ATTRB=(BRT,PROT),                                              X
                   INITIAL='ADDRESS:'
ADDRESS     DFHMDF POS=(9,18),                                                    X
                   LENGTH=30,                                                     X
                   ATTRB=(UNPROT,FSET)
            DFHMDF POS=(9,49),                                                    X
                   LENGTH=1,                                                      X
                   ATTRB=ASKIP
*******************************************************************************
            DFHMDF POS=(10,1),                                                    X
                   LENGTH=15,                                                     X
                   ATTRB=(BRT,PROT),                                              X
                   INITIAL='CITY/STATE/ZIP:'
CITY        DFHMDF POS=(10,18),                                                   X
                   LENGTH=21,                                                     X
                   ATTRB=(UNPROT,FSET)
STATE       DFHMDF POS=(10,40),                                                   X
                   LENGTH=2,                                                      X
                   ATTRB=(UNPROT,FSET)
ZIP         DFHMDF POS=(10,43),                                                   X
                   LENGTH=5,                                                      X
                   ATTRB=(UNPROT,FSET)
            DFHMDF POS=(10,49),                                                   X
                   LENGTH=1,                                                      X
                   ATTRB=ASKIP
*******************************************************************************
ERROR2      DFHMDF POS=(23,1),                                                    X
                   LENGTH=79,                                                     X
                   ATTRB=(BRT,PROT)
MESSAG2     DFHMDF POS=(24,1),                                                    X
                   LENGTH=77,                                                     X
                   ATTRB=(BRT,PROT)
DUMMY2      DFHMDF POS=(24,79),                                                   X
                   LENGTH=1,                                                      X
                   ATTRB=(DRK,PROT,FSET),                                         X
                   INITIAL=' '
*******************************************************************************
            DFHMSD TYPE=FINAL
            END
```

```
  BKEND
01   MT21MP1I.
     02  FILLER PIC X(12).
     02  DATE1L    COMP  PIC  S9(4).
     02  DATE1F     PICTURE X.
     02  FILLER REDEFINES DATE1F.
       03 DATE1A     PICTURE X.
     02  DATE1I  PIC X(8).
     02  CODE1L    COMP  PIC  S9(4).
     02  CODE1F     PICTURE X.
     02  FILLER REDEFINES CODE1F.
       03 CODE1A     PICTURE X.
     02  CODE1I  PIC X(5).
     02  ERROR1L    COMP  PIC  S9(4).
     02  ERROR1F     PICTURE X.
     02  FILLER REDEFINES ERROR1F.
       03 ERROR1A     PICTURE X.
     02  ERROR1I  PIC X(79).
     02  MESSAG1L    COMP  PIC  S9(4).
     02  MESSAG1F     PICTURE X.
     02  FILLER REDEFINES MESSAG1F.
       03 MESSAG1A     PICTURE X.
     02  MESSAG1I  PIC X(77).
     02  DUMMY1L    COMP  PIC  S9(4).
     02  DUMMY1F     PICTURE X.
     02  FILLER REDEFINES DUMMY1F.
       03 DUMMY1A     PICTURE X.
     02  DUMMY1I  PIC X(1).
01   MT21MP1O REDEFINES MT21MP1I.
     02  FILLER PIC X(12).
     02  FILLER PICTURE X(3).
     02  DATE1O  PIC X(8).
     02  FILLER PICTURE X(3).
     02  CODE1O  PIC X(5).
     02  FILLER PICTURE X(3).
     02  ERROR1O  PIC X(79).
     02  FILLER PICTURE X(3).
     02  MESSAG1O  PIC X(77).
     02  FILLER PICTURE X(3).
     02  DUMMY1O  PIC X(1).
01   MT21MP2I.
     02  FILLER PIC X(12).
     02  DATE2L    COMP  PIC  S9(4).
     02  DATE2F     PICTURE X.
     02  FILLER REDEFINES DATE2F.
       03 DATE2A     PICTURE X.
     02  DATE2I  PIC X(8).
     02  CODE2L    COMP  PIC  S9(4).
     02  CODE2F     PICTURE X.
     02  FILLER REDEFINES CODE2F.
       03 CODE2A     PICTURE X.
     02  CODE2I  PIC X(5).
     02  NAMEL    COMP  PIC  S9(4).
     02  NAMEF     PICTURE X.
     02  FILLER REDEFINES NAMEF.
       03 NAMEA     PICTURE X.
     02  NAMEI  PIC X(30).
     02  ADDRESSL    COMP  PIC  S9(4).
     02  ADDRESSF     PICTURE X.
     02  FILLER REDEFINES ADDRESSF.
       03 ADDRESSA     PICTURE X.
     02  ADDRESSI  PIC X(30).
     02  CITYL    COMP  PIC  S9(4).
     02  CITYF     PICTURE X.
     02  FILLER REDEFINES CITYF.
       03 CITYA     PICTURE X.
     02  CITYI  PIC X(21).
     02  STATEL    COMP  PIC  S9(4).
     02  STATEF     PICTURE X.
```

```
        02  FILLER REDEFINES STATEF.
          03 STATEA     PICTURE X.
        02  STATEI  PIC X(2).
        02  ZIPL     COMP  PIC  S9(4).
        02  ZIPF     PICTURE X.
        02  FILLER REDEFINES ZIPF.
          03 ZIPA      PICTURE X.
        02  ZIPI  PIC X(5).
        02  ERROR2L    COMP  PIC  S9(4).
        02  ERROR2F     PICTURE X.
        02  FILLER REDEFINES ERROR2F.
          03 ERROR2A     PICTURE X.
        02  ERROR2I  PIC X(79).
        02  MESSAG2L     COMP  PIC  S9(4).
        02  MESSAG2F     PICTURE X.
        02  FILLER REDEFINES MESSAG2F.
          03 MESSAG2A      PICTURE X.
        02  MESSAG2I  PIC X(77).
        02  DUMMY2L    COMP  PIC  S9(4).
        02  DUMMY2F     PICTURE X.
        02  FILLER REDEFINES DUMMY2F.
          03 DUMMY2A      PICTURE X.
        02  DUMMY2I  PIC X(1).
    01  MT21MP20 REDEFINES MT21MP2I.
        02  FILLER PIC X(12).
        02  FILLER PICTURE X(3).
        02  DATE20  PIC X(8).
        02  FILLER PICTURE X(3).
        02  CODE20  PIC X(5).
        02  FILLER PICTURE X(3).
        02  NAMEO  PIC X(30).
        02  FILLER PICTURE X(3).
        02  ADDRESSO  PIC X(30).
        02  FILLER PICTURE X(3).
        02  CITYO  PIC X(21).
        02  FILLER PICTURE X(3).
        02  STATEO  PIC X(2).
        02  FILLER PICTURE X(3).
        02  ZIPO  PIC X(5).
        02  FILLER PICTURE X(3).
        02  ERROR20  PIC X(79).
        02  FILLER PICTURE X(3).
        02  MESSAG20  PIC X(77).
        02  FILLER PICTURE X(3).
        02  DUMMY20  PIC X(1).
    BKEND
```

```
  BKEND    C.MT21SET

*
 01   ACTION-MAP.
*
      05   FILLER                     PIC X(12).
*
      05   AM-L-DATE                  PIC S9(4)    COMP.
      05   AM-A-DATE                  PIC X.
      05   AM-D-DATE                  PIC 99/99/99.
*
      05   AM-L-CUSTOMER-CODE         PIC S9(4)    COMP.
      05   AM-A-CUSTOMER-CODE         PIC X.
      05   AM-D-CUSTOMER-CODE         PIC X(5).
*
      05   AM-L-ERROR-MESSAGE         PIC S9(4)    COMP.
      05   AM-A-ERROR-MESSAGE         PIC X.
      05   AM-D-ERROR-MESSAGE         PIC X(79).
*
      05   AM-L-OPERATOR-MESSAGE      PIC S9(4)    COMP.
      05   AM-A-OPERATOR-MESSAGE      PIC X.
      05   AM-D-OPERATOR-MESSAGE      PIC X(77).
*
      05   AM-L-DUMMY                 PIC S9(4)    COMP.
      05   AM-A-DUMMY                 PIC X.
      05   AM-D-DUMMY                 PIC X.
*
 01   CUSTOMER-DATA-MAP.
*
      05   FILLER                     PIC X(12).
*
      05   CDM-L-DATE                 PIC S9(4)    COMP.
      05   CDM-A-DATE                 PIC X.
      05   CDM-D-DATE                 PIC 99/99/99.
*
      05   CDM-L-CUSTOMER-CODE        PIC S9(4)    COMP.
      05   CDM-A-CUSTOMER-CODE        PIC X.
      05   CDM-D-CUSTOMER-CODE        PIC X(5).
*
      05   CDM-L-NAME                 PIC S9(4)    COMP.
      05   CDM-A-NAME                 PIC X.
      05   CDM-D-NAME                 PIC X(30).
*
      05   CDM-L-ADDRESS              PIC S9(4)    COMP.
      05   CDM-A-ADDRESS              PIC X.
      05   CDM-D-ADDRESS              PIC X(30).
*
      05   CDM-L-CITY                 PIC S9(4)    COMP.
      05   CDM-A-CITY                 PIC X.
      05   CDM-D-CITY                 PIC X(21).
*
      05   CDM-L-STATE                PIC S9(4)    COMP.
      05   CDM-A-STATE                PIC X.
      05   CDM-D-STATE                PIC XX.
*
      05   CDM-L-ZIP-CODE             PIC S9(4)    COMP.
      05   CDM-A-ZIP-CODE             PIC X.
      05   CDM-D-ZIP-CODE             PIC X(5).
*
      05   CDM-L-ERROR-MESSAGE        PIC S9(4)    COMP.
      05   CDM-A-ERROR-MESSAGE        PIC X.
      05   CDM-D-ERROR-MESSAGE        PIC X(79).
*
      05   CDM-L-OPERATOR-MESSAGE     PIC S9(4)    COMP.
      05   CDM-A-OPERATOR-MESSAGE     PIC X.
      05   CDM-D-OPERATOR-MESSAGE     PIC X(77).
*
      05   CDM-L-DUMMY                PIC S9(4)    COMP.
      05   CDM-A-DUMMY                PIC X.
      05   CDM-D-DUMMY                PIC X.

  BKEND
```

```
000001 IDENTIFICATION DIVISION.
000002*
000003 PROGRAM-ID.   MNT2100.
000004*
000005 ENVIRONMENT DIVISION.
000006*
000007 DATA DIVISION.
000008*
000009 WORKING-STORAGE SECTION.
000010*
000011 01   SWITCHES.
000012*
000013      05  END-SESSION-SW            PIC X       VALUE 'N'.
000014          88  END-SESSION                       VALUE 'Y'.
000015      05  VALID-ACTION-SW           PIC X       VALUE 'Y'.
000016          88  VALID-ACTION                      VALUE 'Y'.
000017      05  CANCEL-ENTRY-SW           PIC X       VALUE 'N'.
000018          88  CANCEL-ENTRY                      VALUE 'Y'.
000019      05  CUSTOMER-FOUND-SW         PIC X       VALUE 'Y'.
000020          88  CUSTOMER-FOUND                    VALUE 'Y'.
000021      05  VALID-DATA-SW             PIC X       VALUE 'Y'.
000022          88  VALID-DATA                        VALUE 'Y'.
000023      05  MODIFY-DATA-SW            PIC X       VALUE 'N'.
000024          88  MODIFY-DATA                       VALUE 'Y'.
000025*
000026 01   WORK-FIELDS.
000027*
000028      05  WS-ZIP-EDIT-FIELDS.
000029          10  WS-ZIP-CODE              PIC X(5).
000030          10  WS-STATE-EDIT-FIELDS.
000031              15  WS-STATE-CODE        PIC XX.
000032              15  WS-VALID-CODE-SW     PIC X.
000033                  88  WS-VALID-CODE    VALUE 'Y'.
000034*
000035 COPY CUSTMAST.
000036*
000037 01   COMMUNICATION-AREA.
000038*
000039      05  CA-PROCESS-FLAG              PIC X.
000040          88  PROCESS-ACTION-SCREEN             VALUE '1'.
000041          88  PROCESS-CUSTOMER-SCREEN           VALUE '2'.
000042          88  PROCESS-VERIFY-SCREEN             VALUE '3'.
000043      05  CA-ACTION-FLAG               PIC X.
000044          88  ADD-RECORD                        VALUE '1'.
000045          88  CHANGE-RECORD                     VALUE '2'.
000046          88  DELETE-RECORD                     VALUE '3'.
000047*
000048 COPY FACDEFN.
000049*
000050 COPY MT21SET.
000051*
000052 LINKAGE SECTION.
000053*
000054 01   DFHCOMMAREA               PIC X(2).
000055*
000056 01   BLL-CELLS.
000057*
000058      05  FILLER                PIC S9(8)    COMP.
000059      05  BLL-CWA               PIC S9(8)    COMP.
000060*
000061 01   COMMON-WORK-AREA.
000062*
000063      05  CWA-DATE              PIC 9(6).
000064*
000065 PROCEDURE DIVISION.
000066*
000067 0000-MAINTAIN-CUSTOMER-FILE SECTION.
000068*
000069      EXEC CICS
000070          ADDRESS CWA(BLL-CWA)
```

```
000071        END-EXEC.
000072        IF EIBCALEN = ZERO
000073            PERFORM 8000-START-TERMINAL-SESSION
000074        ELSE
000075            MOVE DFHCOMMAREA TO COMMUNICATION-AREA
000076            IF PROCESS-ACTION-SCREEN
000077                PERFORM 1000-PROCESS-ACTION-SCREEN
000078            ELSE IF PROCESS-CUSTOMER-SCREEN
000079                PERFORM 2000-PROCESS-CUSTOMER-SCREEN
000080            ELSE
000081                PERFORM 3000-PROCESS-VERIFY-SCREEN.
000082        IF END-SESSION
000083            EXEC CICS
000084                XCTL PROGRAM('MNT2000')
000085            END-EXEC
000086        ELSE
000087            EXEC CICS
000088                RETURN TRANSID('MT21')
000089                       COMMAREA(COMMUNICATION-AREA)
000090                       LENGTH(2)
000091            END-EXEC.
000092*
000093 1000-PROCESS-ACTION-SCREEN SECTION.
000094*
000095        MOVE SPACE TO CA-ACTION-FLAG.
000096        PERFORM 1100-RECEIVE-ACTION-SCREEN.
000097        IF NOT VALID-ACTION
000098            PERFORM 1400-SEND-ACTION-SCREEN
000099        ELSE
000100            IF NOT END-SESSION
000101                PERFORM 1200-EDIT-ACTION-ENTRY
000102                IF VALID-ACTION
000103                    MOVE LOW-VALUE TO CUSTOMER-DATA-MAP
000104                    MOVE AM-D-CUSTOMER-CODE
000105                        TO CDM-D-CUSTOMER-CODE
000106                    MOVE CM-NAME                TO CDM-D-NAME
000107                    MOVE CM-ADDRESS             TO CDM-D-ADDRESS
000108                    MOVE CM-CITY                TO CDM-D-CITY
000109                    MOVE CM-STATE               TO CDM-D-STATE
000110                    MOVE CM-ZIP-CODE            TO CDM-D-ZIP-CODE
000111                    MOVE SPACE                  TO CDM-D-ERROR-MESSAGE
000112                    MOVE -1 TO CDM-L-NAME
000113                    IF          ADD-RECORD
000114                            OR CHANGE-RECORD
000115                        MOVE 'CLEAR = CANCEL ENTRY'
000116                            TO CDM-D-OPERATOR-MESSAGE
000117                        PERFORM 1300-SEND-CUSTOMER-SCREEN
000118                        MOVE '2' TO CA-PROCESS-FLAG
000119                    ELSE
000120                        MOVE 'PF1 = DELETE THIS RECORD; CLEAR = CANCE
000121                             'L ENTRY' TO CDM-D-OPERATOR-MESSAGE
000122                        PERFORM 1500-SEND-VERIFY-SCREEN
000123                        MOVE '3' TO CA-PROCESS-FLAG
000124                ELSE
000125                    PERFORM 1400-SEND-ACTION-SCREEN.
000126*
000127 1100-RECEIVE-ACTION-SCREEN SECTION.
000128*
000129        EXEC CICS
000130            HANDLE AID CLEAR(1100-CLEAR-KEY)
000131                       PF1(1100-PF1-KEY)
000132                       PF2(1100-PF2-KEY)
000133                       PF3(1100-PF3-KEY)
000134                       ANYKEY(1100-ANYKEY)
000135        END-EXEC.
000136        EXEC CICS
000137            RECEIVE MAP('MT21MP1')
000138                    MAPSET('MT21SET')
000139                    INTO(ACTION-MAP)
000140        END-EXEC.
```

```
000141        MOVE 'N'                    TO VALID-ACTION-SW.
000142        MOVE 'INVALID KEY PRESSED' TO AM-D-ERROR-MESSAGE.
000143        GO TO 1100-EXIT.
000144*
000145 1100-CLEAR-KEY.
000146*
000147        MOVE 'Y' TO END-SESSION-SW.
000148        GO TO 1100-EXIT.
000149*
000150 1100-PF1-KEY.
000151*
000152        MOVE '1' TO CA-ACTION-FLAG.
000153        GO TO 1100-EXIT.
000154*
000155 1100-PF2-KEY.
000156*
000157        MOVE '2' TO CA-ACTION-FLAG.
000158        GO TO 1100-EXIT.
000159*
000160 1100-PF3-KEY.
000161*
000162        MOVE '3' TO CA-ACTION-FLAG.
000163        GO TO 1100-EXIT.
000164*
000165 1100-ANYKEY.
000166*
000167        MOVE 'N'                    TO VALID-ACTION-SW.
000168        MOVE 'INVALID KEY PRESSED' TO AM-D-ERROR-MESSAGE.
000169*
000170 1100-EXIT.
000171*
000172        EXIT.
000173*
000174 1200-EDIT-ACTION-ENTRY SECTION.
000175*
000176        MOVE LOW-VALUE        TO AM-D-ERROR-MESSAGE.
000177        MOVE FAC-UNPROT-MDT TO AM-A-CUSTOMER-CODE.
000178        IF         AM-D-CUSTOMER-CODE = SPACE
000179            OR AM-L-CUSTOMER-CODE = ZERO
000180          MOVE 'N'                    TO VALID-ACTION-SW
000181          MOVE FAC-UNPROT-BRT-MDT TO AM-A-CUSTOMER-CODE
000182          MOVE 'YOU MUST ENTER A CUSTOMER CODE'
000183             TO AM-D-ERROR-MESSAGE
000184        ELSE
000185          PERFORM 1210-READ-CUSTOMER-RECORD
000186          IF NOT CUSTOMER-FOUND
000187             IF           CHANGE-RECORD
000188                  OR DELETE-RECORD
000189               MOVE 'N'                    TO VALID-ACTION-SW
000190               MOVE FAC-UNPROT-BRT-MDT TO AM-A-CUSTOMER-CODE
000191               MOVE 'THE CUSTOMER RECORD IS NOT ON FILE.  YOU CA
000192                  'NNOT MODIFY OR DELETE IT.'
000193                  TO AM-D-ERROR-MESSAGE.
000194        IF VALID-ACTION
000195          IF CUSTOMER-FOUND
000196             IF ADD-RECORD
000197               MOVE 'N'                    TO VALID-ACTION-SW
000198               MOVE FAC-UNPROT-BRT-MDT TO AM-A-CUSTOMER-CODE
000199               MOVE 'THE CUSTOMER RECORD IS ALREADY ON FILE.  YO
000200                  'U CANNOT ADD IT.'
000201                  TO AM-D-ERROR-MESSAGE.
000202*
000203 1210-READ-CUSTOMER-RECORD SECTION.
000204*
000205        MOVE 'Y' TO CUSTOMER-FOUND-SW.
000206        EXEC CICS
000207           HANDLE CONDITION NOTFND(1210-NOTFND)
000208        END-EXEC.
000209        EXEC CICS
```

The interactive file-maintenance
program using CICS

```
000210              READ DATASET('CUSTMAS')
000211                   INTO(CUSTOMER-MASTER-RECORD)
000212                   RIDFLD(AM-D-CUSTOMER-CODE)
000213         END-EXEC.
000214         GO TO 1210-EXIT.
000215*
000216 1210-NOTFND.
000217*
000218         MOVE SPACE TO CUSTOMER-MASTER-RECORD.
000219         MOVE 'N'   TO CUSTOMER-FOUND-SW.
000220*
000221 1210-EXIT.
000222*
000223         EXIT.
000224*
000225 1300-SEND-CUSTOMER-SCREEN SECTION.
000226*
000227         PERFORM 1310-SET-ENTRY-FACS.
000228         MOVE CWA-DATE TO CDM-D-DATE.
000229         EXEC CICS
000230             SEND MAP('MT21MP2')
000231                  MAPSET('MT21SET')
000232                  FROM(CUSTOMER-DATA-MAP)
000233                  CURSOR
000234             END-EXEC.
000235*
000236 1310-SET-ENTRY-FACS SECTION.
000237*
000238         MOVE FAC-UNPROT-MDT TO CDM-A-NAME
000239                                CDM-A-ADDRESS
000240                                CDM-A-CITY
000241                                CDM-A-STATE
000242                                CDM-A-ZIP-CODE.
000243*
000244 1400-SEND-ACTION-SCREEN SECTION.
000245*
000246         MOVE CWA-DATE TO AM-D-DATE.
000247         MOVE 'PF1 = ADD; PF2 = CHANGE; PF3 = DELETE; CLEAR = END PROG
000248              'RAM' TO AM-D-OPERATOR-MESSAGE.
000249         EXEC CICS
000250             SEND MAP('MT21MP1')
000251                  MAPSET('MT21SET')
000252                  FROM(ACTION-MAP)
000253                  ERASE
000254         END-EXEC.
000255*
000256 1500-SEND-VERIFY-SCREEN SECTION.
000257*
000258         PERFORM 1510-SET-VERIFY-FACS.
000259         EXEC CICS
000260             SEND MAP('MT21MP2')
000261                  MAPSET('MT21SET')
000262                  FROM(CUSTOMER-DATA-MAP)
000263                  DATAONLY
000264         END-EXEC.
000265*
000266 1510-SET-VERIFY-FACS SECTION.
000267*
000268         MOVE FAC-PROT-MDT TO CDM-A-NAME
000269                              CDM-A-ADDRESS
000270                              CDM-A-CITY
000271                              CDM-A-STATE
000272                              CDM-A-ZIP-CODE.
000273*
000274 2000-PROCESS-CUSTOMER-SCREEN SECTION.
000275*
000276         PERFORM 2100-RECEIVE-CUSTOMER-SCREEN.
000277         IF VALID-DATA
000278             IF NOT CANCEL-ENTRY
```

```
000279                    PERFORM 2200-EDIT-CUSTOMER-DATA
000280                    IF VALID-DATA
000281                        MOVE SPACE TO CDM-D-ERROR-MESSAGE
000282                        MOVE 'PF1 = ACCEPT; PF4 = MODIFY; CLEAR = CANCEL
000283                             'ENTRY' TO CDM D-OPERATOR-MESSAGE
000284                        PERFORM 1500-SEND-VERIFY-SCREEN
000285                        MOVE '3' TO CA-PROCESS-FLAG
000286                    ELSE
000287                        PERFORM 1300-SEND-CUSTOMER-SCREEN
000288                ELSE
000289                    MOVE LOW-VALUE TO ACTION-MAP
000290                    PERFORM 1400-SEND-ACTION-SCREEN
000291                    MOVE '1' TO CA-PROCESS-FLAG
000292            ELSE
000293                PERFORM 1300-SEND-CUSTOMER-SCREEN.
000294*
000295 2100-RECEIVE-CUSTOMER-SCREEN SECTION.
000296*
000297        EXEC CICS
000298            HANDLE AID CLEAR(2100-CLEAR-KEY)
000299                       ANYKEY(2100-ANYKEY)
000300        END-EXEC.
000301        EXEC CICS
000302            RECEIVE MAP('MT21MP2')
000303                    MAPSET('MT21SET')
000304                    INTO(CUSTOMER-DATA-MAP)
000305        END-EXEC.
000306        GO TO 2100-EXIT.
000307*
000308 2100-CLEAR-KEY.
000309*
000310        MOVE 'Y' TO CANCEL-ENTRY-SW.
000311        GO TO 2100-EXIT.
000312*
000313 2100-ANYKEY.
000314*
000315        MOVE 'N'                     TO VALID-DATA-SW.
000316        MOVE 'INVALID KEY PRESSED' TO CDM-D-ERROR-MESSAGE.
000317        MOVE -1                      TO CDM-L-NAME.
000318*
000319 2100-EXIT.
000320*
000321        EXIT.
000322*
000323 2200-EDIT-CUSTOMER-DATA SECTION.
000324*
000325        MOVE LOW-VALUE        TO CDM-D-ERROR-MESSAGE.
000326        MOVE FAC-UNPROT-MDT TO CDM-A-NAME
000327                               CDM-A-ADDRESS
000328                               CDM-A-CITY
000329                               CDM-A-STATE
000330                               CDM-A-ZIP-CODE.
000331        IF      CDM-D-ZIP-CODE = SPACE
000332             OR CDM-L-ZIP-CODE = ZERO
000333            MOVE FAC-UNPROT-BRT-MDT TO CDM-A-ZIP-CODE
000334            MOVE -1                 TO CDM-L-ZIP-CODE
000335            MOVE 'YOU MUST ENTER A ZIP CODE'
000336                TO CDM-D-ERROR-MESSAGE.
000337*
000338        IF      CDM-D-STATE = SPACE
000339             OR CDM-L-STATE = ZERO
000340            MOVE FAC-UNPROT-BRT-MDT TO CDM-A-STATE
000341            MOVE -1                 TO CDM-L-STATE
000342            MOVE 'YOU MUST ENTER A STATE'
000343                TO CDM-D-ERROR-MESSAGE
000344        ELSE
000345            MOVE CDM-D-STATE TO WS-STATE-CODE
000346            EXEC CICS
000347                LINK PROGRAM('STATEDIT')
```

```
000348                     COMMAREA(WS-STATE-EDIT-FIELDS)
000349                     LENGTH(3)
000350              END-EXEC
000351              IF NOT WS-VALID-CODE
000352                  MOVE FAC-UNPROT-BRT-MDT TO CDM-A-STATE
000353                  MOVE -1                 TO CDM-L-STATE
000354                  MOVE 'STATE CODE IS INVALID'
000355                      TO CDM-D-ERROR-MESSAGE.
000356*
000357          IF CDM-D-ERROR-MESSAGE EQUAL LOW-VALUE
000358              MOVE CDM-D-ZIP-CODE TO WS-ZIP-CODE
000359              EXEC CICS
000360                  LINK PROGRAM('ZIPEDIT')
000361                      COMMAREA(WS-ZIP-EDIT-FIELDS)
000362                      LENGTH(8)
000363              END-EXEC
000364              IF NOT WS-VALID-CODE
000365                  MOVE FAC-UNPROT-BRT-MDT TO CDM-A-ZIP-CODE
000366                  MOVE -1                 TO CDM-L-ZIP-CODE
000367                  MOVE 'ZIP CODE DOES NOT AGREE WITH STATE CODE'
000368                      TO CDM-D-ERROR-MESSAGE.
000369*
000370          IF        CDM-D-CITY = SPACE
000371              OR CDM-L-CITY = ZERO
000372              MOVE FAC-UNPROT-BRT-MDT TO CDM-A-CITY
000373              MOVE -1                 TO CDM-L-CITY
000374              MOVE 'YOU MUST ENTER A CITY'
000375                  TO CDM-D-ERROR-MESSAGE.
000376*
000377          IF        CDM-D-ADDRESS = SPACE
000378              OR CDM-L-ADDRESS = ZERO
000379              MOVE FAC-UNPROT-BRT-MDT TO CDM-A-ADDRESS
000380              MOVE -1                 TO CDM-L-ADDRESS
000381              MOVE 'YOU MUST ENTER AN ADDRESS'
000382                  TO CDM-D-ERROR-MESSAGE.
000383*
000384          IF        CDM-D-NAME = SPACE
000385              OR CDM-L-NAME = ZERO
000386              MOVE FAC-UNPROT-BRT-MDT TO CDM-A-NAME
000387              MOVE -1                 TO CDM-L-NAME
000388              MOVE 'YOU MUST ENTER A NAME'
000389                  TO CDM-D-ERROR-MESSAGE.
000390*
000391          IF CDM-D-ERROR-MESSAGE NOT = LOW-VALUE
000392              MOVE 'N' TO VALID-DATA-SW.
000393*
000394   3000-PROCESS-VERIFY-SCREEN SECTION.
000395*
000396          PERFORM 3100-RECEIVE-VERIFY-SCREEN.
000397          IF VALID-DATA
000398              IF        NOT CANCEL-ENTRY
000399                      AND NOT MODIFY-DATA
000400                  IF ADD-RECORD
000401                      PERFORM 3200-ADD-CUSTOMER-MASTER
000402                  ELSE IF CHANGE-RECORD
000403                      PERFORM 3300-CHANGE-CUSTOMER-MASTER
000404                  ELSE IF DELETE-RECORD
000405                      PERFORM 3400-DELETE-CUSTOMER-MASTER.
000406          IF VALID-DATA
000407              IF NOT MODIFY-DATA
000408                  MOVE LOW-VALUE TO ACTION-MAP
000409                  PERFORM 1400-SEND-ACTION-SCREEN
000410                  MOVE '1' TO CA-PROCESS-FLAG
000411              ELSE
000412                  MOVE SPACE                 TO CDM-D-ERROR-MESSAGE
000413                  MOVE 'CLEAR = CANCEL ENTRY' TO CDM-D-OPERATOR-MESSAGE
000414                  MOVE -1                    TO CDM-L-NAME
000415                  PERFORM 1300-SEND-CUSTOMER-SCREEN
000416                  MOVE '2'                   TO CA-PROCESS-FLAG
```

```
000417        ELSE
000418            PERFORM 1500-SEND-VERIFY-SCREEN.
000419*
000420 3100-RECEIVE-VERIFY-SCREEN SECTION.
000421*
000422        EXEC CICS
000423            HANDLE AID CLEAR(3100-CLEAR-KEY)
000424                       PF1(3100-PF1-KEY)
000425                       PF4(3100-PF4-KEY)
000426                       ANYKEY(3100-ANYKEY)
000427        END-EXEC.
000428        EXEC CICS
000429            RECEIVE MAP('MT21MP2')
000430                    MAPSET('MT21SET')
000431                    INTO(CUSTOMER-DATA-MAP)
000432        END-EXEC.
000433        MOVE 'N'                        TO VALID-DATA-SW.
000434        MOVE 'INVALID KEY PRESSED' TO CDM-D-ERROR-MESSAGE.
000435        GO TO 3100-EXIT.
000436*
000437 3100-CLEAR-KEY.
000438*
000439        MOVE 'Y' TO CANCEL-ENTRY-SW.
000440        GO TO 3100-EXIT.
000441*
000442 3100-PF1-KEY.
000443*
000444        GO TO 3100-EXIT.
000445*
000446 3100-PF4-KEY.
000447*
000448        IF NOT DELETE-RECORD
000449            MOVE 'Y' TO MODIFY-DATA-SW
000450        ELSE
000451            MOVE 'N'                        TO VALID-DATA-SW
000452            MOVE 'INVALID KEY PRESSED' TO CDM-D-ERROR-MESSAGE.
000453        GO TO 3100-EXIT.
000454*
000455 3100-ANYKEY.
000456*
000457        MOVE 'N'                        TO VALID-DATA-SW.
000458        MOVE 'INVALID KEY PRESSED' TO CDM-D-ERROR-MESSAGE.
000459*
000460 3100-EXIT.
000461*
000462        EXIT.
000463*
000464 3200-ADD-CUSTOMER-MASTER SECTION.
000465*
000466        MOVE CDM-D-CUSTOMER-CODE TO CM-CUSTOMER-CODE.
000467        MOVE CDM-D-NAME          TO CM-NAME.
000468        MOVE CDM-D-ADDRESS       TO CM-ADDRESS.
000469        MOVE CDM-D-CITY          TO CM-CITY.
000470        MOVE CDM-D-STATE         TO CM-STATE.
000471        MOVE CDM-D-ZIP-CODE      TO CM-ZIP-CODE.
000472        PERFORM 3210-WRITE-CUSTOMER-RECORD.
000473*
000474 3210-WRITE-CUSTOMER-RECORD SECTION.
000475*
000476        EXEC CICS
000477            HANDLE CONDITION DUPREC(3210-DUPREC)
000478        END-EXEC.
000479        EXEC CICS
000480            WRITE DATASET('CUSTMAS')
000481                  FROM(CUSTOMER-MASTER-RECORD)
000482                  RIDFLD(CM-CUSTOMER-CODE)
000483        END-EXEC.
000484        GO TO 3210-EXIT.
000485*
000486 3210-DUPREC.
```

The interactive file-maintenance program using CICS

```
000487*
000488        MOVE 'N' TO VALID-DATA-SW.
000489        MOVE 'ERROR--CUSTOMER RECORD ALREADY EXISTS'
000490            TO CDM-D-ERROR-MESSAGE.
000491*
000492 3210-EXIT.
000493*
000494        EXIT.
000495*
000496 3300-CHANGE-CUSTOMER-MASTER SECTION.
000497*
000498        PERFORM 3310-READ-CUSTOMER-FOR-UPDATE.
000499        IF CUSTOMER-FOUND
000500            MOVE CDM-D-NAME          TO CM-NAME
000501            MOVE CDM-D-ADDRESS       TO CM-ADDRESS
000502            MOVE CDM-D-CITY          TO CM-CITY
000503            MOVE CDM-D-STATE         TO CM-STATE
000504            MOVE CDM-D-ZIP-CODE      TO CM-ZIP-CODE
000505            PERFORM 3320-REWRITE-CUSTOMER-RECORD.
000506*
000507 3310-READ-CUSTOMER-FOR-UPDATE SECTION.
000508*
000509        EXEC CICS
000510            HANDLE CONDITION NOTFND(3310-NOTFND)
000511        END-EXEC.
000512        EXEC CICS
000513            READ DATASET('CUSTMAS')
000514                INTO(CUSTOMER-MASTER-RECORD)
000515                RIDFLD(CDM-D-CUSTOMER-CODE)
000516                UPDATE
000517        END-EXEC.
000518        MOVE 'Y' TO CUSTOMER-FOUND-SW.
000519        GO TO 3310-EXIT.
000520*
000521 3310-NOTFND.
000522*
000523        MOVE 'N' TO VALID-DATA-SW.
000524        MOVE 'ERROR--CUSTOMER RECORD DOES NOT EXIST'
000525            TO CDM-D-ERROR-MESSAGE.
000526        MOVE 'N' TO CUSTOMER-FOUND-SW.
000527*
000528 3310-EXIT.
000529*
000530        EXIT.
000531*
000532 3320-REWRITE-CUSTOMER-RECORD SECTION.
000533*
000534        EXEC CICS
000535            REWRITE DATASET('CUSTMAS')
000536                    FROM(CUSTOMER-MASTER-RECORD)
000537        END-EXEC.
000538*
000539 3400-DELETE-CUSTOMER-MASTER SECTION.
000540*
000541        PERFORM 3310-READ-CUSTOMER-FOR-UPDATE.
000542        IF CUSTOMER-FOUND
000543            PERFORM 3410-DELETE-CUSTOMER-RECORD.
000544*
000545 3410-DELETE-CUSTOMER-RECORD SECTION.
000546*
000547        EXEC CICS
000548            DELETE DATASET('CUSTMAS')
000549        END-EXEC.
000550*
000551 8000-START-TERMINAL-SESSION SECTION.
000552*
000553        MOVE LOW-VALUE TO ACTION-MAP.
000554        PERFORM 1400-SEND-ACTION-SCREEN.
000555        MOVE '1' TO CA-PROCESS-FLAG.
```

```
      CBL LIB,APOST,LANGLVL(1),NOTRUNC,CLIST,VERB
00001     000001 IDENTIFICATION DIVISION.
00002     000002*
00003     000003 PROGRAM-ID.   MNT2100.
00004     000004*
00005     000005 ENVIRONMENT DIVISION.
00006     000006*
00007     000007 DATA DIVISION.
00008     000008*
00009     000009 WORKING-STORAGE SECTION.
00010     000010*
00011     000011 01   SWITCHES.
00012     000012*
00013     000013      05   END-SESSION-SW          PIC X       VALUE 'N'.
00014     000014           88   END-SESSION                    VALUE 'Y'.
00015     000015      05   VALID-ACTION-SW         PIC X       VALUE 'Y'.
00016     000016           88   VALID-ACTION                   VALUE 'Y'.
00017     000017      05   CANCEL-ENTRY-SW         PIC X       VALUE 'N'.
00018     000018           88   CANCEL-ENTRY                   VALUE 'Y'.
00019     000019      05   CUSTOMER-FOUND-SW       PIC X       VALUE 'Y'.
00020     000020           88   CUSTOMER-FOUND                 VALUE 'Y'.
00021     000021      05   VALID-DATA-SW           PIC X       VALUE 'Y'.
00022     000022           88   VALID-DATA                     VALUE 'Y'.
00023     000023      05   MODIFY-DATA-SW          PIC X       VALUE 'N'.
00024     000024           88   MODIFY-DATA                    VALUE 'Y'.
00025     000025*
00026     000026 01   WORK-FIELDS.
00027     000027*
00028     000028      05   WS-ZIP-EDIT-FIELDS.
00029     000029           10   WS-ZIP-CODE        PIC X(5).
00030     000030           10   WS-STATE-EDIT-FIELDS.
00031     000031                15   WS-STATE-CODE      PIC XX.
00032     000032                15   WS-VALID-CODE-SW   PIC X.
00033     000033                     88   WS-VALID-CODE     VALUE 'Y'.
00034     000034*
00035     000035 COPY CUSTMAST.
00036 C        *
00037 C           01   CUSTOMER-MASTER-RECORD.
00038 C        *
00039 C             05   CM-CUSTOMER-CODE          PIC X(5).
00040 C             05   CM-NAME                   PIC X(30).
00041 C             05   CM-ADDRESS                PIC X(30).
00042 C             05   CM-CITY                   PIC X(21).
00043 C             05   CM-STATE                  PIC XX.
00044 C             05   CM-ZIP-CODE               PIC X(5).
00045     000036*
00046     000037 01   COMMUNICATION-AREA.
00047     000038*
00048     000039      05   CA-PROCESS-FLAG         PIC X.
00049     000040           88   PROCESS-ACTION-SCREEN          VALUE '1'.
00050     000041           88   PROCESS-CUSTOMER-SCREEN        VALUE '2'.
00051     000042           88   PROCESS-VERIFY-SCREEN          VALUE '3'.
00052     000043      05   CA-ACTION-FLAG          PIC X.
00053     000044           88   ADD-RECORD                     VALUE '1'.
00054     000045           88   CHANGE-RECORD                  VALUE '2'.
00055     000046           88   DELETE-RECORD                  VALUE '3'.
00056     000047*
00057     000048 COPY FACDEFN.
00058 C        *
00059 C           01   FIELD-ATTRIBUTE-CHARACTERS.
00060 C        *
00061 C             05   FAC-UNPROT               PIC X       VALUE ' '.
00062 C             05   FAC-UNPROT-MDT           PIC X       VALUE 'A'.
00063 C             05   FAC-UNPROT-BRT           PIC X       VALUE 'H'.
00064 C             05   FAC-UNPROT-BRT-MDT       PIC X       VALUE 'I'.
00065 C             05   FAC-UNPROT-DARK          PIC X       VALUE '<'.
00066 C             05   FAC-UNPROT-DARK-MDT      PIC X       VALUE '('.
```

```
00067 C             05    FAC-UNPROT-NUM                  PIC X           VALUE 'ε'.
00068 C             05    FAC-UNPROT-NUM-MDT              PIC X           VALUE 'J'.
00069 C             05    FAC-UNPROT-NUM-BRT             PIC X           VALUE 'Q'.
00070 C             05    FAC-UNPROT-NUM-BRT-MDT          PIC X           VALUE 'R'.
00071 C             05    FAC-UNPROT-NUM-DARK            PIC X           VALUE '≑'.
00072 C             05    FAC-UNPROT-NUM-DARK-MDT         PIC X           VALUE ')'.
00073 C             05    FAC-PROT                        PIC X           VALUE '-'.
00074 C             05    FAC-PROT-MDT                    PIC X           VALUE '/'.
00075 C             05    FAC-PROT-BRT                    PIC X           VALUE 'Y'.
00076 C             05    FAC-PROT-BRT-MDT               PIC X           VALUE 'Z'.
00077 C             05    FAC-PROT-DARK                   PIC X           VALUE 'x'.
00078 C             05    FAC-PROT-DARK-MDT              PIC X           VALUE ' '.
00079 C             05    FAC-PROT-NUM                    PIC X           VALUE 'o'.
00080 C             05    FAC-PROT-NUM-MDT               PIC X           VALUE '1'.
00081 C             05    FAC-PROT-NUM-BRT               PIC X           VALUE '8'.
00082 C             05    FAC-PROT-NUM-BRT-MDT           PIC X           VALUE '9'.
00083 C             05    FAC-PROT-NUM-DARK              PIC X           VALUE 'a'.
00084 C             05    FAC-PROT-NUM-DARK-MDT          PIC X           VALUE QUOTE.
00085     000049≑
00086     000050 COPY MT21SET.
00087 C          ≑
00088 C          01   ACTION-MAP.
00089 C          ≑
00090 C             05    FILLER                          PIC X(12).
00091 C          ≑
00092 C             05    AM-L-DATE                       PIC S9(4)       COMP.
00093 C             05    AM-A-DATE                       PIC X.
00094 C             05    AM-D-DATE                       PIC 99/99/99.
00095 C          ≑
00096 C             05    AM-L-CUSTOMER-CODE              PIC S9(4)       COMP.
00097 C             05    AM-A-CUSTOMER-CODE              PIC X.
00098 C             05    AM-D-CUSTOMER-CODE              PIC X(5).
00099 C          ≑
00100 C             05    AM-L-ERROR-MESSAGE              PIC S9(4)       COMP.
00101 C             05    AM-A-ERROR-MESSAGE              PIC X.
00102 C             05    AM-D-ERROR-MESSAGE              PIC X(79).
00103 C          ≑
00104 C             05    AM-L-OPERATOR-MESSAGE           PIC S9(4)       COMP.
00105 C             05    AM-A-OPERATOR-MESSAGE           PIC X.
00106 C             05    AM-D-OPERATOR-MESSAGE           PIC X(77).
00107 C          ≑
00108 C             05    AM-L-DUMMY                      PIC S9(4)       COMP.
00109 C             05    AM-A-DUMMY                      PIC X.
00110 C             05    AM-D-DUMMY                      PIC X.
00111 C          ≑
00112 C          01   CUSTOMER-DATA-MAP.
00113 C          ≑
00114 C             05    FILLER                          PIC X(12).
00115 C          ≑
00116 C             05    CDM-L-DATE                      PIC S9(4)       COMP.
00117 C             05    CDM-A-DATE                      PIC X.
00118 C             05    CDM-D-DATE                      PIC 99/99/99.
00119 C          ≑
00120 C             05    CDM-L-CUSTOMER-CODE             PIC S9(4)       COMP.
00121 C             05    CDM-A-CUSTOMER-CODE             PIC X.
00122 C             05    CDM-D-CUSTOMER-CODE             PIC X(5).
00123 C          ≑
00124 C             05    CDM-L-NAME                      PIC S9(4)       COMP.
00125 C             05    CDM-A-NAME                      PIC X.
00126 C             05    CDM-D-NAME                      PIC X(30).
00127 C          ≑
00128 C             05    CDM-L-ADDRESS                   PIC S9(4)       COMP.
00129 C             05    CDM-A-ADDRESS                   PIC X.
00130 C             05    CDM-D-ADDRESS                   PIC X(30).
00131 C          ≑
00132 C             05    CDM-L-CITY                      PIC S9(4)       COMP.
00133 C             05    CDM-A-CITY                      PIC X.
```

```
00134 C              05   CDM-D-CITY                    PIC X(21).
00135 C        ≠
00136 C              05   CDM-I-STATE                   PIC S9(4)    COMP.
00137 C              05   CDM-A-STATE                   PIC X.
00138 C              05   CDM-D-STATE                   PIC XX.
00139 C        ≠
00140 C              05   CDM-L-ZIP-CODE                PIC S9(4)    COMP.
00141 C              05   CDM-A-ZIP-CODE                PIC X.
00142 C              05   CDM-D-ZIP-CODE                PIC X(5).
00143 C        ≠
00144 C              05   CDM-L-ERROR-MESSAGE           PIC S9(4)    COMP.
00145 C              05   CDM-A-ERROR-MESSAGE           PIC X.
00146 C              05   CDM-D-ERROR-MESSAGE           PIC X(79).
00147 C        ≠
00148 C              05   CDM-L-OPERATOR-MESSAGE        PIC S9(4)    COMP.
00149 C              05   CDM-A-OPERATOR-MESSAGE        PIC X.
00150 C              05   CDM-D-OPERATOR-MESSAGE        PIC X(77).
00151 C        ≠
00152 C              05   CDM-L-DUMMY                   PIC S9(4)    COMP.
00153 C              05   CDM-A-DUMMY                   PIC X.
00154 C              05   CDM-D-DUMMY                   PIC X.
00155    000051≠
00156          01   DFHEIVAR COPY DFHEIVAR.
00157 C        01   DFHEIVAR.
00158 C              02   DFHEIV0   PICTURE X(26).
00159 C              02   DFHEIV1   PICTURE X(8).
00160 C              02   DFHEIV2   PICTURE X(8).
00161 C              02   DFHEIV3   PICTURE X(8).
00162 C              02   DFHEIV4   PICTURE X(6).
00163 C              02   DFHEIV5   PICTURE X(4).
00164 C              02   DFHEIV6   PICTURE X(4).
00165 C              02   DFHEIV7   PICTURE X(2).
00166 C              02   DFHEIV8   PICTURE X(2).
00167 C              02   DFHEIV9   PICTURE X(1).
00168 C              02   DFHEIV10  PICTURE S9(7) USAGE COMPUTATIONAL-3.
00169 C              02   DFHEIV11  PICTURE S9(4) USAGE COMPUTATIONAL.
00170 C              02   DFHEIV12  PICTURE S9(4) USAGE COMPUTATIONAL.
00171 C              02   DFHEIV13  PICTURE S9(4) USAGE COMPUTATIONAL.
00172 C              02   DFHEIV14  PICTURE S9(4) USAGE COMPUTATIONAL.
00173 C              02   DFHEIV15  PICTURE S9(4) USAGE COMPUTATIONAL.
00174 C              02   DFHEIV16  PICTURE S9(9) USAGE COMPUTATIONAL.
00175 C              02   DFHEIV17  PICTURE X(4).
00176 C              02   DFHEIV18  PICTURE X(4).
00177 C              02   DFHEIV19  PICTURE X(4).
00178 C              02   DFHEIV20  PICTURE X(8).
00179 C              02   DFHEIV97  PICTURE S9(7) USAGE COMPUTATIONAL-3 VALUE ZERO.
00180 C              02   DFHEIV98  PICTURE S9(4) USAGE COMPUTATIONAL VALUE ZERO.
00181 C              02   DFHEIV99  PICTURE X(1)  VALUE SPACE.
00182    000052 LINKAGE SECTION.
00183    000053≠
00184          01   DFHEIBLK COPY DFHEIBLK.
00185 C        ≠    EIBLK EXEC INTERFACE BLOCK
00186 C        01   DFHEIBLK.
00187 C        ≠         EIBTIME      TIME IN 0HHMMSS FORMAT
00188 C              02 EIBTIME       PICTURE S9(7) USAGE COMPUTATIONAL-3.
00189 C        ≠         EIBDATE      DATE IN 00YYDDD FORMAT
00190 C              02 EIBDATE       PICTURE S9(7) USAGE COMPUTATIONAL-3.
00191 C        ≠         EIBTRNID     TRANSACTION IDENTIFIER
00192 C              02 EIBTRNID      PICTURE X(4).
00193 C        ≠         EIBTASKN     TASK NUMBER
00194 C              02 EIBTASKN      PICTURE S9(7) USAGE COMPUTATIONAL-3.
00195 C        ≠         EIBTRMID     TERMINAL IDENTIFIER
00196 C              02 EIBTRMID      PICTURE X(4).
00197 C        ≠         DFHEIGDI     RESERVED
00198 C              02 DFHEIGDI      PICTURE S9(4) USAGE COMPUTATIONAL.
00199 C        ≠         EIBCPOSN     CURSOR POSITION
00200 C              02 EIBCPOSN      PICTURE S9(4) USAGE COMPUTATIONAL.
```

The interactive file-maintenance program using CICS

```
00201 C       ¢          EIBCALEN     COMMAREA LENGTH
00202 C          02 EIBCALEN    PICTURE S9(4) USAGE COMPUTATIONAL.
00203 C       ¢          EIBAID       ATTENTION IDENTIFIER
00204 C          02 EIBAID      PICTURE X(1).
00205 C       ¢          EIBFN        FUNCTION CODE
00206 C          02 EIBFN       PICTURE X(2).
00207 C       ¢          EIBRCODE     RESPONSE CODE
00208 C          02 EIBRCODE    PICTURE X(6).
00209 C       ¢          EIBDS        DATASET NAME
00210 C          02 EIBDS       PICTURE X(8).
00211 C       ¢          EIBREQID     REQUEST IDENTIFIER
00212 C          02 EIBREQID    PICTURE X(8).
00213 C       ¢          EIBRSRCE     RESOURCE NAME
00214 C          02 EIBRSRCE    PICTURE X(8).
00215 C       ¢          EIBSYNC      SYNCPOINT REQUIRED
00216 C          02 EIBSYNC     PICTURE X.
00217 C       ¢          EIBFREE      TERMINAL FREE REQUIRED
00218 C          02 EIBFREE     PICTURE X.
00219 C       ¢          EIBRECV      DATA RECEIVE REQUIRED
00220 C          02 EIBRECV     PICTURE X.
00221 C       ¢          EIBSEND      RESERVED
00222 C          02 EIBSEND     PICTURE X.
00223 C       ¢          EIBATT       ATTACH DATA EXISTS
00224 C          02 EIBATT      PICTURE X.
00225 C       ¢          EIBEOC       GOTTEN DATA IS COMPLETE
00226 C          02 EIBEOC      PICTURE X.
00227 C       ¢          EIBFMH       GOTTEN DATA CONTAINS FMH
00228 C          02 EIBFMH      PICTURE X.
00229   000054 01  DFHCOMMAREA                 PIC X(2).
00230   000055¢
00231   000056 01  BLL-CELLS.
00232   000057¢
00233   000058     05  FILLER                  PIC S9(8)    COMP.
00234   000059     05  BLL-CWA                 PIC S9(8)    COMP.
00235   000060¢
00236   000061 01  COMMON-WORK-AREA.
00237   000062¢
00238   000063     05  CWA-DATE                PIC 9(6).
00239   000064¢
00240   000065 PROCEDURE DIVISION USING DFHEIBLK DFHCOMMAREA.
00241          CALL 'DFHEI1'.
00242   000066¢
00243   000067 000-MAINTAIN-CUSTOMER-FILE SECTION.
00244   000068¢
00245      ¢    EXEC CICS
00246      ¢        ADDRESS CWA(BLL-CWA)
00247      ¢    END-EXEC.
00248   000069     MOVE '                    ' TO DFHEIV0 CALL 'DFHEI1' USING
00249             DFHEIV0 BLL-CWA.
00250
00251   000072     IF EIBCALEN = ZERO
00252   000073         PERFORM 8000-START-TERMINAL-SESSION
00253   000074     ELSE
00254   000075         MOVE DFHCOMMAREA TO COMMUNICATION-AREA
00255   000076         IF PROCESS-ACTION-SCREEN
00256   000077             PERFORM 1000-PROCESS-ACTION-SCREEN
00257   000078         ELSE IF PROCESS-CUSTOMER-SCREEN
00258   000079             PERFORM 2000-PROCESS-CUSTOMER-SCREEN
00259   000080         ELSE
00260   000081             PERFORM 3000-PROCESS-VERIFY-SCREEN.
00261   000082     IF END-SESSION
00262      ¢        EXEC CICS
00263      ¢            XCTL PROGRAM('MNT2000')
00264      ¢        END-EXEC
00265   000083         MOVE 'MNT2000' TO DFHEIV3 MOVE '       ' TO DFHEIV0
00266             CALL 'DFHEI1' USING DFHEIV0 DFHEIV3
00267
```

```
00268    000086        ELSE
00269      ✿              EXEC CICS
00270      ✿                 RETURN TRANSID('MT21')
00271      ✿                         COMMAREA(COMMUNICATION-AREA)
00272      ✿                         LENGTH(2)
00273      ✿              END-EXEC.
00274    000087          MOVE 'MT21' TO DFHEIV5 MOVE 2 TO DFHEIV11 MOVE '
00275              ' ' TO DFHEIV0 CALL 'DFHEI1' USING DFHEIV0 DFHEIV5
00276              COMMUNICATION-AREA DFHEIV11.
00277
00278
00279    000092✿
00280    000093 1000-PROCESS-ACTION-SCREEN SECTION.
00281    000094✿
00282    000095        MOVE SPACE TO CA-ACTION-FLAG.
00283    000096        PERFORM 1100-RECEIVE-ACTION-SCREEN.
00284    000097        IF NOT VALID-ACTION
00285    000098            PERFORM 1400-SEND-ACTION-SCREEN
00286    000099        ELSE
00287    000100            IF NOT END-SESSION
00288    000101                PERFORM 1200-EDIT-ACTION-ENTRY
00289    000102                IF VALID-ACTION
00290    000103                    MOVE LOW-VALUE TO CUSTOMER-DATA-MAP
00291    000104                    MOVE AM-D-CUSTOMER-CODE
00292    000105                        TO CDM-D-CUSTOMER-CODE
00293    000106                    MOVE CM-NAME              TO CDM-D-NAME
00294    000107                    MOVE CM-ADDRESS           TO CDM-D-ADDRESS
00295    000108                    MOVE CM-CITY              TO CDM-D-CITY
00296    000109                    MOVE CM-STATE             TO CDM-D-STATE
00297    000110                    MOVE CM-ZIP-CODE          TO CDM-D-ZIP-CODE
00298    000111                    MOVE SPACE                TO CDM-D-ERROR-MESSAGE
00299    000112                    MOVE -1 TO CDM-L-NAME
00300    000113                    IF        ADD-RECORD
00301    000114                          OR CHANGE-RECORD
00302    000115                        MOVE 'CLEAR = CANCEL ENTRY'
00303    000116                            TO CDM-D-OPERATOR-MESSAGE
00304    000117                        PERFORM 1300-SEND-CUSTOMER-SCREEN
00305    000118                        MOVE '2' TO CA-PROCESS-FLAG
00306    000119                    ELSE
00307    000120                        MOVE 'PF1 = DELETE THIS RECORD; CLEAR = CANCE
00308      -              'L ENTRY' TO CDM-D-OPERATOR-MESSAGE
00309    000122                        PERFORM 1500-SEND-VERIFY-SCREEN
00310    000123                        MOVE '3' TO CA-PROCESS-FLAG
00311    000124                ELSE
00312    000125                    PERFORM 1400-SEND-ACTION-SCREEN.
00313    000126✿
00314    000127 1100-RECEIVE-ACTION-SCREEN SECTION.
00315    000128✿
00316      ✿        EXEC CICS
00317      ✿            HANDLE AID CLEAR(1100-CLEAR-KEY)
00318      ✿                       PF1(1100-PF1-KEY)
00319      ✿                       PF2(1100-PF2-KEY)
00320      ✿                       PF3(1100-PF3-KEY)
00321      ✿                       ANYKEY(1100-ANYKEY)
00322      ✿        END-EXEC.
00323    000129        MOVE '    8                ' TO DFHEIV0 CALL 'DFHEI1' USING
00324              DFHEIV0 GO TO 1100-CLEAR-KEY 1100-PF1-KEY 1100-PF2-KEY
00325              1100-PF3-KEY 1100-ANYKEY DEPENDING ON DFHEIGDI.
00326
00327
00328
00329
00330      ✿        EXEC CICS
00331      ✿            RECEIVE MAP('MT21MP1')
00332      ✿                    MAPSET('MT21SET')
00333      ✿                    INTO(ACTION-MAP)
00334      ✿        END-EXEC.
```

```
00335    000136        MOVE 'MT21MP1' TO DFHEIV1 MOVE 'MT21SET' TO DFHEIV2 MOVE '
00336       -          '         ' TO DFHEIV0 CALL 'DFHEI1' USING DFHEIV0
00337                  DFHEIV1 ACTION-MAP DFHEIV98 DFHEIV2.
00338
00339
00340    000141        MOVE 'N'                    TO VALID-ACTION-SW.
00341    000142        MOVE 'INVALID KEY PRESSED' TO AM-D-ERROR-MESSAGE.
00342    000143        GO TO 1100-EXIT.
00343    000144*
00344    000145 1100-CLEAR-KEY.
00345    000146*
00346    000147        MOVE 'Y' TO END-SESSION-SW.
00347    000148        GO TO 1100-EXIT.
00348    000149*
00349    000150 1100-PF1-KEY.
00350    000151*
00351    000152        MOVE '1' TO CA-ACTION-FLAG.
00352    000153        GO TO 1100-EXIT.
00353    000154*
00354    000155 1100-PF2-KEY.
00355    000156*
00356    000157        MOVE '2' TO CA-ACTION-FLAG.
00357    000158        GO TO 1100-EXIT.
00358    000159*
00359    000160 1100-PF3-KEY.
00360    000161*
00361    000162        MOVE '3' TO CA-ACTION-FLAG.
00362    000163        GO TO 1100-EXIT.
00363    000164*
00364    000165 1100-ANYKEY.
00365    000166*
00366    000167        MOVE 'N'                    TO VALID-ACTION-SW.
00367    000168        MOVE 'INVALID KEY PRESSED' TO AM-D-ERROR-MESSAGE.
00368    000169*
00369    000170 1100-EXIT.
00370    000171*
00371    000172        EXIT.
00372    000173*
00373    000174 1200-EDIT-ACTION-ENTRY SECTION.
00374    000175*
00375    000176        MOVE LOW-VALUE      TO AM-D-ERROR-MESSAGE.
00376    000177        MOVE FAC-UNPROT-MDT TO AM-A-CUSTOMER-CODE.
00377    000178        IF        AM-D-CUSTOMER-CODE = SPACE
00378    000179           OR AM-L-CUSTOMER-CODE = ZERO
00379    000180        MOVE 'N'                    TO VALID-ACTION-SW
00380    000181        MOVE FAC-UNPROT-BRT-MDT TO AM-A-CUSTOMER-CODE
00381    000182        MOVE 'YOU MUST ENTER A CUSTOMER CODE'
00382    000183            TO AM-D-ERROR-MESSAGE
00383    000184        ELSE
00384    000185           PERFORM 1210-READ-CUSTOMER-RECORD
00385    000186           IF NOT CUSTOMER-FOUND
00386    000187              IF        CHANGE-RECORD
00387    000188                     OR DELETE-RECORD
00388    000189                 MOVE 'N'                    TO VALID-ACTION-SW
00389    000190                 MOVE FAC-UNPROT-BRT-MDT TO AM-A-CUSTOMER-CODE
00390    000191                 MOVE 'THE CUSTOMER RECORD IS NOT ON FILE.  YOU CA
00391       -          'NNOT MODIFY OR DELETE IT.'
00392    000193                    TO AM-D-ERROR-MESSAGE.
00393    000194        IF VALID-ACTION
00394    000195           IF CUSTOMER-FOUND
00395    000196              IF ADD-RECORD
00396    000197                 MOVE 'N'                    TO VALID-ACTION-SW
00397    000198                 MOVE FAC-UNPROT-BRT-MDT TO AM-A-CUSTOMER-CODE
00398    000199                 MOVE 'THE CUSTOMER RECORD IS ALREADY ON FILE.  YO
00399       -          'U CANNOT ADD IT.'
00400    000201                    TO AM-D-ERROR-MESSAGE.
```

```
00401   000202*
00402   000203 1210-READ-CUSTOMER-RECORD SECTION.
00403   000204*
00404   000205        MOVE 'Y' TO CUSTOMER-FOUND-SW.
00405        *        EXEC CICS
00406        *            HANDLE CONDITION NOTFND(1210-NOTFND)
00407        *        END-EXEC.
00408   000206        MOVE '                    ' TO DFHEIVO CALL 'DFHEI1' USING
00409                  DFHEIVO GO TO 1210-NOTFND DEPENDING ON DFHEIGDI.
00410
00411        *        EXEC CICS
00412        *            READ DATASET('CUSTMAS')
00413        *                 INTO(CUSTOMER-MASTER-RECORD)
00414        *                 RIDFLD(AM-D-CUSTOMER-CODE)
00415        *        END-EXEC.
00416   000209        MOVE 'CUSTMAS' TO DFHEIV3 MOVE '       ' TO DFHEIVO CALL '
00417        -        'DFHEI1' USING DFHEIVO DFHEIV3 CUSTOMER-MASTER-RECORD
00418                 DFHEIV98 AM-D-CUSTOMER-CODE.
00419
00420
00421   000214        GO TO 1210-EXIT.
00422   000215*
00423   000216 1210-NOTFND.
00424   000217*
00425   000218        MOVE SPACE TO CUSTOMER-MASTER-RECORD.
00426   000219        MOVE 'N'   TO CUSTOMER-FOUND-SW.
00427   000220*
00428   000221 1210-EXIT.
00429   000222*
00430   000223        EXIT.
00431   000224*
00432   000225 1300-SEND-CUSTOMER-SCREEN SECTION.
00433   000226*
00434   000227        PERFORM 1310-SET-ENTRY-FACS.
00435   000228        MOVE CWA-DATE TO CDM-D-DATE.
00436        *        EXEC CICS
00437        *            SEND MAP('MT21MP2')
00438        *                 MAPSET('MT21SET')
00439        *                 FROM(CUSTOMER-DATA-MAP)
00440        *                 CURSOR
00441        *        END-EXEC.
00442   000229        MOVE 'MT21MP2' TO DFHEIV1 MOVE 'MT21SET' TO DFHEIV2 MOVE -1
00443                  TO DFHEIV11 MOVE '   J        \   ' TO DFHEIVO CALL 'DFHEI1'
00444                  USING DFHEIVO DFHEIV1 CUSTOMER-DATA-MAP DFHEIV98 DFHEIV2
00445                  DFHEIV99 DFHEIV99 DFHEIV99 DFHEIV11.
00446
00447
00448   000235*
00449   000236 1310-SET-ENTRY-FACS SECTION.
00450   000237*
00451   000238        MOVE FAC-UNPROT-MDT TO CDM-A-NAME
00452   000239                               CDM-A-ADDRESS
00453   000240                               CDM-A-CITY
00454   000241                               CDM-A-STATE
00455   000242                               CDM-A-ZIP-CODE.
00456   000243*
00457   000244 1400-SEND-ACTION-SCREEN SECTION.
00458   000245*
00459   000246        MOVE CWA-DATE TO AM-D-DATE.
00460   000247        MOVE 'PF1 = ADD; PF2 = CHANGE; PF3 = DELETE; CLEAR = END PROG
00461        -        'RAM' TO AM-D-OPERATOR-MESSAGE.
00462        *        EXEC CICS
00463        *            SEND MAP('MT21MP1')
00464        *                 MAPSET('MT21SET')
00465        *                 FROM(ACTION-MAP)
00466        *                 ERASE
00467        *        END-EXEC.
```

The interactive file-maintenance program using CICS

```
00468    000249          MOVE 'MT21MP1' TO DFHEIV1 MOVE 'MT21SET' TO DFHEIV2 MOVE '
00469       -        '      S    ' TO DFHEIV0 CALL 'DFHEI1' USING DFHEIV0
00470                     DFHEIV1 ACTION-MAP DFHEIV98 DFHEIV2.
00471
00472
00473
00474    000255*
00475    000256 1500-SEND-VERIFY-SCREEN SECTION.
00476    000257*
00477    000258          PERFORM 1510-SET-VERIFY-FACS.
00478       *       EXEC CICS
00479       *           SEND MAP('MT21MP2')
00480       *               MAPSET('MT21SET')
00481       *               FROM(CUSTOMER-DATA-MAP)
00482       *               DATAONLY
00483       *       END-EXEC.
00484    000259          MOVE 'MT21MP2' TO DFHEIV1 MOVE 'MT21SET' TO DFHEIV2 MOVE '
00485       -        '                ' TO DFHEIV0 CALL 'DFHEI1' USING DFHEIV0
00486                     DFHEIV1 CUSTOMER-DATA-MAP DFHEIV98 DFHEIV2.
00487
00488
00489
00490    000265*
00491    000266 1510-SET-VERIFY-FACS SECTION.
00492    000267*
00493    000268          MOVE FAC-PROT-MDT TO CDM-A-NAME
00494    000269                              CDM-A-ADDRESS
00495    000270                              CDM-A-CITY
00496    000271                              CDM-A-STATE
00497    000272                              CDM-A-ZIP-CODE.
00498    000273*
00499    000274 2000-PROCESS-CUSTOMER-SCREEN SECTION.
00500    000275*
00501    000276          PERFORM 2100-RECEIVE-CUSTOMER-SCREEN.
00502    000277          IF VALID-DATA
00503    000278              IF NOT CANCEL-ENTRY
00504    000279                  PERFORM 2200-EDIT-CUSTOMER-DATA
00505    000280                  IF VALID-DATA
00506    000281                      MOVE SPACE TO CDM-D-ERROR-MESSAGE
00507    000282                      MOVE 'PF1 = ACCEPT; PF4 = MODIFY; CLEAR = CANCEL
00508       -        'ENTRY' TO CDM-D-OPERATOR-MESSAGE
00509    000284                      PERFORM 1500-SEND-VERIFY-SCREEN
00510    000285                      MOVE '3' TO CA-PROCESS-FLAG
00511    000286                  ELSE
00512    000287                      PERFORM 1300-SEND-CUSTOMER-SCREEN
00513    000288              ELSE
00514    000289                  MOVE LOW-VALUE TO ACTION-MAP
00515    000290                  PERFORM 1400-SEND-ACTION-SCREEN
00516    000291                  MOVE '1' TO CA-PROCESS-FLAG
00517    000292          ELSE
00518    000293              PERFORM 1300-SEND-CUSTOMER-SCREEN.
00519    000294*
00520    000295 2100-RECEIVE-CUSTOMER-SCREEN SECTION.
00521    000296*
00522       *       EXEC CICS
00523       *           HANDLE AID CLEAR(2100-CLEAR-KEY)
00524       *                      ANYKEY(2100-ANYKEY)
00525       *       END-EXEC.
00526    000297          MOVE '                  ' TO DFHEIV0 CALL 'DFHEI1' USING
00527                     DFHEIV0 GO TO 2100-CLEAR-KEY 2100-ANYKEY DEPENDING ON
00528                     DFHEIGDI.
00529
00530       *       EXEC CICS
00531       *           RECEIVE MAP('MT21MP2')
00532       *                   MAPSET('MT21SET')
00533       *                   INTO(CUSTOMER-DATA-MAP)
```

```
00534          ✻        END-EXEC.
00535   000301          MOVE 'MT21MP2' TO DFHEIV1 MOVE 'MT21SET' TO DFHEIV2 MOVE '
00536       -                    ' TO DFHEIVO CALL 'DFHEI1' USING DFHEIVO
00537                   DFHEIV1 CUSTOMER-DATA-MAP DFHEIV98 DFHEIV2.
00538
00539
00540   000306          GO TO 2100-EXIT.
00541   000307✻
00542   000308 2100-CLEAR-KEY.
00543   000309✻
00544   000310          MOVE 'Y' TO CANCEL-ENTRY-SW.
00545   000311          GO TO 2100-EXIT.
00546   000312✻
00547   000313 2100-ANYKEY.
00548   000314✻
00549   000315          MOVE 'N'                    TO VALID-DATA-SW.
00550   000316          MOVE 'INVALID KEY PRESSED' TO CDM-D-ERROR-MESSAGE.
00551   000317          MOVE -1                     TO CDM-L-NAME.
00552   000318✻
00553   000319 2100-EXIT.
00554   000320✻
00555   000321          EXIT.
00556   000322✻
00557   000323 2200-EDIT-CUSTOMER-DATA SECTION.
00558   000324✻
00559   000325          MOVE LOW-VALUE        TO CDM-D-ERROR-MESSAGE.
00560   000326          MOVE FAC-UNPROT-MDT TO CDM-A-NAME
00561   000327                                 CDM-A-ADDRESS
00562   000328                                 CDM-A-CITY
00563   000329                                 CDM-A-STATE
00564   000330                                 CDM-A-ZIP-CODE.
00565   000331          IF         CDM-D-ZIP-CODE = SPACE
00566   000332             OR CDM-L-ZIP-CODE = ZERO
00567   000333             MOVE FAC-UNPROT-BRT-MDT TO CDM-A-ZIP-CODE
00568   000334             MOVE -1                 TO CDM-L-ZIP-CODE
00569   000335             MOVE 'YOU MUST ENTER A ZIP CODE'
00570   000336                 TO CDM-D-ERROR-MESSAGE.
00571   000337✻
00572   000338          IF         CDM-D-STATE = SPACE
00573   000339             OR CDM-L-STATE = ZERO
00574   000340             MOVE FAC-UNPROT-BRT-MDT TO CDM-A-STATE
00575   000341             MOVE -1                 TO CDM-L-STATE
00576   000342             MOVE 'YOU MUST ENTER A STATE'
00577   000343                 TO CDM-D-ERROR-MESSAGE
00578   000344          ELSE
00579   000345             MOVE CDM-D-STATE TO WS-STATE-CODE
00580       ✻            EXEC CICS
00581       ✻                LINK PROGRAM('STATEDIT')
00582       ✻                        COMMAREA(WS-STATE-EDIT-FIELDS)
00583       ✻                        LENGTH(3)
00584       ✻            END-EXEC
00585   000346             MOVE 'STATEDIT' TO DFHEIV3 MOVE 3 TO DFHEIV11 MOVE '
00586       -         '        ' TO DFHEIVO CALL 'DFHEI1' USING DFHEIVO DFHEIV3
00587                   WS-STATE-EDIT-FIELDS DFHEIV11
00588
00589
00590   000351             IF NOT WS-VALID-CODE
00591   000352                 MOVE FAC-UNPROT-BRT-MDT TO CDM-A-STATE
00592   000353                 MOVE -1                 TO CDM-L-STATE
00593   000354                 MOVE 'STATE CODE IS INVALID'
00594   000355                     TO CDM-D-ERROR-MESSAGE.
00595   000356✻
00596   000357          IF CDM-D-ERROR-MESSAGE EQUAL LOW-VALUE
00597   000358             MOVE CDM-D-ZIP-CODE TO WS-ZIP-CODE
00598       ✻            EXEC CICS
00599       ✻                LINK PROGRAM('ZIPEDIT')
```

The interactive file-maintenance
program using CICS

```
00600            *                    COMMAREA(WS-ZIP-EDIT-FIELDS)
00601            *                    LENGTH(8)
00602            *              END-EXEC
00603    000359          MOVE 'ZIPEDIT' TO DFHEIV3 MOVE 8 TO DFHEIV11 MOVE '
00604       -          ' ' TO DFHEIV0 CALL 'DFHEI1' USING DFHEIV0 DFHEIV3
00605                WS-ZIP-EDIT-FIELDS DFHEIV11
00606
00607
00608    000364          IF NOT WS-VALID-CODE
00609    000365              MOVE FAC-UNPROT-BRT-MDT TO CDM-A-ZIP-CODE
00610    000366              MOVE -1                 TO CDM-L-ZIP-CODE
00611    000367              MOVE 'ZIP CODE DOES NOT AGREE WITH STATE CODE'
00612    000368                  TO CDM-D-ERROR-MESSAGE.
00613    000369*
00614    000370      IF      CDM-D-CITY = SPACE
00615    000371          OR CDM-L-CITY = ZERO
00616    000372          MOVE FAC-UNPROT-BRT-MDT TO CDM-A-CITY
00617    000373          MOVE -1                 TO CDM-L-CITY
00618    000374          MOVE 'YOU MUST ENTER A CITY'
00619    000375              TO CDM-D-ERROR-MESSAGE.
00620    000376*
00621    000377      IF      CDM-D-ADDRESS = SPACE
00622    000378          OR CDM-L-ADDRESS = ZERO
00623    000379          MOVE FAC-UNPROT-BRT-MDT TO CDM-A-ADDRESS
00624    000380          MOVE -1                 TO CDM-L-ADDRESS
00625    000381          MOVE 'YOU MUST ENTER AN ADDRESS'
00626    000382              TO CDM-D-ERROR-MESSAGE.
00627    000383*
00628    000384      IF      CDM-D-NAME = SPACE
00629    000385          OR CDM-L-NAME = ZERO
00630    000386          MOVE FAC-UNPROT-BRT-MDT TO CDM-A-NAME
00631    000387          MOVE -1                 TO CDM-L-NAME
00632    000388          MOVE 'YOU MUST ENTER A NAME'
00633    000389              TO CDM-D-ERROR-MESSAGE.
00634    000390*
00635    000391      IF CDM-D-ERROR-MESSAGE NOT = LOW-VALUE
00636    000392          MOVE 'N' TO VALID-DATA-SW.
00637    000393*
00638    000394 3000-PROCESS-VERIFY-SCREEN SECTION.
00639    000395*
00640    000396      PERFORM 3100-RECEIVE-VERIFY-SCREEN.
00641    000397      IF VALID-DATA
00642    000398          IF        NOT CANCEL-ENTRY
00643    000399              AND NOT MODIFY-DATA
00644    000400          IF ADD-RECORD
00645    000401              PERFORM 3200-ADD-CUSTOMER-MASTER
00646    000402          ELSE IF CHANGE-RECORD
00647    000403              PERFORM 3300-CHANGE-CUSTOMER-MASTER
00648    000404          ELSE IF DELETE-RECORD
00649    000405              PERFORM 3400-DELETE-CUSTOMER-MASTER.
00650    000406      IF VALID-DATA
00651    000407          IF NOT MODIFY-DATA
00652    000408              MOVE LOW-VALUE TO ACTION-MAP
00653    000409              PERFORM 1400-SEND-ACTION-SCREEN
00654    000410              MOVE '1' TO CA-PROCESS-FLAG
00655    000411          ELSE
00656    000412              MOVE SPACE                  TO CDM-D-ERROR-MESSAGE
00657    000413              MOVE 'CLEAR = CANCEL ENTRY' TO CDM-D-OPERATOR-MESSAGE
00658    000414              MOVE -1                     TO CDM-L-NAME
00659    000415              PERFORM 1300-SEND-CUSTOMER-SCREEN
00660    000416              MOVE '2'                    TO CA-PROCESS-FLAG
00661    000417      ELSE
00662    000418          PERFORM 1500-SEND-VERIFY-SCREEN.
00663    000419*
00664    000420 3100-RECEIVE-VERIFY-SCREEN SECTION.
00665    000421*
```

```
00666          ✷    EXEC CICS
00667          ✷        HANDLE AID CLEAR(3100-CLEAR-KEY)
00668          ✷                   PF1(3100-PF1-KEY)
00669          ✷                   PF4(3100-PF4-KEY)
00670          ✷                   ANYKEY(3100-ANYKEY)
00671          ✷    END-EXEC.
00672   000422      MOVE ' 0                       ' TO DFHEIV0 CALL 'DFHEI1' USING
00673               DFHEIV0 GO TO 3100-CLEAR-KEY 3100-PF1-KEY 3100-PF4-KEY
00674               3100-ANYKEY DEPENDING ON DFHEIGDI.
00675
00676
00677
00678          ✷    EXEC CICS
00679          ✷        RECEIVE MAP('MT21MP2')
00680          ✷                MAPSET('MT21SET')
00681          ✷                INTO(CUSTOMER-DATA-MAP)
00682          ✷    END-EXEC.
00683   000428      MOVE 'MT21MP2' TO DFHEIV1 MOVE 'MT21SET' TO DFHEIV2 MOVE '
00684       -        '          ' TO DFHEIV0 CALL 'DFHEI1' USING DFHEIV0
00685               DFHEIV1 CUSTOMER-DATA-MAP DFHEIV98 DFHEIV2.
00686
00687
00688   000433      MOVE 'N'                     TO VALID-DATA-SW.
00689   000434      MOVE 'INVALID KEY PRESSED' TO CDM-D-ERROR-MESSAGE.
00690   000435      GO TO 3100-EXIT.
00691   000436✷
00692   000437 3100-CLEAR-KEY.
00693   000438✷
00694   000439      MOVE 'Y' TO CANCEL-ENTRY-SW.
00695   000440      GO TO 3100-EXIT.
00696   000441✷
00697   000442 3100-PF1-KEY.
00698   000443✷
00699   000444      GO TO 3100-EXIT.
00700   000445✷
00701   000446 3100-PF4-KEY.
00702   000447✷
00703   000448      IF NOT DELETE-RECORD
00704   000449          MOVE 'Y' TO MODIFY-DATA-SW
00705   000450      ELSE
00706   000451          MOVE 'N'                     TO VALID-DATA-SW
00707   000452          MOVE 'INVALID KEY PRESSED' TO CDM-D-ERROR-MESSAGE.
00708   000453      GO TO 3100-EXIT.
00709   000454✷
00710   000455 3100-ANYKEY.
00711   000456✷
00712   000457      MOVE 'N'                     TO VALID-DATA-SW.
00713   000458      MOVE 'INVALID KEY PRESSED' TO CDM-D-ERROR-MESSAGE.
00714   000459✷
00715   000460 3100-EXIT.
00716   000461✷
00717   000462      EXIT.
00718   000463✷
00719   000464 3200-ADD-CUSTOMER-MASTER SECTION.
00720   000465✷
00721   000466      MOVE CDM-D-CUSTOMER-CODE TO CM-CUSTOMER-CODE.
00722   000467      MOVE CDM-D-NAME          TO CM-NAME.
00723   000468      MOVE CDM-D-ADDRESS       TO CM-ADDRESS.
00724   000469      MOVE CDM-D-CITY          TO CM-CITY.
00725   000470      MOVE CDM-D-STATE         TO CM-STATE.
00726   000471      MOVE CDM-D-ZIP-CODE      TO CM-ZIP-CODE.
00727   000472      PERFORM 3210-WRITE-CUSTOMER-RECORD.
00728   000473✷
00729   000474 3210-WRITE-CUSTOMER-RECORD SECTION.
00730   000475✷
```

The interactive file-maintenance program using CICS

```
00731              *        EXEC CICS
00732              *            HANDLE CONDITION DUPREC(3210-DUPREC)
00733              *        END-EXEC.
00734     000476            MOVE '                       ' TO DFHEIVO CALL 'DFHEI1' USING
00735                       DFHEIVO GO TO 3210-DUPREC DEPENDING ON DFHEIGDI.
00736
00737              *        EXEC CICS
00738              *            WRITE DATASET('CUSTMAS')
00739              *                FROM(CUSTOMER-MASTER-RECORD)
00740              *                RIDFLD(CM-CUSTOMER-CODE)
00741              *        END-EXEC.
00742     000479            MOVE 'CUSTMAS' TO DFHEIV3 MOVE '         ' TO DFHEIVO CALL '
00743        -             'DFHEI1' USING DFHEIVO DFHEIV3 CUSTOMER-MASTER-RECORD
00744                       DFHEIV98 CM-CUSTOMER-CODE.
00745
00746
00747     000484            GO TO 3210-EXIT.
00748     000485*
00749     000486 3210-DUPREC.
00750     000487*
00751     000488            MOVE 'N' TO VALID-DATA-SW.
00752     000489            MOVE 'ERROR--CUSTOMER RECORD ALREADY EXISTS'
00753     000490                TO CDM-D-ERROR-MESSAGE.
00754     000491*
00755     000492 3210-EXIT.
00756     000493*
00757     000494            EXIT.
00758     000495*
00759     000496 3300-CHANGE-CUSTOMER-MASTER SECTION.
00760     000497*
00761     000498            PERFORM 3310-READ-CUSTOMER-FOR-UPDATE.
00762     000499            IF CUSTOMER-FOUND
00763     000500                MOVE CDM-D-NAME            TO CM-NAME
00764     000501                MOVE CDM-D-ADDRESS         TO CM-ADDRESS
00765     000502                MOVE CDM-D-CITY            TO CM-CITY
00766     000503                MOVE CDM-D-STATE           TO CM-STATE
00767     000504                MOVE CDM-D-ZIP-CODE        TO CM-ZIP-CODE
00768     000505                PERFORM 3320-REWRITE-CUSTOMER-RECORD.
00769     000506*
00770     000507 3310-READ-CUSTOMER-FOR-UPDATE SECTION.
00771     000508*
00772              *        EXEC CICS
00773              *            HANDLE CONDITION NOTFND(3310-NOTFND)
00774              *        END-EXEC.
00775     000509            MOVE '                    ' TO DFHEIVO CALL 'DFHEI1' USING
00776                       DFHEIVO GO TO 3310-NOTFND DEPENDING ON DFHEIGDI.
00777
00778              *        EXEC CICS
00779              *            READ DATASET('CUSTMAS')
00780              *                INTO(CUSTOMER-MASTER-RECORD)
00781              *                RIDFLD(CDM-D-CUSTOMER-CODE)
00782              *                UPDATE
00783              *        END-EXEC.
00784     000512            MOVE 'CUSTMAS' TO DFHEIV3 MOVE '         ' TO DFHEIVO CALL '
00785        -             'DFHEI1' USING DFHEIVO DFHEIV3 CUSTOMER-MASTER-RECORD
00786                       DFHEIV98 CDM-D-CUSTOMER-CODE.
00787
00788
00789
00790     000518            MOVE 'Y' TO CUSTOMER-FOUND-SW.
00791     000519            GO TO 3310-EXIT.
00792     000520*
00793     000521 3310-NOTFND.
00794     000522*
00795     000523            MOVE 'N' TO VALID-DATA-SW.
00796     000524            MOVE 'ERROR--CUSTOMER RECORD DOES NOT EXIST'
```

```
00797    000525            TO CDM-D-ERROR-MESSAGE.
00798    000526       MOVE 'N' TO CUSTOMER-FOUND-SW.
00799    000527*
00800    000528 3310-EXIT.
00801    000529*
00802    000530       EXIT.
00803    000531*
00804    000532 3320-REWRITE-CUSTOMER-RECORD SECTION.
00805    000533*
00806       *      EXEC CICS
00807       *          REWRITE DATASET('CUSTMAS')
00808       *                  FROM(CUSTOMER-MASTER-RECORD)
00809       *      END-EXEC.
00810    000534     MOVE 'CUSTMAS' TO DFHEIV3 MOVE '        ' TO DFHEIVO CALL '
00811       -    'DFHEI1' USING DFHEIVO DFHEIV3 CUSTOMER-MASTER-RECORD
00812            DFHEIV98.
00813
00814    000538*
00815    000539 3400-DELETE-CUSTOMER-MASTER SECTION.
00816    000540*
00817    000541       PERFORM 3310-READ-CUSTOMER-FOR-UPDATE.
00818    000542       IF CUSTOMER-FOUND
00819    000543           PERFORM 3410-DELETE-CUSTOMER-RECORD.
00820    000544*
00821    000545 3410-DELETE-CUSTOMER-RECORD SECTION.
00822    000546*
00823       *      EXEC CICS
00824       *          DELETE DATASET('CUSTMAS')
00825       *      END-EXEC.
00826    000547     MOVE 'CUSTMAS' TO DFHEIV3 MOVE '        ' TO DFHEIVO CALL '
00827       -    'DFHEI1' USING DFHEIVO DFHEIV3.
00828
00829    000550*
00830    000551 8000-START-TERMINAL-SESSION SECTION.
00831    000552*
00832    000553       MOVE LOW-VALUE TO ACTION-MAP.
00833    000554       PERFORM 1400-SEND-ACTION-SCREEN.
00834    000555       MOVE '1' TO CA-PROCESS-FLAG.
```

The interactive file-maintenance program using CICS

Index

Comment Form

Your opinions count

Your opinions today will affect our future products and policies. So if you have questions, criticisms, or suggestions, I'm eager to get them. You can expect a response within a week of the time we receive your comments.

Also, if you discover any errors in this book, typographical or otherwise, please point them out. We'll correct them when the book is reprinted.

Thanks for your help!

Mike Murach, President
Mike Murach and Associates, Inc.

Book title: The COBOL Programmer's Handbook

Dear Mike: _____

_____

_____

_____

_____

_____

_____

_____

_____

_____

_____

_____

_____

_____

_____

_____

_____

Name and Title _____

Company (if any) _____

Address _____

City, State, Zip _____

Fold where indicated and staple.
No postage necessary if mailed in the U.S.

fold

fold

fold

fold

BUSINESS REPLY MAIL

FIRST-CLASS MAIL   PERMIT NO. 3063   FRESNO, CA

POSTAGE WILL BE PAID BY ADDRESSEE

Mike Murach & Associates, Inc.

4697 West Jacquelyn Avenue
Fresno, CA 93722-9986

Order Form

Our Unlimited Guarantee

To our customers who order directly from us: You must be satisfied. Our books must work for you, or you can send them back for a full refund...no matter how many you buy, no matter how long you've had them.

Name & Title _____

Company (if company address) _____

Address_____

City, State, Zip _____

Phone number (including area code) _____

Qty	Product code and title	Price
COBOL Program Development		
_____ DDCP	How to Design and Develop COBOL Programs	$30.00
_____ CPHB	The COBOL Programmer's Handbook	20.00
_____ CPCS	Program Development Case Studies	6.00
_____ CPIG	Program Development Instructor's Guide	75.00
_____ MODS	LISTMODS, the structure listing program	250.00
_____ LMUG	LISTMODS User's Guide (price will be applied to later purchase of LISTMODS)	5.00
COBOL Language Elements		
_____ SC1R	Structured ANS COBOL: Part 1	$25.00
_____ SC2R	Structured ANS COBOL: Part 2	25.00
_____ RW	Report Writer	13.50
System Development		
_____ DDBS	How to Design and Develop Business Systems	$20.00
_____ SDCS	System Development Case Studies	6.00
_____ SDIG	System Development Instructor's Guide	75.00

Qty	Product code and title	Price
CICS		
_____ CIC1	CICS for the COBOL Programmer: Part 1	$25.00
_____ CIC2	CICS for the COBOL Programmer: Part 2	25.00
_____ CREF	The CICS Programmer's Desk Reference	32.50
Data Base Processing		
_____ IMS1	IMS for the COBOL Programmer Part 1: DL/I Data Base Processing	$30.00
_____ IMS2	IMS for the COBOL Programmer Part 2: Data Communications and MFS	30.00
VSAM		
_____ VSAM	VSAM for the COBOL Programmer	$15.00
_____ VSMX	VSAM: Access Method Services and Application Programming	25.00

☐ Bill me the appropriate price plus UPS shipping and handling (and sales tax in California) for each book ordered.

☐ Bill the appropriate book prices plus UPS shipping and handling (and sales tax in California) to my _____VISA _____MasterCard:

Card number_____
Valid thru (month/year)_____
Cardowner's signature_____
(not valid without signature)

☐ I want to **save** UPS shipping and handling charges. Here's my check or money order for $_____. California residents, please add 6% sales tax to your total. (Offer valid in the U.S. only.)

To order more quickly,

Call **toll-free** 1-800-221-5528

(Weekdays, 9 to 4 Pacific Std. Time)

In California, call 1-800-221-5527

Mike Murach & Associates, Inc.

4697 West Jacquelyn Avenue
Fresno, California 93722
(209) 275-3335